Ideology, Conflict, and Leadership in Groups and Organizations

Ideology, Conflict, and Leadership in Groups and Organizations

Otto F. Kernberg, M.D.

Yale University Press

New Haven and London

Copyright © 1998 by Otto F. Kernberg.
All rights reserved.
This book may not be reproduced, in whole or in part, including illustrations, in any form (beyond that copying permitted by Sections 107 and 108 of the U.S. Copyright Law and except by reviewers for the public press), without written permission from the publishers.

Set in Garamond and Stone Sans types by The Composing Room of Michigan, Inc.
Printed in the United States of America.

Library of Congress Cataloging-in-Publication Data

Kernberg, Otto F., 1928–
    Ideology, conflict, and leadership in groups and organizatons / Otto F. Kernberg.
      p.   cm.
    Includes bibliographical references and index.
    ISBN 0–300–07355–0 (alk. paper)
     1. Organizational behavior. 2. Group psychoanalysis. 3. Social groups. 4. Political psychology. 5. Psychoanalysis—Study and teaching. I. Title.
HD58.7.K465 1998
158.2'6—dc21
97–32793
CIP

A catalogue record for this book is available from the British Library.

The paper in this book meets the guidelines for permanence and durability of the Committee on Production Guidelines for Book Longevity of the Council on Library Resources.

10 9 8 7 6 5 4 3 2 1

To the memory of Ignacio Matte-Blanco of Santiago, Chile, and of Ernst Ticho, of Vienna, Austria, my friends and teachers

Contents

Preface

My interest in the treatment of severe personality disorders confronted me very early with the pervasive destructive and self-destructive currents that are an essential aspect of the unconscious conflicts and interpersonal difficulties of these patients. Treating them in the context of a hospital setting provided much information about the expression of their unconscious intrapsychic conflicts within the social life of the hospital environment. What came as a surprise was how the conflicts of these patients resonated with preexisting conflicts within the social matrix of the hospital and, at times, permitted the clarification of silent but troublesome undercurrents of the hospital's administrative conflicts.

From a complementary vantage point, my experiences over more than twenty-five years—first as medical director of the C. F. Menninger Memorial Hospital, then as director of General Inpatient Services at the New York State Psychiatric Institute, and, more recently, as medical director of the New York Hospital-Cornell Medical Center, Westchester Division, gave me an opportunity to observe the activation of regressive group processes marked by destructive and self-destructive conflicts as a virtually unavoidable aspect of organizational functioning, the shadowy counterpart to the productive work carried out by effective task groups and organizational structures in these institutions.

I became aware that the dynamic interplay of libidinal and aggressive impulses is enacted not only within the dynamic unconscious of the individual but also at the level of groups and social institutions. Defensive and sublimatory processes expressing the vicissitudes of erotism and aggression, of creativity, and of self-destructiveness can be observed at both the individual and the organizational level. The striking, mutual influences of individual, group, and organizational processes clearly require an integrated theory of these crosscurrents.

Perhaps the most dramatic illustration of the interaction between individual and group dynamics is the observation that very sick patients may perform quite normally in groups whose structure is sound and whose tasks are clearly defined and maintained. By contrast, perfectly healthy and well-adjusted professionals, working in the context of regressive groups with an inadequate task structure, may rapidly regress into abnormal behaviors. At times, it is as though the most severely destructive and self-destructive forces of the dynamic unconscious are unleashed within such dysfunctional group situations.

My experiences as a member and leader of psychiatric and psychoanalytic organizations and as an organizational consultant to hospitals and educational institutions, provided further evidence of the relation between the unconscious conflicts of the individual, regressive group processes, and the influences of organizational leadership in reducing or exacerbating primitive aggression within a social context.

I gradually developed a theoretical frame that integrates our present-day knowledge regarding the psychodynamics of individuals, groups, and organizations. In this volume I spell out this integrative frame and apply it to the analysis of the regressive processes in groups, to the nature of institutional leadership, and to the conditions of rational organizational functioning that may protect the organization from the most dangerous consequences of regressive group processes. The application of this frame of reference to group therapy and the therapeutic community illustrates the therapeutic uses of this model, while a section on problems in psychoanalytic institutes illustrates the consultative potential of this theory. Finally, in proposing some contributions to the psychology of ideology formation, bureaucracy, conventionality, and the political process, I open this theoretical frame to interface with the social sciences beyond the realm of specific organizational functioning.

I hope that what follows will shed new light on the turbulent nature of human interactions in groups and organizations, while at the same time avoiding a utopian overextension of this knowledge. I have attempted to point out where and to what extent such understanding may help to resolve conflicts at the group and institutional level and the model's potential for therapeutic effectiveness in achieving institutional change.

For the development of my formulations, I am deeply indebted to a distinguished group of colleagues and friends, some of them pioneers in the contemporary studies of organizational psychology. Harry Levinson, former director of the Department of Industrial Psychology at the Menninger Foundation and more recently president of the Harry Levinson Institute in Boston, first inspired me to use a psychoanalytic perspective in the study of organizational conflict. The late Thomas Dolgoff, former senior administrator and teacher of administrative theory at the Menninger Foundation, provided me with the luxury of his personal consultations during the first year of my directorship of the C. F. Menninger Memorial Hospital. The late John Sutherland, former director of the Tavistock Clinic, editor of the *International Journal of Psycho-Analysis,* and for many years senior consultant to the Menninger Foundation, introduced me to both the object-relations theory of Ronald Fairbairn and the group-dynamic approach of the Tavistock Institute of Group Relations and stimulated me to develop bridging concepts between the psychopathology of the individual and the psychopathology of groups and organizations.

My early learning in group dynamics and group psychotherapy evolved under the inspired teaching and supervision of Ramón Ganzaraín, former director of Group Dynamics and Psychosomatic Medicine at the Department of Psychiatry of the School of Medicine at the University of Chile and, later, of group psychotherapy at the Menninger Foundation. Jerome Frank, professor of psychiatry at the Johns Hopkins Medical School and a pioneer in research on group psychotherapy at the Henry Phipps Clinic of Johns Hopkins Hospital, helped expand my experience in group psychotherapy and psychotherapy research. Professional interactions with Leonard Horwitz at the Menninger Foundation, Howard Kibel at the New York Hospital-Cornell Medical Center, Westchester Division, and Saul Scheidlinger, former editor of the *International Journal of Group Psychotherapy,* helped me significantly to expand my knowledge about group psychotherapy.

The work of Didier Anzieu in France and of Rene Käes in Switzerland; of Pierre Turquet, Malcolm Pines, and Earl Hopper in Great Britain; of Abraham

Zalesnick in the United States; and the experience of participating as a member and staff at conferences of the A. K. Rice Institute were important sources for learning about group dynamics and the theory of organization. I was particularly helped by stimulating contacts with Margaret Rioch and Roger Shapiro.

Throughout the course of my professional work and writings in recent years I have been deeply indebted to a group of friends and colleagues who have provided me with an ongoing, challenging, and stimulating critique of my work. They include Harold Blum, Arnold Cooper, William Grossman, Paulina Kernberg, Robert Michels, Ethel Person, Gertrude Ticho, and Robert Wallerstein.

The encouragement and support of my present work by Jack Barchas, professor and chair of the Department of Psychiatry at the Cornell University Medical College, have been an invaluable stimulus for this book. My colleagues at the Personality Disorders Institute at the Westchester Division of the New York Hospital continue to provide me with opportunities for therapeutic exploration in both the group and individual therapeutic settings. I am extremely indebted to them all, in particular to Ann Appelbaum, Stephen Bauer, John Clarkin, Pamela Foelsch, Kay Haran, Paulina Kernberg, Harold Koenigsberg, Sonia Kulchycky, Lawrence Rockland, Michael Stone, and Frank Yeomans.

My profound gratitude to my two recently deceased teachers and friends, Ignacio Matte Blanco, former chair of the Department of Psychiatry of the School of Medicine of the University of Chile and one of the most original contributors to psychoanalytic theory in recent years, and Ernst Ticho, former director of the Psychotherapy Service of the Menninger Foundation and the most gifted psychotherapist and psychotherapy teacher of my professional experience. Both helped me to keep my faith in moments of adversity and to maintain an unwavering optimism about the power of ideas.

As in the past, I wish to express my gratitude to Gladys Topkis, senior editor at Yale University Press, whose encouraging and critical thought has stimulated me in the publication of several books, and to Lorraine Alexson, who carefully edited this volume. Becky Whipple patiently and efficiently typed many versions of the chapters of this book, and I greatly appreciate her work and dedication. Finally, I wish to thank Louise Taitt, the secretary of the Institute for Personality Disorders at the Westchester Division of the New York Hospital, who throughout the years of our collaborative work has creatively handled the many tasks she is in charge of, contributed in major ways to protecting the time and space for my professional writing by bringing order into what at times seemed unmanageable chaos, and seen to it that all the details of the work with this book were taken care of.

Part One Psychoanalytic Studies of Group Processes: Theory and Application

Chapter 1 Psychoanalytic Theories of Group Psychology

THE PSYCHOLOGY OF LARGE AND SMALL GROUPS

Freud (1921) initiated the psychoanalytic study of group processes and explained them in terms of ego psychology, which he had recently developed. In Freud's view, people in mobs have an immediate sense of intimacy with one another that is derived from the projection of their ego ideal onto the leader and from their identification with the leader as well as with their fellows. The projection of the ego ideal onto the idealized leader eliminates moral constraints as well as the superego-mediated functions of self-criticism and responsibility, and the sense of unity and belonging protects the members of the mob from losing their sense of identity. This projection is accompanied by a severe reduction in ego functioning. As a result, primitive, ordinarily unconscious needs take over, and the mob functions under the sway of drives and affects, excitement and rage, all of which are stimulated and directed by the leader.

In works written in the 1940s and early 1950s, Bion (1961) described the regressive processes he had noted when the leader of unstructured groups of seven to twelve members consistently refused to participate in group decision making but only observed and commented on the group's behavior. Bion explained these processes in terms of three basic group emotional assumptions (basic-assumptions groups), which are the foundation for group reactions that potentially exist at all times but that are activated when the task structure or "work group" breaks down.

The first is the basic group assumption of "dependency." Members perceive the leader as omnipotent and omniscient and themselves as inadequate, immature, and incompetent. They match their idealization of the leader with efforts to extract knowledge, power, and goodness from him. The group members are thus both forever greedy and forever dissatisfied. When the leader fails to live up to their ideal, they react first with denial and then by rapidly and completely devaluing the leader and searching for a substitute. Thus, primitive idealization, projected omnipotence, denial, envy, and greed, together with their accompanying defenses, characterize the basic dependency group.

The second basic-assumptions group operates under a "fight-flight" assumption, united against what it vaguely perceives to be external enemies. This group expects the leader to direct the fight against such enemies and also to protect the group from infighting. Because the members cannot tolerate opposition to their shared ideology, they easily split into subgroups, which fight with one other. Frequently, one subgroup becomes subservient to the idealized leader while another either attacks the subservient group or flees from it. Prevalent features include the group's tendencies to try to control the leader or to experience itself as being controlled by the leader, to experience closeness through shared denial of intragroup hostility, and to project aggression onto an out-group. In short, splitting, projection of aggression, and projective identification prevail. In the fight-flight group, the search for nurture and dependency that characterizes the dependency group is replaced by conflicts over aggressive control, suspiciousness, fighting, and dread of annihilation.

The third basic-assumptions group operates under a "pairing" assumption. Members tend to focus on a couple within the group, one that is usually but not necessarily heterosexual. The focal couple symbolizes the group's positive expectation that it will, in effect, reproduce itself and thus preserve the group's threatened identity and ensure its survival. The pairing group experiences general intimacy and sexual developments as potential protections against the dangerous conflicts over dependency and aggression that characterize the dependency and fight-flight groups. Although the latter two groups have a pregenital character, the pairing group has a genital character.

Both Le Bon (1969 [1895]) and Freud (1921) referred to the direct manifestations of violent aggression in mobs. By contrast, the potential for violence is generally under control in small groups, which not only make use of the mechanisms just described but are helped to maintain a certain civilized attitude by the context of eye contact and mutual acquaintance. An external enemy serves to absorb the aggression generated within the group. Occasionally, however, an outside enemy cannot be defined or located, and this creates much stronger tensions, which threaten the internal cohesion of the group.

Rice (1965) and Turquet (1975) studied the behavior of large unstructured groups (40–120 members), using methods similar to Bion's for smaller group processes. Turquet described the complete loss of identity felt by the individual member of a large (unstructured) group. Concomitantly, the individual's capacity for realistically evaluating the effects of his or her words and actions decreased dramatically within the large group, where the ordinary social feedback to individual verbal communication disappears. In large, unstructured groups, nobody seems to be able to listen to anybody else, dialogue is stifled by the subsequent discontinuity of communication, and efforts to establish small subgroups usually fail. Even projective mechanisms fail, because no one can realistically evaluate another's behavior. In this context, projections become multiple and unstable, and the individual must find some kind of "skin" that will differentiate him or her from the others.

Turquet also described the individual's fears of aggression from other members, loss of control, and violent behavior—fears that can emerge at any time in the large group. Fear is the counterpart of the provocative behaviors that group members sometimes express at random but usually direct at the leader. Gradually, it becomes evident that those who try to maintain a semblance of individuality in this atmosphere are the ones who are most frequently attacked. At the same time, efforts of homogenization are prevalent; any simplistic generalization or ideology that permeates the group may be easily transformed into a conviction of absolute truth. In contrast to the rationalization of violence that characterizes the mob, however, the vulgar or commonsense philosophy of the large group functions as a calming, reassuring doctrine that reduces all thought to cliché. For the most part, aggression in the large group takes the form of envy—envy of thinking, of individuality, and of rationality.

Anzieu (1971) proposed that under conditions of regression in the unstructured group, the relationship of individuals to the group would acquire the characteristics of fusion. In his view, individual instinctual needs would be fused with a fantastic conception of the group as a primitive ego ideal, that

Anzieu equated with an all-gratifying primary object, the mother of the earliest stages of development. The psychology of the group, then, reflects three sets of shared illusions: (1) that the group is composed of individuals who are all equal, thus denying sexual differences and castration anxiety; (2) that the group is self-engendered—that is, as a powerful mother of itself; and (3) that the group itself can repair all narcissistic lesions because it becomes an idealized "breast-mother."

Chasseguet-Smirgel (1975) expanded on Anzieu's observations, suggesting that under these conditions any group, small or large, tends to select leaders who represent not the paternal aspects of the prohibitive superego but a pseudopaternal "merchant of illusions." A leader of this kind provides the group with an ideology, a unifying system of ideas; in this case, the ideology is an illusion that confirms the individual's narcissistic aspirations of fusing with the group as a primitive ego ideal—the all-powerful and all-gratifying preoedipal mother. Basically, the small- or large-group members' identification with one another permits them to experience a primitive narcissistic gratification of greatness and power. When violent groups operate under the influence of ideologies that have been adopted under such psychological conditions, their violence reflects their need to destroy any external reality that interferes with the group's illusionary ideology. The losses of personal identity, cognitive discrimination, and differentiating individuality within the group are compensated for by the shared sense of omnipotence. In this conceptualization, the regressed ego, the id, and the primitive (preoedipal) ego ideal of each individual are fused in the group illusion.

AN OBJECT-RELATIONS APPROACH TO GROUP PSYCHOLOGY

In earlier work (Kernberg, 1976, 1980b, 1980c), I proposed that we might better understand the strikingly regressive features of small groups, large groups, and mobs by using the concept of the internalized object relations that predate object constancy and the consolidation of the ego, the superego, and the id. From this viewpoint, one might consider two levels of internalized object relations. A basic level would be characterized by multiple self- and object representations that correspond to primitive fantasy formations linked with primitive impulse derivatives. The second and higher level would be characterized by sophisticated, integrated self- and object representations linked with higher levels of affect dispositions. These higher-level object relations reflect the early childhood experiences of the individual and his or her conflicts with real parental figures and siblings more accurately than do the basic-level object relations. At the higher level, the integrated self-concept, together with realistically integrated object representations that are related to the self-concept, constitute ego identity. When integrated concepts of the self and others are lacking, the syndrome of identity diffusion develops.

Impressive clinical evidence indicates that regardless of the individual's maturity and psychological integration, certain group conditions tend to bring on regression and activate primitive psychological levels. Small, closed, and unstructured groups—as well as groups that are large, minimally structured, and lacking clearly defined tasks to relate them to their environment—tend to bring about an immediate regression in the individual, a regression that consists in the activation of defensive operations and interpersonal processes that reflect primitive object relations. The potential for this regression exists within us all. When we lose our ordinary social structure, when our customary social roles are suspended, and when multiple objects are present simultaneously in an unstructured relationship, reproducing a multiplicity of primitive intrapsychic object relations in the interpersonal field, primitive levels of psychological functioning may be activated.

On the basis of observations of small groups, large groups, and mobs, I propose that group processes in general pose a basic threat to personal identity, a threat linked to the proclivity in group situations for primitive psychological levels to be activated, including primitive object relations, primitive defensive operations, and primitive aggression with predominantly pregenital features (Kernberg, 1980b, 1980c). Turquet's explanation of what happens in large groups describes the basic situation for the activation of defenses in a group of any size. The horde's idealization of the leader described by Freud; the group's idealization of the group ideology and of leaders who promote its narcissistic self-aggrandizement described by Anzieu and Chasseguet-Smirgel; and the small-group processes described by Bion are all ways of defending against the situation Turquet defined. Obviously, large-group processes can be obscured or controlled by rigid social structuring. Bureaucratization, ritualization, and well-organized task performance are different methods with similar immediate effects.

Large-group processes also highlight the intimate connection between threats to the individual's identity and the individual's fear that primitive aggressions and aggressively infiltrated sexuality will emerge. Through group and organization processes, an important part of nonintegrated and unsublimated aggression is expressed in vicarious ways. In the group processes of organizations and institutions, for example, the exercise of power constitutes a channel for expressing the aggression that in dyads and triads would ordinarily be under control. Aggression emerges more directly and intensely when group processes are relatively unstructured.

Narcissistic personalities, as I have pointed out elsewhere (Kernberg, 1980b, 1984c), are ideally constituted for the assumption of leadership under the conditions of large-group processes. Such peoples' lack of deep conviction regarding their own values makes it easy for them to go along with the group. A narcissistic personality who can communicate effectively can provide the large group with an acceptable ideology and convey a sense of certainty without triggering the group's envy against individualized thinking. These abilities make such a leader the soother of the large group's tensions. By the same token, the large-group members' identification with the narcissistic leader reinforces some of the pathologically narcissistic characteristics of "static" crowds (Canetti, 1960). These groups are conventional, ideologically simplistic, conformist, and able to indulge themselves without guilt or gratitude; they lack a sense of personal responsibility or a deep investment in others.

Another striking characteristic of group life is the activation of infantile sexual features. In the small group, sexuality emerges when the basic assumption of pairing serves as a defense against primitive aggression. In the large group, sexuality is either denied or expressed in sadistically infiltrated sexual allusions. In the large group, sexuality usually goes "underground," or is "split off": couples form secretly as a direct reaction to and defense against large-group processes. In the horde, the unchallenged idealization of the leader has its counterpart in the group's intolerance of any couple that attempts to preserve its identity as one. Freud (1913) saw the crowd's intolerance of sexuality as a result of something akin to the original danger that faces the primitive horde: namely, the sons' rivalry for their mothers and sisters. He proposed that totemic exogamy protected the social structure at the cost of repressing sexual urges within it. Anzieu (1971) and Chasseguet-Smirgel (1975) both stressed the denial of oedipal sexuality in unstructured group processes.

The projection of superego functions onto the group and its leader and the related submission to authoritarian leadership do protect against both violence and the destruction of couples within the group. It is condensed, however, with the prohibition against incest and the most infantile aspects of sexuality. Thus, group morality veers toward a conventionalized desexualization of heterosexual relations, toward the suppression of erotic fantasy insofar as it involves infantile polymorphous trends, and toward acknowledging and sanctioning only the more permissible love relations. In large groups, the alternative to these defensive efforts—and to their miscarriage in repressive ideologies—is the eruption of a crude and anally tinged sexuality that is reminiscent of the sexualized group formations of latency and early adolescence. (See chapters 2 and 3.)

APPLICATIONS TO GROUP PSYCHOTHERAPY

The following summary is significantly influenced by several overviews of the literature (Foulkes and Anthony, 1957; de Mare, 1972; Whiteley and Gordon, 1979; Scheidlinger, 1982).

The Psychoanalytic Psychotherapy of Individuals in Groups

In the 1930s Slavson (1959, 1962, 1964) pioneered psychoanalytic group psychotherapy in the United States. He attempted to stimulate individual patients in the group to free associate, and he analyzed resistances and transferences directed toward both the group leader and other members of the group. Slavson believed that the multiple expression of transferences toward other group members would dilute or decrease transference intensity and that this could facilitate working with the transference. In fact, because Slavson considered group processes to be potentially detrimental to the therapeutic use of groups, he came to place his emphasis on working with individuals within the group. Similarly, Wolf and Schwartz (1962) originally stressed the psychoanalytically based treatment of the individual in the group, but they gradually came to concentrate on the group process itself, focusing on the interacting patterns of the members.

Expanding upon the contributions of these pioneers, an entire school of psychoanalytic group psychotherapy developed, based on first applying psychoanalytic theory and technique to individual psychotherapy and then carrying out individual psychoanalytic psychotherapy in a group setting. Gradually, other theoretical and technical principles from sociological analyses of small-group processes were incorporated. In particular, systems theory was applied to the interrelationships between the individual, the group, and the social environment. Finally, psychoanalytic theories of group processes proper were developed and incorporated. Bach (1954), Durkin (1964), and Scheidlinger (1982) offer outstanding syntheses of psychoanalytic concepts, systems theory, and Lewin's (1951) contributions to the social dynamics of small groups.

The Psychoanalytically Oriented Treatment of the Whole Group

Group therapists in Britain developed a theoretical and technical approach that focused on the psychoanalytic meaning of group processes rather than on the psychopathology of individual patients within the group. They based their theory on the British psychoanalytic schools of Fairbairn and Melanie Klein and particularly on Bion's works of the 1940s and early 1950s (Bion, 1961). The most radical of these approaches is reflected in Bion's own method. Here, the group psychotherapist interprets the dominant basic assumptions of dependency, fight-flight, and pairing as aspirations, fantasies, and behaviors shared by the entire group. The defensive functions of these basic assumptions are interpreted as protections against the experienced danger that "psychotic anxieties" could erupt, anxieties related to primitive levels of aggression and the corresponding threats to the self and internalized objects.

Bion assumed that each patient has a particular "valence" toward the conflicts and fantasies of these basic-assumptions groups and that the dominant group mentality at any time is a consequence of the moment-to-moment summation of the members' valences. Implicitly, the individual patient's psychopathology would be explored at points when his or her valences were dominant in the atmosphere of the entire group. Working through is therefore carried out in terms of the repetitive activation of alternating basic-assumptions phenomena rather than in terms of the intrapsychic structures of individual patients.

Ezriel (1950) and Sutherland (1952) modified Bion's approach to small groups by focusing on the individual patient's particular reactions to the predominant group tension. Accordingly, they expanded the interpretation of the dominant group mentality to include the individual patient's specific ways of expressing or reacting to it. Ezriel's concept of the "common group tension" corresponds roughly to Bion's "dominant group mentality." Both express the moment-to-moment summation of members' predisposition to participate in a particular group theme. In Ezriel's view, this theme can be interpreted as a dominant "required relationship," established as a defense against an "avoided relationship." The avoided relationship, in turn, is feared because of the fantasied disastrous consequences of yet another relationship, a "calamitous relationship."

The approaches of Bion, Ezriel, and Sutherland call for the therapist to maintain a basic distance. The therapist interprets all communications, even those directed to him or her by individual patients, in terms of common group features. The group therapist's role is exclusively interpretive, and the interpretations are focused on the meaning of the group situation as a whole and on transferences. Moreover, regardless of whether these are individual or group transferences, they are interpreted only in terms of the here and now, not in terms of an individual patient's past or of any genetic reconstructions. The free-floating verbal communications within the group, which are similar but not equivalent to the free associations of an individual patient, are used as primary data. The effect of this particular technique—maximally in the case of Bion and significantly less so with Ezriel and Sutherland—is to reduce the usual role relationships between patients and therapist. And this prevents the group structuring that ordinarily develops through socially acceptable and reassuring roles and interactions.

This technique has both advantages and dangers. Among the advantages are the sharp highlighting of primitive modes of mental operations and the possibility of jointly examining the unconscious processes that influence group behavior. On the negative side, a number of questions have been raised about the artificial distance of the group leader, the elimination of the ordinary supportive features of group interactions, and the fact that cognitive instruments for self-understanding are not offered to individual patients regarding their particular psychopathology (Scheidlinger, 1960; Malan et al., 1976). These features of the technique may be too demanding for the individual patient and thus therapeutically counterproductive.

Psychoanalytic Psychotherapy of Individuals Through the Analysis of Group Processes

Foulkes and Anthony (1957) developed a technique of group psychotherapy that was based on the promotion of a group culture characterized by free-floating discussions. They considered these discussions to be analogous to free association and as offering the raw material for interpretive work. Within the group culture, a network of interpersonal communication, or "group matrix," develops.

Foulkes's approach is less centered on the group leader than are those of Bion, Ezriel, and Sutherland, but his understanding of group processes is derived from their work. Technically, though, his use and stimulation of individual patients' observing ego functions and the growth-promoting and supportive potential of the group process is closer to the approaches that are characteristic of American psychoanalytic group psychotherapy. Other features of Foulkes's techniques are closer to the Bion, Ezriel, and Sutherland models: he focuses only on the transferences in the here and now and on group processes at large.

When the psychoanalytic theory of group processes is applied to group psychotherapy, it seems that the more the technique focuses on the analysis of group processes per se, the more it approaches a purely Bionian model. Consequently, primitive group phenomena and transferences may emerge more dramatically, giving rise to the possibility of concrete learning by the group members about deep anxieties and fantasies that are close to what dominates in the psychopathology of borderline conditions. Clearly, all this has enormous heuristic value for the study of regressive processes in groups. The risk, however, is that the individual nature of each patient's psychopathology will be neglected and the ego-supportive group processes will be downplayed. Furthermore, the individual patient's responsibility for participating in the psychotherapeutic process may not receive sufficient attention. Highlighting primitive transferences does not guarantee that they will be resolved.

On the other hand, bypassing the analysis of group processes and focusing on individualized psychoanalytic exploration within the group also has its advantages and disadvantages. Among the apparent advantages is that the individually oriented application may maximize the supportive aspect of group functioning and minimize the phenomena of basic-assumptions groups. This application may also highlight dominant pathological character traits in the context of activating triadic, "high-level" transferences. Finally, it may have the advantage of facilitating what may in practice resemble a supportive-expressive psychotherapy, making full use of group socialization for reeducative purposes. The risks of individually oriented application include intellectualizing the interpretations of intrapsychic dynamics, underutilizing the psychoanalytic understanding of deeper aspects of unconscious intrapsychic conflicts, and facilitating a supportive-reeducative effect on character pathology without at the same time facilitating its deep resolution.

HOSPITAL TREATMENT AND THERAPEUTIC COMMUNITY MODELS

Main (1957) studied the group reactions of hospital nursing staff who were treating predominantly borderline and psychotic patients ("special" cases) and found that the nurses were experiencing phenomena similar to those Bion observed in the basic-assumptions groups. He suggested that regressed patients, borderline patients in particular, may under certain conditions activate their own intrapsychic object relations in the interpersonal relations of the hospital staff. In effect, these patients induce in their social fields a reenactment of the conflicts within their intrapsychic worlds. The massive projection, omnipotent control, denial, primitive idealization, and, above all, splitting observed in the nursing staff reflect both their own intrapsychic mechanisms and the behavioral means by which the patients' intrapsychic worlds distort staff relationships. Stanton and Schwartz (1954) demonstrated the corollary—splits and covert conflicts in the interpersonal and social fields of the hospital may likewise intensify the intrapsychic conflict and disorganization of the special patients. The pathology that the patient induces in the social field uses preexisting cleavages in that field, cleavages that reflect conflicts in the administrative structure of the social organization. Intrapsychic conflict and social conflict thus reinforce each other.

If channels of communication within the staff group and between the staff and the patients are kept open, the interpersonal conflicts generated around each patient can be explored; this can illuminate the individual patient's psychopathology. The hospital therapist can explore psychoanalytically the patient's evolving deployment of primitive object relations in the hospital's social field by systematically examining with the patient his or her interpersonal experiences in the hospital.

The techniques of therapeutic community approaches may help the therapist strengthen the diagnosis and therapeutic use of the patient's interactions within the immediate social field. Although different authors have variously described the essential aspects of this approach, the basic orientation stems from Jones (1953) and Main (1946) and emphasizes the following features: staff and patients must function jointly as an organized community to carry out the treatment of the patient population; all activities and interactions must relate to the goal of reeducating and socially rehabilitating the patients; and finally, the living-learning-confrontation model must be used to open the flow of communication between patients and staff and provide immediate feedback about observed behaviors and reactions.

Three specific kinds of meetings facilitate the therapeutic community and are common to all models. This typology is different from the small-, large-, and task-group types of meetings, but principles from the latter typology may apply as well. The community meeting includes all patients and the entire staff.

With a free flow of communication, this meeting aims to examine the whole staff-patient social environment; any distortions or interferences, regardless of source; and the development and possible resolution of antidemocratic or authoritarian processes. Patient-government meetings are a second common type. Regardless of the specific form patient government takes, therapeutic community models tend to foster patients' organization, allowing the patients to participate in the social and decision-making processes. The third type of meeting is the staff meeting. Complementing patient government, this meeting expresses the concept of democratic decision making among staff. It allows staff members to explore how they are influenced by administrative and other pressures, as well as by their interactions with patients.

The most important precondition for the development of a therapeutic community is that it be functionally integrated with the administrative structure of the hospital within which it operates. If the therapeutic community openly explores the social system actualized by the patient-staff community, it will of necessity also activate the stress and latent conflicts in the system. It will thus influence the political dimensions of the institutional decision-making process.

Therapeutic communities can powerfully reinforce the therapeutic utilization of the hospital's social milieu. They can also become a real or perceived threat to the patient's treatment. Patient meetings, staff meetings, and particularly the community meeting easily acquire the characteristics of large-group processes. The regressive effects of large-group processes can in turn affect the individual patient's development in the community in antitherapeutic ways.

I have previously pointed to the dangers that arise when patients as a group regress to the functioning of a basic-assumptions group (Kernberg, 1976, chap. 9; 1980c). Under such regressive circumstances, patient groups may become intolerant of individuals, establishing a group dictatorship that acquires the characteristics of a primitive morality and fosters the leadership of narcissistic and antisocial personalities. Staff may contribute to this regression by their ideologically determined denial of differences between individual patients, their implicit expectation that all patients have the same needs, and their consequent expectation that all patients will react or participate in similar ways. The most regressed patients, including chronic monopolizers, manipulators, and the violent, gain control of unstructured group processes and significantly distort first the content of meetings and later the allocation of resources, thus reducing many patients' treatment time. Elsewhere (Kernberg, 1981, 1982) I proposed a model that attempts to maximize the advantages and control the potential liabilities of the therapeutic community.

APPLICATIONS TO GROUP AND
ORGANIZATIONAL DYNAMICS

Underlying this discussion of applications to group and organizational dynamics are the contributions of Jaques (1955, 1976, 1982), Menzies (1967), Rioch (1970a, 1970b), and, fundamentally, Rice (1963, 1965, 1969; Miller and Rice, 1967). (Bion [1970] has also explored the area of relations between individuals, groups, and institutions, but I shall not focus on his work here.) Other significant contributions to this expanding field are the works of Colman and Bexton (1975), Kreeger (1975), Miller (1976), and Lawrence (1969) and the overview by De Board (1978).

Rice's work employs a systems theory of organizations, in which the individual, the group, and the social organization are seen as a continuum of open systems. Rice (1965) integrates this open-systems theory with Bion's theories of small-group functioning and Turquet's understanding of large-group functioning. His perspective represents the core set of concepts that circumscribe organizational applications of psychoanalytic thinking. From Rice's theoretical perspective, all open systems carry out their tasks in exchange with the environment. A task that the system must perform in order to survive is called a primary task. Each system must include a control function that will permit it to analyze the environment, the internal reality of the system, and the executive organization of task performance within this internal and external reality. Because open systems must by definition carry out exchanges with their environment in order to survive, this control function must lie at the boundary between the system and its environment. A breakdown of system boundaries implies a breakdown of the open system's control, and this in turn brings about a breakdown in the performance of the primary task and threatens the survival of the system. In the field of clinical psychiatry, this open-systems theory may be applied to individual patients, to groups, and to the hospital as a social system.

In the psychic life of an individual, the ego may be conceived of as the control function, ego boundaries as the system boundaries defined and protected by the ego functions, and the person's intrapsychic world of object relations as the inner space or inner world of the system. The individual's primary task is to satisfy the instinctual and object-oriented needs of his or her internal world by means of interactions with the social environment. In the performance of this task, the individual adapts to and creatively modifies his or her interpersonal world in terms of intrapsychic needs and in turn elaborates intrapsychic needs in terms of external realities.

In the life of the group, the group leader may be seen as the control function, and the primary task of the group is whatever determined its existence in the first place. The activation of primitive object relations within the group structure (Bion's basic-assumptions group) represents the group's internal world of object relations (Rice, 1969). The equilibrium between the group focusing on the task (task group) and the group focusing on the activation of primitive object relations in its social field (basic-assumptions group) depends on such factors as the extent to which the task is clear and defined, the adequacy of task leadership, and the examination of the basic assumptions within the task or considered as task constraints.

In a social organization like an industry, an educational establishment, or a hospital, the administration represents the leader or manager of system-control functions. The purposes for which the organization was established represent the primary tasks of the system. For example, the primary tasks of a psychiatric teaching hospital are patient care, education, and research. The organization must create and protect an optimal social atmosphere in order to carry out its primary tasks. This requirement reflects a basic constraint of organizational functioning: human needs must be gratified in the course of carrying out the specific tasks of the organization. A further constraint of organizational systems is that they must organize task systems so that intragroup and intergroup processes facilitate rather than interfere with task performance. Group processes reflect the inner space or inner world of the organization as an open system. Effective organizational management requires the administrators to adequately define the primary organizational task or tasks and constraints and to establish priorities and constraints on a functional basis. Management needs adequate control over organization boundaries, and this need implies a stable, fully delegated authority over all organizational functions, from the managing board to the director or managing team.

Within this model, psychopathology may be conceptualized as a breakdown of the control function, a failure to carry out the primary task, and a threat to the survival of the system. In the case of the individual, we see the breakdown of the ego and emotional regression; in the group, the breakdown of leadership and paralysis in basic assumptions; in the institution, the breakdown of the administration, failure to carry out the institutional tasks, and loss of morale.

The breakdown of boundary control is the principal manifestation of a breakdown in the control function.

Rice's theories have served as the basis for the group-relations conferences sponsored by the Tavistock Clinic in Leicester, England, and their offshoots in the United States, the A. K. Rice Group Relations Conferences organized by the Washington School of Psychiatry. These conferences are designed to teach group, organizational, administrative, and leadership functions. They usually last from a few days to two weeks and are organized around specific events. Small-group meetings (study groups) of seven to twelve members follow a strictly Bionian model, and large-group meetings of thirty to eighty members use the same technique with the corresponding leadership functions as described by Rice and Turquet. Intergroup exercises bring together the entire conference membership or students to organize ad hoc tasks, interact with other groups, and relate spontaneously with the management or staff as a group. In addition, theoretical conferences or lectures serve to expand on the experiential learning, offering brief overviews of key concepts. Finally, application groups give individual members or students the opportunity to discuss the problems of their home organizations and to apply their learning to those problems.

I have participated in these conferences both as a member and on staff. Several processes have emerged with impressive regularity and intensity. First, intense anxieties and primitive fantasies are activated in the small study groups. Second, a primitive group functioning and potential individual aggression are activated in the large groups, dramatically illustrating the observations of Bion, Rice, and Turquet. Ad hoc myths about the conference or its leadership and the search for a comprehensive, simplistic ideology develop rapidly and contrast with discriminating reason, illustrating in one stroke what happens during a breakdown of organizational functioning. The crucial functions of boundaries in task performance and of task-oriented leadership become apparent as groups confront the temptation, at points of regression, to select the most dysfunctional members of subgroups to become leaders of basic-assumptions groups.

One important drawback to these temporary group-relations conferences is their relative neglect of the functions that time and personality issues have in stable social organizations. Katz and Kahn (1966) point out that the staffs of social and industrial organizations frequently fail to learn new attitudes in the context of exploring the irrational aspects of group processes in an experiential setting because they fail to analyze the stable features of organizational structures and because of their relation to the real (in contrast to fantasied or irrational) conflicts of interests that such structures mediate.

In addition, short-term learning experiences in groups may make it difficult to study the impact of the members' personality structures, particularly those of key leaders, a drawback that may lead to distortions in the organization's administrative structure. These distortions can be compensated for by structural rearrangements in the organization. Although the rearrangements may not seem functional in a short-term, cross-sectional analysis, in the long run they may represent the most functional compromise between the optimal organizational use of the leader's personality and an effort to reduce or control his or her distortion of administrative structures.

Several specific areas have been explored more recently within the general framework of psychoanalytic approaches to organization and leadership. The efforts by large groups to develop organizing myths and ideologies stimulated Arlow (1979) to study the characteristic contents of ideology as a group process. Similarly, Kaes (1980) and Anzieu (1981) applied Bion's, Rice's, and Turquet's techniques to explorations of the ideology of small and large groups. Their groundbreaking studies highlight the formation of group ideologies and ways of understanding them in terms of the emerging dominant unconscious themes.

Braunschweig and Fain (1971) explored typical group-formation processes in terms of the relationships of male and female members from earliest childhood through adulthood. Using socially prevalent myths about various age groups, they illustrate a developmental sequence of culturally framed relationships between the sexes.

Levinson (1972) and Zaleznik (1979) used psychoanalytic theory to analyze organizational conflicts. Levinson focused on how transference phenomena influence the relationships between hierarchical superiors and subordinates as well as those of peers within organizations, and he examined the nature of the drive gratifications and superego controls expressed in the context of work and organizational structures. Zaleznik focused on the distribution of power and the function of organizational ideology in protecting the stability of the institution.

In my own work (see chapters 4 and 5), I analyzed the connection between particular personality types as organization leaders and the regressive processes within their organizations.

Shapiro (1979) applied the psychoanalytic theories of group processes to the study of family processes and family therapy. Skynner (1976) used a systems approach to relate the psychoanalytic understanding of group processes to the analysis of family dynamics and family therapy.

APPLICATIONS TO LEADERSHIP, CULTURE, AND SOCIETY

As mentioned earlier, Freud (1921) explained that the emotional climate of hordes or mobs, their sense of immediate closeness, and their impulse-ridden behavior all derive from the projection of their ego ideal onto the leader and their identification with the leader as well as with one another. Freud linked these concepts to his hypotheses regarding the historical origin of the primal horde (1913). He suggested that the totemic law that regulates the life of the horde and protects it from both self-destructive rivalry and incestuous endogamy derives from the alliance of the sons, who have killed their father—an act he sees as endemic to the primal horde. Because of their unconscious guilt, the sons replace the father's living laws with the totemic law that symbolizes the father's law. The idealized leader therefore represents both the oedipal hero who killed his father and the alliance of the sons. Ultimately, he also symbolizes the father and his law, which the horde obeys out of unconscious guilt over the patricide.

This concept, as Lasch (1981) pointed out, has provided a theoretical underpinning for generations of Marxists and other socialist philosophers, from Reich (1962 [1935]) to Althusser (1976). The patriarchal bourgeois family was seen as the locus of introjection for the repressive ideology of capitalism, which was associated with the sexual prohibitions of the oedipal father. Where Freud thought that the repression of sexuality was the price of cultural evolution, Reich thought that it represented the effect of a pathological superego that was determined by the social structure of capitalism. The Soviet Union's sexual repressiveness, he proposed, similarly reflected the development of a Soviet authoritarian power structure. As Robinson (1959) pointed out, Marcuse (1955) agreed with Reich that overrepression of sexuality could engender overaggressiveness. Marcuse differed from Reich in other respects, however. For him, it was not genital sexuality but pregenital polymorphous infantile sexuality that the capitalist system repressed. As Marcuse saw it, the system aimed its repression at restricting sexual functions to the genital zone so that it could channel the broader unsatisfied erotism of human beings into social production.

Foucault (1978) criticized the idea that the capitalist state and bourgeois society foster the repression of sexuality. On the contrary, he suggested, bourgeois society has a keen interest in studying sexual phenomena and reclassifying them from moral to scientific and medical issues. Foucault added, however, that this interest has been accompanied by a desire to control sexual behavior and through it, the family structure; bourgeois society has an equal interest in manipulating sexual behavior to suit the state's requirements.

Althusser (1976) has come up with another application of Freud's formulations about the oedipal father. As Anderson (1976) points out, Althusser used Freud's concept of the unconscious to construct a new theory of ideology, one in which ideology is defined as a system of unconsciously determined illusory representations of reality. Specifically, the ideological system derives from internalization of the dominant illusion harbored by a social class about the conditions of its own existence. This dominant illusion stems from the internalization of the paternal law, which in turn is part of the internalization of the superego.

Unlike these models, which all make use of Freud's concept of the leader as the symbolic oedipal father, the theories of Bion, Rice, Turquet, Anzieu, and Chasseguet-Smirgel focus on the infiltration of preoedipal conflicts in regressive group formation and propose a more primitive nature of leadership. In contrast to their predecessors, these theorists focused specifically on the psychology of regression in groups. That regression, as they saw it, reflected the fantasies of merger that are linked to the preoedipal conflicts of the separation-individuation stage or even of the symbiotic merger of earliest infancy.

Mitscherlich (1963) examined the cultural consequences of the absence of the father at the social and familial level. He described the rejection of the father in contemporary society as part of the rejection of traditional cultural values brought about by the intoxicating effects of mass production, which promises immediate gratification and consequently fosters a psychology of demand and a rejection of individual responsibility. Mitscherlich described the new "mass person" as classless. He stressed the absence of the father in the contemporary family that had been brought about by the industrial revolution, and he pointed out that the individualized functions of the father were lost in the large contemporary institution.

Writing under the pseudonym André Stephane, Chasseguet-Smirgel and Grunberger (1969) analyzed the social psychology of both French fascism and the New Left in light of the 1968 student rebellion. They described several characteristics that the Left and Right have in common. Both, for example, reject such traditional values as the nuclear family and individual responsibility. Chasseguet-Smirgel and Grunberger interpret this as a symbolic rejection of both paternal and maternal principles and as a search for gratification in a primary, diffuse, maternal group. The group symbolizes a preoedipal mother who provides love and sexual gratification without demands for either individual differentiation or commitment within couples. The destruction of both authority and highly individualized and exclusive forms of sexuality thus reflects a rejection of the oedipal couple; it also denies the oedipal stage of development and demonstrates a regression to an early form of narcissism.

Lasch (1978) even described the correspondence between characteristics of the narcissistic personality and those of current Western society. The family no longer serves as a source of moral guidance, he wrote; instead of demanding that children accept responsibility for their behavior, parents try to avoid conflict by compromising and offering instinctual gratification. This attitude serves to corrode the development of a mature superego in the child. The child must thus depend internally on sadistic and primitive superego forerunners, and it overindulges in impulse gratification. This dynamic entails not only the lack of superego restrictions but also the lack of internal superego approval, and it leads to a secondary overdependence on external sources for the gratification of self-esteem. The corrosion of authority within the family is amplified by the general societal shift from a traditional mode of social leadership, which derived from ethical principles and intellectual consistency, to a mode of leadership that is without a moral justification or basis of control. The new, weaker mode of control is based primarily on power; controlling techniques take the form of manipulation and pseudohumanization of the interpersonal relationships and working conditions within the social organizations.

Lasch (1981) later expanded his ideas to include parts of Chasseguet-Smirgel's theory of group processes, particularly her use of the preoedipal mother to symbolize large-group psychology. The all-embracing and inexhaustible breast-mother gratifies the voracious, greedy, self-centered infant, whose characteristics symbolize those of crowds. Like Lasch, I find Chasseguet-Smirgel and Grunberger convincing in their explanation of regressive phenomena in crowds (phenomena Ortega y Gasset [1976 (1929)] described beautifully in *La Rebelión de las Masas*). This symbolic preoedipal mother is very different from the reasonable, differentiated oedipal mother who is separate from the child and in a private union with the oedipal father. The condition for which the latter is an image is one that regressive groups cannot tolerate.

A curious circumstance emerges here. Under conditions of large-group functioning, the dominant sexual ideology tends, on the one hand, to be marked by an excessive projection of superego function onto the authoritarian leadership of the group, a process that makes it conventional and sexually repressive. On the other hand, it can be marked by a preoedipal ideology that is expressed in the condensation of a random aggressive propensity with preoedipal forms of sexuality, manifesting trends toward polymorphous perverse infantile sexuality. Both extremes produce a similar outcome, a conventional morality directed against the private sexual fulfillment of the autonomous couple.

Chapter 2 Identity, Alienation, and Ideology in Adolescent Group Processes

IDENTITY CRISIS, IDENTITY DIFFUSION, AND ALIENATION

The physical and emotional changes of puberty and early adolescence and the corresponding loss of congruence between the adolescent's concept of himself and the concept that significant others have of him bring about a temporary loss of what Erikson (1950, 1956) called the *confirmation* of ego identity by the social group and, with it, an identity crisis. As I stressed in earlier work (Kernberg, 1976), I restrict the concept of identity crisis to the loss of correspondence between a subjective sense of ego identity and the objective psychosocial environment—which is a normal development in early adolescence. It predisposes the adolescent to feel estranged or alienated when there is an acute discrepancy between his subjective sense of identity and the objective reactions to him.

In contrast, the syndrome of identity diffusion, which is characteristic of borderline personality organization, consists of a lack of integration of the self-concept and the concept of significant others and, by the same token, a loss of the sense of continuity of the self-concept, cross-sectionally as well as longitudinally, and of the capacity for understanding oneself and others in depth. Identity diffusion may be reflected in chronic feelings of emptiness and alienation but, as we shall see, under different circumstances from those activating the acute sense of alienation in normal adolescents.

Even for adolescents in emotional turmoil (a condition that is far less prevalent than used to be thought [see Offer et al., 1981]); for those in whom relatively rapid shifts in identifications with a social group, an ideology, or a lifestyle are reflected in dramatic changes in their external appearance; or for those in whom severe conflicts with their parents produce regressive behavior, it is possible to differentiate the normal and neurotic adolescent with an identity crisis and a sense of alienation from the borderline adolescent with identity diffusion. The normal or neurotic adolescent in an identity crisis retains the capacity to describe the most important people in his life in depth, even his parents (with whom he may be having intense conflicts) and highly idealized teachers or friends. He cares about people and has social and cultural interests, value systems, and intellectual pursuits beyond the gratification of immediate narcissistic needs. He is also able to experience feelings of guilt and concern for himself and others, reflecting the capacity for experiencing ambivalence and for tolerating superego pressures in addition to the development of a normal ego ideal. All this reflects a solid ego identity and a corresponding consolidation of the self-concept and of object relations in depth.

This sense of alienation, then, is normal; it reinforces the adolescent's need to protect himself from the intensification of his emotional interactions with parents and siblings under the influence of reactivated oedipal and preoedipal urges. At the same time, this development fosters the adolescent's tendency to overidentify with his peers and explains the homogeneity in appearance, behavior, and preferences of the early-adolescent same-sex group.

The borderline personality does not usually experience this sense of alienation in early adolescence. On the contrary, he or she may externalize intense conflicts around sex and aggression at home and at school and within the peer group. Splitting mechanisms, denial, and projective identification permit the adolescent to rationalize aggression while attributing its causes to a hostile environment. The same primitive defenses facilitate the expression of sexual urges in temporary experiences that bypass the profound emotional challenges of being part of a couple.

All but the most severe cases of borderline and narcissistic personalities manage to go underground in early adolescence precisely because the groups they join provide them with a social structure that stabilizes their functioning. In mid- and late adolescence, however, when normal and neurotic adolescents are beginning to form couples, those with borderline and narcissistic personalities typically show severe behavior disturbances and a growing subjective sense of alienation.

Adapting to a conventional peer group enables the normal youth to bring the experience of alienation under control in the context of the identity crisis of early adolescence. But a new development then arises, relating to the establishment of sexual couples in mid- and late adolescence. The sexual couple always experiences itself, and is experienced by the social group surrounding it, as symbolizing an act of defiance. The group admires and envies the couple and struggles with wishes both to emulate and destroy it. It makes little difference whether the formal culture and ideology of the mixed-sex group in mid- and late adolescence is sexually "liberated" or conventionally "puritanical"; the sexually promiscuous adolescent groups of the 1960s facilitated powerful constraints on sexual intimacy by subscribing to an ideology that reduced sexual behavior to a mechanical act lacking emotional commitment or responsibility. The constraints were equal to those imposed by the proverbial small-town social groups, who reinforced superego prohibitions against sexual intimacy (and social hypocrisy).

Toward the end of adolescence, the same-sex group of latency and early adolescence and the mixed-sex group of middle and late adolescence are replaced by a loosely associated network of couples, signaling the successful transformation of adolescence into adulthood. Now the shared experience of the couple, who are creating a new, private world of sexual intimacy and emotional experiences and values—and thereby freeing themselves from the conventionality of their immediate social environment—may generate a new sense of alienation. Each member of the couple and both jointly may engage in a search for emotional understanding not only of the beloved but of all human relationships, a search for the encounter with and realization of the value systems and ideals they establish in their union.

I referred in chapter 1 to Freud's (1921) observation that by projecting their ego ideal onto the leader, the members of a mob are able to eliminate individual moral constraints as well as the higher functions of self-criticism and responsibility that are mediated by the superego. As a result, primitive, ordinarily unconscious needs take over. And I described Bion's (1961) categorization of the regressive processes he observed in small groups in terms of three basic emotional assumptions, which determined how the group operated: the fight-flight assumption, the dependency assumption, and the pairing assumption. The fight-flight group expects the leader to direct a fight against what it vaguely perceives as external enemies and to protect the group from in-fighting. The group, however, cannot tolerate any opposition to the "ideology" shared by the majority of its members and easily splits into subgroups that fight one another. Small groups of this type, often of mixed sex, may temporarily bind borderline adolescents in an unstable and conflictual social subgroup, unlike the conventional one-sex group of normal early adolescence. Such groups do not usually develop a coherent ideology, although idealization of and submission to the leader of a street gang may stabilize the group within a generally chaotic social subculture.

NORMAL AND PATHOLOGICAL ALIENATION

The concept of alienation has had an important place in American psychosocial studies. It is particularly highlighted in Keniston's *The Uncommitted* (1965), a study of alienated youth in American society. As Keniston himself remarks, however, the meaning of the term *alienation* is ambiguous: it first acquired a significant sociological connotation in the early writings of Karl Marx, who coined the term to refer to the objective estrangement of humans from their social reality—that is, their subjugation by their own works, which have assumed the guise of independent entities (Ollman, 1976; Kolakowski, 1978a, 1978b).

In *The Sane Society,* Erich Fromm (1955) transformed the Marxist conception of alienation into the "self-alienation" of the individual who experiences a lack of contact between his or her conscious self and his or her "productive" potential. According to Fromm, this was a central feature of the "marketing personality" that was characteristic of capitalism. In the usage of Fromm and other social psychologists, the subjective experience of alienation from society is predominant, rather than the objective nature of the workers' alienation, which Marx stressed.

I see the sense of alienation as a basic alarm signal that alerts the normal member of a large group of the danger threatening her sense of identity as well as of the dangers inherent in the emergence of primitive emotions, particularly aggression, and the primitivization of thinking and judgment concomitant to large groups. The pathological, chronic sense of alienation experienced under ordinary social circumstances by patients with borderline personality organization and narcissistic personalities is strikingly similar to the alienation experienced by the normal personality when confronted by the activation of large-group processes or, to speak more generally, under social conditions in which ordinary role functions are suspended. A feeling of alienation may therefore express both severe psychopathology and a normal response to the threat to individual identity posed by the regressive effects of large-group processes.

This sense of alienation in the large group is responsible for the longing to transform the static nature of unstructured large-group processes into the action-oriented horde or mob described by Freud. The immediate solutions provided by idealization of the leader are amplified by the sense of power and the safe gratification of aggression in a mob that has found its external enemy. The large group, in contrast to the mob, propels its members to join in its search for a soothing ideology or the establishment of a rigid bureaucracy. A leader whose idealization transforms the large group into a mob or horde can also achieve control by the idealization of an ideology. Those who resist this pressure must be willing to pay the price of alienation and powerlessness within the mob in order to maintain their sense of identity.

The alienation of the patient with identity diffusion in relating to a normal social environment and that of the individual with a well-defined identity faced with large-group processes and mobs differ not simply in terms of duration. The temporary alienation of normal people in large groups and mobs in a free society may become permanent in totalitarian societies. When a society is transformed into one huge, regressive mob, the capacity to feel subjectively alienated may be considered an adaptive warning signal to protect ego identity. This brings us to the function of ideology as an expression not only of regressive group processes but also of normal value systems.

IDEOLOGY IN ADOLESCENCE

I use the term *ideology* in a broad sense, following a definition proposed by Althusser (as found in Green, 1969, p. 212): "An ideology is a system (with its corresponding logic and rigor) of representations (images, myths, ideas, or concepts) that possess a historical existence or function within a given society" (translation mine). Ideology, for Althusser, was an unconsciously determined system of illusory representations of reality, derived from the dominant conceptions a social group harbors about its own existence and internalized as part of the consolidation of the oedipal superego.

Two related aspects of ideologies require emphasis: the content of the ideology and the nature of the individual's commitment to it. Green suggests that the developmental stages of idealization may provide an important means of determining the level of psychological maturity involved in ideological commitments. From earliest narcissistic omnipotence through the intermediary stages of idealization of parental objects and the final consolidation of the ego ideal, the nature of the individual's commitment to ideologies would be determined by the extent to which they reflect the projection of an omnipotent self or the externalization of a mature ego ideal. The nature of the commitment may also influence the type of ideology selected, or the subtype within an ideological spectrum.

I agree with Green that the developmental stages of the mechanism of idealization, from the primitive idealization of good objects (split off from bad objects) to the projection of a pathological grandiose self to the idealization of objects out of an unconscious sense of guilt and, finally, to the establishment of ideal value systems as a reflection of the consolidation of the ego ideal determine the level of commitment to ideologies. The incapacity to commit oneself to any value system beyond self-serving needs usually indicates severe narcissistic pathology. Commitment to an ideology that includes sadistic demands for perfection and tolerates primitive aggression or a conventional naïveté in value judgments indicates an immature ego ideal and the lack of integration of a mature superego. Accordingly, identification with a messianic system and acceptance of social clichés and trivialities are commensurate with narcissistic and borderline pathology. By contrast, identification with more differentiated, open-ended, nontotalistic ideologies that respect individual discrimination, autonomy, and privacy and that tolerate sexuality while rejecting collusion with the expression of primitive aggression are characteristics of the mature ego ideal.

An ideology that respects individual differences and the complexity of human relations and leaves room for a mature attitude toward sexuality will appeal to those with a more mature ego ideal. Here, the liberation of the late adolescent from group mores as he or she moves toward couple formation becomes crucial. The capacity for falling in love and the development of love relations in late adolescence lead the couple to search for a shared system of values, an ideology that transcends the group and cements the couple. The romantic attitude of the single adolescent who is capable of falling in love leads her in the same direction. Thus, the search for an encompassing system of beliefs and for an ideology the couple can share in middle and late adolescence compensates for the sense of alienation that arises as the individual and the couple emerge from the group and links the late adolescent to the cultural and historical values of her society.

Simultaneously, the mutual need of the couple and the group for one another, a need that tends to diminish as the group gradually becomes transformed into a network of couples, also fosters a search for an ideology that is broad and universal, open and flexible, that respects individual thinking and differentiation, tolerates the differentiation of couples within the group, and formulates a task-oriented attitude toward society. The development of such an ideology further fosters the maturity of the individual, couples, and the group. Here I am referring to the search for an ideology that is broader and more task-oriented than the beliefs, values, and convictions of the adolescent couple or the romantic adolescent, an ideology that often centers around shared life goals in the arts, sciences, or social and political areas. The organization of civil defense in London during the air raids of World War II, the Peace Corps, and the organized campaigns for voter registration in the United States in the 1960s showed these qualities. The ideology represented by this kind of activity is characterized by open-ended values, restricted aims, a task-oriented interaction with the community, and a search for functional leadership. The activities themselves channel the sublimatory aspects of the search for new meanings and the organization of a worldview, the search for the enrichment of personal identity through historical context, and the search for group cohesion that respects the intimacy of couples; they also lead young adults toward participation in cultural and political processes in the adult community.

The development of this kind of ideology within a group requires a socially propitious atmosphere as well as an intelligent adaptation of adolescent groups to their society. There are historical moments when an entire country appeals to its youth in the context of a shared task, and there are dramatic moments when a social catastrophe brings out the best in everybody in the context of such group formation. In contrast, the rigid social structure of totalitarian societies leads to highly bureaucratized group structures that can tolerate only conventional and simplistic ideologies: adult couples frequently have to go underground and an Orwellian atmosphere prevails. Here, the capacity of the normal individual and couple to tolerate alienation from the social system may be the cost of preserving a sense of personal and moral integrity.

Paradoxically, however, an open society can also foster the development of overconventionalized adolescent groups in two very different ways. One way, already preformed in the normal group formation of latency and early adolescence, is represented by relatively unstructured, large-group formation, such as schools, factories, social organizations, and community clubs, where tolerance of individuals and of couples is guaranteed by certain rigid social conventions and a simplistic ideology of clichés that provides a minimal sociocultural structure and facilitates the projection of infantile superego features on the leadership at large. This relatively benign type of group—benign in the sense that it tolerates individual freedom and even couples—may become a haven for people with narcissistic personality structure. The loosely structured groups permit individuals to adapt socially without being threatened by excessive intimacy; these groups thus constitute an acceptable solution for a large number of people. Lasch's *Culture of Narcissism* (1978) describes the dominant ideology of such groups.

The other way an open society might lead to overconventional adolescent groups is by making available social subgroups or even subcultures that profess a messianic ideology.

MESSIANIC IDEOLOGIES, GANGS, AND TERRORISM

A messianic ideology is particularly attractive as a solution for the experience of alienation for many patients with borderline personality organization, including those narcissistic personalities who function on an overt borderline level.

In late adolescence the borderline personality cannot tolerate the loss of the protection of the conventional group as his normal and neurotic peers form into couples. The resulting exacerbation of his interpersonal conflicts, both in his home and in his immediate social group, might force him to withdraw socially while experiencing severe alienation or to reorganize the conventional large adolescent group into a small fight-flight group with antisocial behavior.

Severe feelings of alienation usually emerge in mid- and late adolescents with borderline personality organization. Alienation may take the form of schizoid withdrawal (see chapter 8), the adoption of a lonely and rebellious stance ("a negative identity" [Erikson, 1956]), severe polysymptomatic neurosis, or chronic impulsive acting out and self-destructive behavior. Narcissistic personalities may, in addition, arrogantly reject their environment.

An alternative solution is to move into a messianic cult that both reinforces and controls primitive defense operations, replaces the lack of internal controls by firm social control, and gratifies dependency needs by allowing identification with the group and its idealized leader. The extent to which the adolescent can freely express his aggression and the messianic group can rationalize it will determine the extent to which the group either legitimizes his sadism and criminality or protects him from them. The channeling of aggression in messianic cults takes various forms. In one, the devaluation of the parental home and its culture is rationalized, which may allow violent attacks against the parents while masking the aggression. Similarly, masochistic submission to cultist demands for obedience, including requirements to beg in the streets and the like, may foster reaction formations against aggression. The direct physical attack on enemies of the group socializes primitive aggression in its crudest forms.

Groups that form around a messianic ideology usually present the following characteristics: they divide the world into good and evil, which promotes the splitting of interpersonal relations into good (within the group) and bad (with rejected out-groups); they stress the totalistic quality of their belief system in the sense that they claim that it will resolve either all the problems of the world or all the problems of the group; they promote an enormous sense of power and meaning by promising a golden future while demanding complete submission to group rules and regulations in addition to full obedience and submission to the group's leader or his representatives. This kind of ideology requires a total commitment. Typically, it does not tolerate couples that have not been sanctioned and do not submit to the strict regulation of their private life, and it is often subtly or crudely antisexual in its ideology. In addition, it regulates many of the details of the members' daily lives.

Messianic group ideologies constitute a closed system of beliefs that is binding on all group members; all other values are reorganized in terms of the group's ideology. Messianic groups typically condense the personal lives of members with their political and ideological endeavors so as to eliminate individual boundaries, and they discourage private thinking and the acquisition of any knowledge that might threaten their belief system.

Such ideologies and their corresponding group formations transform the unstructured large group of social conventionality into the basic-assumptions group of fight-flight and/or dependency. If several such groups coalesce into a mass movement, they simultaneously acquire the quality of a horde or of a stabilized mob as well. Propitious social conditions may transform these groups into mass movements with significant historical impact, as happened, for example, in Germany during the 1920s and 1930s and in the Cultural Revolution in China. It is important to consider the extent to which the ideology rationalizes the use of aggression and actually fosters it against out-groups. When this occurs—as, for example, in the Marxist terrorist groups in Germany, Peru, and the Middle East—there is a great need to dehumanize all relationships other than those of the in-group. Hence, the constituency of such groups veers from the ordinary borderline to the outright antisocial personalities. The characteristics of the fundamentalist People's Temple of Jim Jones and the sociopsychological characteristics Dicks (1972) found in SS killers illustrate the relation between mass murder and institutionalized dehumanization.

Other groups with totalistic ideologies maintain relatively firm control over their members' expression of primitive aggression. Many religious cults in the United States, for example, serve as protective havens for adolescents with severe identity diffusion, borderline personality organization, and the incapacity to maintain relations with a large social group or even with a single other person. The religious cult provides controls over the individual's daily life, and these improve ego functions and gratify needs for dependency, closeness, and feelings of power and significance. The greed that motivates the leaders of many cults is usually unknown to the cult members, who may beg in the street and whose self-sacrifice serves sublimatory functions and as a defense against aggression by masochistic reaction formations.

The emotional security provided by a religious cult—protection against the painful alienation related to identity diffusion and the denial or restriction of aggression—compensate borderline adolescents for what they are renouncing in terms of personal privacy, freedom of thought, and a meaningful love relationship. Relatively normal adolescents, however, soon find the vague and simplistic ideology of cults insulting to their intelligence and rebel against the restrictions. Practically all the patients I have examined who have long-term commitments to religious cults presented severe types of character pathology. Because the early adolescent with borderline personality finds it easy to adjust to peer groups, he gives the impression of normalcy. Later on, however, his adherence to a cultist ideology may surprise those who knew him in earlier life.

There are group-centered ideologies that do not present the totalistic characteristics of religious cults and political terrorism. Street-gang psychology prevails when the group ideology directly affirms the indiscriminate expression of sexuality and aggression in combination with antisocial behavior. A group bound by this type of ideology may be socially the most maladaptive, the kind of group from which a member can free himself most easily, for it provides a milieu for its members without compensating them for the symptom of identity diffusion, and it tolerates the eruption of primitive sexuality and aggression.

The disappearance of the leader or the end of the group's illusion of his omnipotence may end the individual's emotional commitment to the group as well. The way leftist terrorist groups both in the United States and abroad have disintegrated into bands of ordinary criminals illustrates what can happen when the group's omnipotence is destroyed.

ALIENATION, AUTONOMY, AND THE COUPLE

In the small group, sexuality emerges in the basic assumption of pairing as a defense against primitive aggression. Here, the "oedipal couple" represents the longing for a sexual resolution of preoedipal conflicts expressed in the wishes, fears, and fantasies of the dependency and fight-flight groups. In the large group, sexuality is either denied or expressed in sadistically infiltrated sexual allusions. More mature forms of sexuality usually go underground, and the secret formation of couples occurs as a direct reaction to and defense against large-group processes. In the horde, unchallenged idealization of the leaders is the counterpart of the horde's intolerance of couples that attempt to preserve their identity as a couple. In the large group, the dominant sexual ideology tends to be marked by an excessive projection of primitive superego functions onto the group leader. Two curious alternatives emerge here: either a sexually repressive conventional ideology or a propensity to dissociate sexual fantasies from emotional relations, to combine devaluative and aggressive attitudes toward sex with fantasies in which preoedipal forms of sexuality—that is, polymorphous perverse infantile sexual trends—clearly predominates. The psychology of group sex illustrates the latter alternative. The two ideologies are similar, however, in that they produce a conventional morality that is directed against the sexual fulfillment of the autonomous couple. It is no coincidence that historically there have been oscillations between sexually repressive and sexually promiscuous ideologies: both aim to conventionalize and flatten the sexual experience of the couple.

Braunschweig and Fain (1971) described how furtive sexual play during the oedipal period is replaced by the antisexual groups of latency, groups where sexuality is tolerated in a depreciative, anal fashion. This depreciation becomes part of the early group mores of adolescent male sexuality. In late adolescence, open, collectively sanctioned affirmation of an aggressive promiscuity replaces the depreciatory, despised anal sexuality of early male adolescence. Among girls, the pseudomaturity of a formal, collectively shared ideology in early adolescence that demands that erotic sensuality be rejected—that is, that represses urges for direct sexual encounters with men—contrasts sharply with the simultaneous, collectively shared hysteriform idealization of an erotized male figure. Only in the latter half of female adolescence do these fantasies break down. The emerging mixed-gender group of late adolescence usually reflects a jointly accepted ideology of sexuality.

This adolescent ideology may reflect an identification with the conventional sexual morality of the adult society, as, for example, the celibacy adopted by adolescents in certain religious subcultures or the youth organizations of communist countries. Even when adolescents rebel against the conventional morality and advocate liberalized sex, their rebellion often hides a fear of commitment to a relationship between a man and a woman in which erotism and tenderness are combined.

There is a built-in, complex, and dangerous relationship between the couple and the group. A couple in isolation can destroy itself because it has no outlet other than itself for the aggression that is generated in all intimate relations (Kernberg, 1976). Because the couple's stability ultimately depends on its successfully establishing its autonomy within a group setting, it cannot escape from its relation to the group. Because the couple enacts and maintains the group's hope for sexual union and love in the face of the potential destructiveness of regressive large-group processes, the group needs the couple. But the group cannot escape its internal hostility and envy toward the couple, which derive, fundamentally, from envy of the happy, private union of the parents and from deep, unconscious guilt against forbidden oedipal strivings.

The inevitable conflicts between the couple and the group lead us back to the concept of alienation. As we have seen, this is both a normal and a pathological phenomenon. The alienated borderline patient has not achieved an integrated sense of identity and lacks a mature, integrated superego. The establishment of a pathological grandiose self to compensate for this identity diffusion results in a narcissistic personality. Both the identity diffusion of the borderline patient and pathological narcissism lead to a wish to submerge the self in large groups and mobs, because such groups offer the illusion of power and meaning that patients with these pathological character formations desperately seek. The patients' incapacity to achieve a stable sexual union with another that maintains firm boundaries separating it from the surrounding social group complements the pathological alienation of these patients.

But alienation is also felt by the normal individual whose integrated sense of identity and firmly established superego permit him to transcend the conventionality of the group, its restrictions of sexuality, and its cultural and intellectual flatness. This normal individual, as we have seen, experiences alienation where the emotionally disturbed person feels relief. The establishment of the autonomous couple that overcomes the oedipal restriction of each of the partners transforms the normal alienation of the individual into that of the couple. The achievement of this developmental stage is a crucial indicator of a successful completion of one of the tasks of adolescence.

Chapter 3 Mass Psychology Through the Analytic Lens

Freud's "Massenpsychologie und Ich-Analyse" (1921) is a bold outline of the contribution of psychoanalysis to mass psychology; its very title includes the term *mass psychology* (although it is usually translated "group psychology," as in the *Standard Edition*). Close to eighty years after its original publication, the book still offers an extremely rich contribution to readers interested in the psychoanalytic theory of organizational and group dynamics.

Mass psychology, although foreshadowed in some of Freud's earlier works ("Totem and Taboo," 1913; "On Narcissism," 1914; and "Beyond the Pleasure Principle," 1920), is developed fully only in this work. He returned to issues of mass psychology briefly in 1927, 1930, and 1939, but he neither added to nor modified the central concepts contained in the earlier work.

Reaching beyond the restricted psychoanalytic community, "Group Psychology and the Analysis of the Ego" has had an impressive, even fundamental, impact on philosophers, particularly the Frankfurt school; on sociologists, particularly Mitscherlich in Germany, Moscovici in France, and Lasch in the United States; and, finally, on another of the great twentieth-century humanists, Elias Canetti, whose book *Masse und Macht* (Crowds and power [1960]), which helped earn him the Nobel Prize for literature in 1980, was conceived under the direct challenge and stimulation of Freud's publication.

Perhaps the most comprehensive use of "Group Psychology" and its update to the present was achieved in Moscovici's *L'Age des foules* (The age of the crowds [1981]). There Moscovici critically retraces the background of Freud's book, as well as Freud's contribution to mass psychology, and illustrates Freud's theory of the historical origin of the primal horde in his analysis of the hero cult that was established in Soviet Russia after Lenin's death and its development during Stalin's totalitarian regime. Moscovici enriches Freud's perspective with his statement that "communication is the Valium of the people." He describes the combined effect of the activation of a pseudocommunity by mass communication that affects masses simultaneously and of the actual expansion of concentrated areas with large populations, thus creating conditions that foster the development of mass psychology. Moscovici agrees with Freud that mass psychology is as fundamental as individual psychology in determining cultural phenomena and considers Freud's contribution a crucial step in the development of mass psychology as a rigorous science.

Whereas Freud looks at mass psychology from the perspective of a concerned outsider who has not only recognized the dangerous, irrational, and violent power of mobs and mass movements but also discovered the intrapsychic dynamics that foster the individual's participation in and creation of mass psychology, Canetti (1960) explores it from the intoxicating perspective of being a participant in the mob—from the seductive, exciting, destructive inside. Moscovici adds the sociological perspective, the social and cultural factors contributing to the condensation of real and imaginary masses by means of modern communication systems and the population explosion. He thus takes up, at a deeper level, what Ortega y Gasset (1976 [1929]) had intuitively observed in his *La Rebelión de las Masas* (The rebellion of the masses). In fact, looking again at Freud's work from the perspective of these two "outsiders," the depth and scope of Freud's discoveries emerge in even sharper focus.

FREUD'S CENTRAL THESIS

In defining mass psychology, Freud (1921) proposed "to isolate as the subject of inquiry the influencing of an individual by a large number of people simultaneously, people with whom he is connected by something, though otherwise they may in many respects be strangers to him. Mass psychology is therefore concerned with the individual man as a member of a race, of a nation, of a caste, of a profession, of an institution, or as a component part of a crowd of people who have been organized into a mass at some particular time for some definite purpose" (p. 70, my translation). It is puzzling that although Freud himself clearly recognized McDougall's (1920) pivotal distinction between crowds and more organized types of group formation, the *Standard Edition* homogenizes all these concepts under the term *group*. A crowd is a large collection of people who have no formal organization; a horde or mob is a crowd that has a rudimentary but visible organization of direction, purpose, or motivation, usually characterized by a high emotional intensity. One might say that mobs are temporary hordes and that certain social and political conditions may transform a crowd into a mob.

Insofar as Freud was referring to the psychology of large collections of people characterized by some organized but highly emotional and irrational behavior, he was describing hordes or mobs. The term *mob,* however, has disparaging connotations that are absent in the German *Masse.* These connotations are inappropriate and irrelevant and should not be implied in the discussion that follows. Finally, Freud used the term *artificial masses* in referring to the Church and the army (see chapter 6), groups that correspond to what would now be designated specialized social organizations. Freud's treatise, therefore, deals with a vast spectrum of mass psychology, including that of crowds, mobs, social and political movements, and stable institutions or social organizations that are characterized by an organizational structure and leadership.

In this work, Freud described the primitive, emotionally driven, unreflective behavior of hordes or mobs. He explained the sense of immediate closeness or intimacy in mobs as being derived from the projection of members' ego ideals onto the leader and their identification with the leader as well as with one another. The projection of the ego ideal onto the idealized leader eliminates individual constraints along with the higher functions of self-criticism and responsibility that are mediated by the superego. (Throughout his essay, Freud used the term *ego ideal* rather than *superego,* which had not yet become part of his theoretical vocabulary.) The mutual identifications by the members of the mob bring about a sense of unity and belonging (which protects them, we might say today, from losing their sense of identity) but are accompanied by a severe reduction in ego functioning. As a result, primitive, ordinarily unconscious, needs take over, and the mob functions under the sway of emotions that are stimulated and directed by the leader. For Freud, the influence of the leader on the members of the mob is the primary cause of the mob's consolidation. By projecting their individual ego ideals onto the leader, the members of the mob create the precondition for their mutual identifications.

LIBIDO AS A BINDING FORCE
AND THE ROLE OF AGGRESSION

At first, Freud was explicit in stressing that the ties of all mass formations are libidinal (1921, pp. 94–95). He went to great lengths to point out that the projection of the ego ideal onto the leader and the attachment to the leader that replaces the attachment to the individual's own ego ideal clearly imply libidinal ties, while the mutual ties with the others reflect an identification, that is, the earliest form of object tie in a libidinal relationship.

In the second part of his essay (pp. 120–121), however, Freud argued against the origin of mass formation in the absence of a leader by pointing to the rivalry and envy between siblings and to the secondary, reactive nature of mutual identification in group formation in early childhood. Here, the earliest ties of the potential group formation of childhood (ties that, in Freud's view, are the basis of group and mass formations later on) are based on the reaction formation against aggression: the earliest ties, then, are aggressive, not libidinal. Also, as Freud describes the relationship between the primal horde and the primal father as its leader, the uncanny nature of this relationship parallels the uncanny aspect of the relationship that occurs in hypnosis. Freud describes the individual's fear of looking into the eyes of the leader, reflecting the representation of an all-powerful, dangerous, deified personality to whom the individual must react passively and masochistically. The horde wishes to be dominated by a personality with unlimited power, to bend and submit masochistically to that person's will. In his postscript, Freud reexamines the myth of the father of the primal horde, stressing that he was the ideal for each group member, simultaneously feared and admired, and that he thus gave rise to a community of brothers who had to deal with their guilt over his murder.

Only a year earlier, Freud had published "Beyond the Pleasure Principle" (1920), where he formulated for the first time the dual drive theory of libido and aggression; yet he does not apply the ideas contained there to his theory of mass psychology. In his description of the dynamics of mass formation he points to the importance of both aggression and libido, but in his theoretical formulation he confines himself to the libido theory alone. Even when describing how mobs break up when their members panic, he refers only to the fear of an outbreak of hostility and to the dissolution of libidinal ties.

From the perspective of contemporary psychoanalytic theory concerning the entire spectrum of group formation—from small and large groups to transitory and stable organizations—one would stress the importance of both libido and aggression, the functions of splitting processes that give rise to idealization and to persecutory fears, and other primitive defensive mechanisms that deal with this complex dialectic.

DYNAMIC CHARACTERISTICS OF VARIOUS GROUP FORMATIONS

In chapter 1, I suggested that some of the strikingly regressive features of small groups, large groups, and mobs might be better understood in light of our present knowledge of the internalized object relations that predate object constancy and the consolidation of the ego, superego, and id. Owing to the nature of the regression that occurs in groups, group processes pose a basic threat to members' personal identity, a threat that is linked to the tendency for primitive object relations, primitive defensive operations, and primitive aggression with predominantly pregenital features to be activated in group situations. These processes, particularly the activation of primitive aggression, are dangerous to the survival of the individual in the group, as well as to any task the group needs to perform.

I proposed that Turquet's (1975) description of what happens in large groups constitutes the basic situation against which both the idealization of the leader in the horde described by Freud and the small-group processes described by Bion (1961) defend. To follow the idealized leader of the mob blindly, as described by Freud, reconstitutes a sort of identity by identification with the leader, protects the individual from intragroup aggression by this common identity and the shared projection of aggression to external enemies, and gratifies dependency needs through submission to the leader. The sense of power experienced by individuals in a mob also gratifies primitive narcissistic needs. Paradoxically, the essentially irrational quality of mobs (that is, of crowds that are temporarily organized into groups by a shared idealization of a leader and a corresponding ad hoc ideology) better protects the individual against awareness of aggression than what obtains in large-group situations where there are no defined external enemies or in small groups where the enemy is part of the group itself.

Large-group processes also highlight the intimate connection between threats to identity and the fear that primitive aggression and aggressively infiltrated sexuality will emerge. My observations from the study of individual patients, small groups, and group processes in organizational and institutional life confirm the overwhelming nature of human aggression in unstructured group situations.

An important part of nonintegrated and nonsublimated aggression is expressed in vicarious ways by group and organizational processes. When relatively well-structured group processes evolve in a task-oriented organization, aggression is channeled toward the decision-making process, particularly when primitive leadership characteristics are evoked in people in positions of authority. Similarly, the exercise of power in organizational and institutional life constitutes an important channel for the expression of aggression in group processes that would ordinarily be under control in a dyadic or triadic relation. Aggression emerges more directly and intensely when group processes are relatively unstructured.

The multiplicity of primitive self- and object representations that predominate as intrapsychic structures of the individual before the consolidation of ego, superego, and id (and, therefore, before the consolidation of ego identity) and the regressive features of part-object relations that evolve when normal ego identity disintegrates parallel the relationships that exist between individuals in a large group.

There is a striking tendency in large groups to project superego functions on the group as a whole in an effort to prevent violence and protect ego identity by means of a shared ideology. The concomitant need of all group members to project and externalize superego functions onto the leader reflects not only sadistic and idealized aspects of primitive superego precursors but also the realistic and protective aspects of more mature superego functioning. The indissoluble union of primitive and advanced aspects of the superego makes this a tragic externalization: the morality of groups and institutions that are influenced by projection of primitive superego features comes closer to the primitive morality of the unconscious superego than to the conscious morality of the mature individual. (See chapter 15.)

In earlier work (Kernberg, 1984a, 1986, 1989a, 1989b, 1991), I examined the nature of the defensive activation of idealization processes under various group conditions in relation to the activation of paranoid developments in them. In contrast to the dominant characteristics of the unstable, threatening, potentially violent, and identity-diffusion-fostering large group, small groups reveal the idealization-persecution dichotomy in their respective activation of Bion's (1961) dependency and fight-flight groups. The activation of the pairing assumption may be considered an effort to escape the primitive conflicts involved with aggression, primitive object relations, and primitive defenses through ambivalent idealization of a selected sexual pair. The large group does not usually split into small groups but rather becomes a static large group that has the quality of what Canetti (1960) described as the typical feasting crowd, engaged, we might say, in dependent and narcissistic behavior and in a corresponding search for a calming, narcissistic, reassuring mediocrity in their leader.

I have described this level of regression as characteristic of the mass psychology of conventionality (see chapter 15); it reflects the ideology characteristic of a latency child superego and represented typically by mass entertainment. As an alternative, the large group evolves into a dynamic mob characterized by predominantly paranoid features and the selection of paranoid leaders; it is typically represented by the mass psychology of revolutionary movements. Conventional culture, on the one hand, and violent revolutionary movements with totalitarian ideology, on the other, may be considered the corresponding mass psychological outcomes of idealization and persecution as basic group phenomena.

At a more advanced level of organization, which involves more mature forms of mass psychology as described by McDougall (1920) and Freud, Bion characterizes the army as the institutional structuralization of the fight-flight group and the Church as the institutional structuralization of the dependency group. Functional social organizations in government, industry, education, and health care represent the maximum control, reduction, and sublimation of mass psychology as part of organizational task systems. Here, the interesting issue is that, regardless of the protective and corrective measures instituted by social organizations—such as functional leadership and appropriate bureaucratic organizational systems (with means for redressing grievances and other measures geared to reduce *paranoiagenesis;* see chapter 8)—aggression, in the form of sadistic behavior, will inevitably develop in institutions and will infiltrate the institutional process at various points, including through the very mechanisms that usually protect the institution from excessive paranoiagenesis.

In summary, then, the unavoidable activation of primitive aggression in the individual's functioning within social groups reflects a universal latent disposition for regression to preoedipal levels of intrapsychic organization. Within this regression, the projection of aggression onto parental figures, the reintrojection of such parental figures under the distorted conditions of projected aggression, and the consequent vicious circles involving the projection and introjection of aggression are dealt with by massive splitting mechanisms, which lead to idealization processes on the one hand and to paranoid, persecutory processes on the other. These primitive psychic operations, derived ultimately from the earliest dyadic relationship with the mother, resonate with later triangular problems, reflecting the oedipal situation, and transform the disposition to multiple preoedipal transferences into a displacement into typical triangular oedipal ones that become dominant in the relationship with authority. The distortion of rational authority resulting from these projective processes, in turn, leads to the defensive activation of narcissistic affirmation, regressive relationships to feared or idealized parental leadership, and finally a generalized tendency to reproject the more advanced aspects of superego functioning onto the total institution.

The projection of superego functions onto the entire institution increases the subjective dependency of the individual on the institution's evaluation of him or her, decreases the individual's capacity to rely on internalized value systems, and provides a trigger for the individual's contamination by ideological crosscurrents, rumors, and regression into primitive depressive and persecutory anxieties when objective feedback and reassurance in the organization fail. Under these conditions, there is a threat not only of emotional and characterological regression in the personality but also of regression in the moral dimension of individual functioning. Here the "paranoid urge to betray" (Jacobson, 1971a) is merely a logical consequence.

Reexamining Freud's essay in light of these contributions, we see that his description of mass psychology corresponds chiefly to the characteristics of large groups and to mob and horde formation. Freud's emphasis on the libidinal links between members as a defense against envious rivalry corresponds precisely to the condensation of and defense against preoedipal, and particularly oral, envy and oedipal rivalry that characterizes the activation of primitive object relations during large-group processes. Freud's description of the ambivalent relation to leadership—the combination of idealization and what might be called paranoid fears of the leader with submission and subservience to him—reflect the struggle between idealizing and persecutory processes that is characteristic of large groups and mobs.

In fact, when Freud (1921, pp. 129–133) points to the remarkable lack of differentiation between the ego and the ego ideal under many circumstances, and to the consequent implication that the relation to the leader becomes in essence an identification of the individual's ego with the leader, he is describing the narcissistic gratification of the exercise of power as part of mass psychology, the sense of freedom from moral constraints, and omnipotence given by what Canetti (1960) described as the *density* of the dynamic mob. The mob, by means of libidinal gratification in the form of primitive narcissism and aggressive gratification in the infiltration of the leader's and the mob's grandiosity and omnipotence with aggression, acquires characteristics analogous to the patient with the syndrome of malignant narcissism (see chapters 7, 8, and 15). Freud comes close to defining the aggressive as well as libidinal sources of mutual identification of the mob as a profound motivation for the way mobs behave.

I question Freud's assertion that it is the personality of the leader that consolidates the mob. Rice's and Turquet's experiences with large groups illustrate the immediate regression into a primitive type of mass psychology of the unstructured large group. Anzieu's and Chasseguet-Smirgel's findings suggest that there is always an implicit primitive leadership in the fantasy of small- and large-group formation, a leadership closer to the primitive maternal ego ideal than to the father of the primal horde. Yet even granting this fantasy structure, it would seem to defend against the basic threats to identity and of violence in the large group. In short, mass psychology predates the crystallization of the identification with the leader.

IDENTIFICATION PROCESSES AND THE NATURE OF LEADERSHIP

Throughout his discussion of identification and the ego ideal, Freud focuses almost exclusively on the father as object, mentioning the mother only in connection with male homosexuality, as in his paper on narcissism (1914). He proposes that identification is the first type of object relations and that becoming like the object will evolve into a potential regression from the wish to have an object. He does not, however, explore the male and the female infants' identifying themselves with mother as the earliest object. Today, thanks to Freud's subsequent full-fledged conceptualization of the superego (1923), we are aware of the various developmental levels of identification processes and can differentiate earliest introjections from later partial identifications and from complex identity formation.

Above all, the dyadic nature of all identification processes, that is, that identification occurs not with an object but with a relation between self and object, is a concept that emerged years after Freud's death as a result of the contributions of Fairbairn (1954), Klein (1946), Erikson (1956), Jacobson (1964), and Mahler (Mahler and Furer, 1968).

The nature of primitive, part-object relations related to splitting processes and expressed by primitive projective and introjective mechanisms in the group situation can be differentiated from more advanced types of internalized whole or integrated object relations that more clearly reproduce the dyadic and triangular relations of early family life. I propose that one can consider two levels of internalized object relations: A basic level would be characterized by multiple self- and object representations that correspond to primitive fantasy formations linked with primitive impulse derivatives. Each unit of self- and object representation carries a particular affect state and is split off from corresponding units with diametrically opposed affect states. The second and higher level of internalized object relations would be characterized by sophisticated, integrated self- and object representations that are linked with higher levels of affect dispositions. These higher level object relations reflect more accurately than do the basic level object relations of infancy and early childhood the experiences and conflicts between the individual and his or her real parental figures and siblings. At the higher level, the integrated self-concept, together with integrated, related, and realistically invested object representations constitute ego identity.

Regardless of the individual's maturity and psychological integration, unstructured small and large groups that lack an operational leadership or clearly defined tasks that can relate them to their environment tend to cause an immediate regression in the individual. This regression consists of the activation of defensive operations and interpersonal processes that reflect primitive object relations. The potential for such regression exists within all of us. When we lose our ordinary social structure, when our ordinary social roles are suspended, and when multiple objects are present simultaneously in an unstructured relationship, reproducing in the interpersonal field the multiplicity of primitive intrapsychic object relations, then primitive levels of psychological functioning tend to be reactivated. It is this propensity to regress that determines the threat to personal identity and the fear that primitive aggression will be activated in unstructured group situations and that motivates the typical defensive operations in the groups I have described. This is the basic dynamic that promotes group psychology and underlies mass psychology at all levels.

Another proposed modification of Freud's views concerns the nature of the symbolic meaning of the leadership of small and large groups. Here I draw on the work of Jacobson (1964) and Chasseguet-Smirgel (1975). In summary, the projection of superego constituents on group leadership depends on both the level of organization of an individual's superego structure and on the nature and extent of regression under which a group operates. Typically, under conditions of advanced types of large-group regressions in the static large group with either benign narcissistic leadership or a leadership that fosters an ambivalent narcissistic dependency and a moderately moralistic ideology, the individual's regression is to the latency period, and the projection is of the latency-period superego, with its typical infantile value systems. These values embrace a simplistic, conventional, black-or-white morality. In addition, oedipal prohibitions are in place, as is the corresponding dissociation of affective engagement from genital erotism. Mass culture also corresponds to this ideology and to its dominant artistic expression, kitsch; the corresponding leadership is perceived as akin to the oedipal father from the advanced oedipal stage of childhood.

When regression develops further, from the narcissistic-dependent to the persecutory-paranoid type of leadership, the activation is of the early, prohibitive oedipal superego, the father who potentially threatens the child with castration for his untamed oedipal rivalry and violence. Here the leader is seen as the prohibitive—in contrast to the generous—father. Even further regression in the group situation brings us to the pseudopaternal promoter of illusions described by Chasseguet-Smirgel (1975), who is characteristic of the primitive ego ideal that depends mostly on the introjection of the preoedipal, all-giving, all-gratifying maternal image. This ego ideal, in turn, protects the individual and the group against archaic aggression toward the mother and toward the distorted maternal image (resulting from projection), which is viewed as extremely threatening. This archaic level of aggression is typically expressed as violence against an external world that threatens the utopia of the gratifying group-breast described by Anzieu (1971). Finally, we may point to the mature superego derived from the postoedipal parental couple—that performs the rational, protective, moral functions of the parents—as the symbolic meaning of the rational leadership of functional organizations, the polarity opposite to large-group regression.

In contrast to Freud's description of the prototypical leader of the mob as the symbolic father of the primal horde, we may now formulate a spectrum of different types of symbolic leaders, each of whom reflects the level of regression in the group. Bion (1961) first pointed to the "role suction" of small groups, where the dependency group tends to promote infantile narcissistic (and even psychopathic) leaders, in contrast to the fight-flight group, which seeks a leader with paranoid characteristics. Freud described some qualities that are required of the leader of the mob that are relevant here. He pointed out (1921, p. 123) that the leader needs to be free from needing the love of others, able to love himself and thus to crystallize, in his narcissistic self-love, the aspirations of the crowd for a jointly projected ego ideal. The leader must be self-confident, independent, and self-assured; he may be dominant and absolutely narcissistic. Freud notes (p. 127) that the leader must also be able to evoke fear and convey an unlimited power to control the group.

In light of contemporary contributions to the analysis of leadership functions, including those stemming from a psychoanalytic background, and in light of the nature of the regressive group processes I have examined, I propose five major, desirable personality characteristics for rational leadership: (1) intelligence; (2) personal honesty and incorruptibility; (3) a capacity for establishing and maintaining object relations in depth; (4) a healthy narcissism; and (5) a healthy, justifiable anticipatory paranoid attitude, in contrast to naïveté. The latter two characteristics are perhaps the most surprising and yet the most important aspects of task leadership, already pointed to in Freud's 1921 essay. A healthy narcissism protects the leader from an overdependency on the approval of others and strengthens her capacity for autonomous functioning; a healthy paranoid attitude makes her alert to the dangers of corruption and paranoiagenic regression (the acting out of diffuse aggression unconsciously activated in all organizational processes) and protects her from a naïveté that would make her unable to analyze the motivational aspects of institutional conflicts.

The danger is that organizational regression will accentuate the narcissistic and paranoid features of leadership and will constitute powerful regressive forces that mobilize further regression along narcissistic-dependent or paranoid-sadistic lines. This regressive development, however, is precisely what characterizes mass psychology at all levels: the always present danger that the aggressive drive derivatives that infiltrate social and institutional life will corrupt the very mechanisms established to control them. I suggest a modified formulation of mass psychology. In essence, both leaders and the people in groups regress along two axes: dependency, narcissism, primitive hedonism, psychopathy; and moralism, paranoid-persecutory control, sadism, violence.

Part Two **Institutional Dynamics and Leadership**

Chapter 4 Leadership and Organizational Functioning

This chapter is a continuation of earlier efforts to apply psychoanalytic object-relations theory, a psychoanalytic theory of group processes, and an open-systems theory of social organizations to the study of psychiatric institutions and of the therapeutic methods carried out there (Kernberg, 1973, 1975b). I focus on the connection between the administrator's personality, the organizational structure, group processes occurring in the organization, and organizational tasks.

Sometimes, the performance of all tasks related to treatment, research, and education seems to be limited by the leader's personality. Often the staff see the leader as arbitrary and authoritarian, a person who uses his power to impose courses of action that are detrimental to commonly shared goals. But this perception may be a misperception. There is often a shared conception—or fantasy—among staff of the leader as lacking in understanding, as arrogant and revengeful, but outside consultants, particularly those who employ modern approaches to organizational diagnosis, may find a different situation, sometimes quite a complex one.

The effectiveness of the leadership of the organization does not depend exclusively or even predominantly on the leader's personality. The first requirement for effective functioning of an organization—including its leadership—is the adequate relation between the organization's overall task and its administrative structure; the task must be meaningful rather than trivial, and feasible, given the available resources, rather than overwhelming. Psychiatric institutions operate within various environments, and their effectiveness in carrying out therapeutic, educational, and research tasks depends on the adequacy of their human and material resources, as well as on the nature of their interaction with the environment. When these resources are insufficient to the tasks or when the normal flow of resources and "products" across the boundaries of the institution breaks down or when contradictory goals or failure to clarify priorities interfere with the functional relation between task and administrative structure, the task-group structures in the organization deteriorate, morale breaks down, and the group processes within the organization regress. This regression, in turn, powerfully affects the quality and effectiveness of leadership.

The development of group fight-flight or dependency assumptions moves the leaders of what were task-oriented groups to take stands that complement the emotional needs of their members or staff. A staff that expects a primitive kind of leadership from an omnipotent, giving figure (in the dependent group) or a powerful or dangerous, controlling authority (in the fight-flight group) tempts or provokes the task leader to regress to that role.

A breakdown in the ability to do the work that is caused by various internal factors and relations between the organization and the environment, then, first induces regressive group processes and then leads to regression in the functioning of the leadership. If these group processes remain undiagnosed, only their end product may be visible, in the form of what appear to be primitive, inadequate leadership and, more specifically, negative effects on the organization created by the leader's personality.

The group processes occurring in psychiatric institutions are, however, influenced by more than the level of task orientation or the appropriateness of the task with regard to administrative and therapeutic structures. The nature of the task carried out in psychiatric institutions, particularly in settings where severely regressed patients are treated, also exerts a powerful influence on these group processes. I am referring here to the replication of the pathological internal world of object relations induced by borderline and psychotic patients in the group processes involving staff and patients. At certain times, severely regressed patients may induce basic-assumptions–group processes in both formal and informal patient-staff groups on a service, and this negatively affects group leadership and possibly the administrative structure of the entire service. In this regard, one might say that the nature of the "product" handled by psychiatric institutions, namely, primitive and deep human conflict, deeply influences the functioning of such institutions.

Again, in this case, only the end product of a process may be visible, and the administrator of the service or of the hospital may appear arbitrary, threatening, and irrational. Only a careful organizational analysis may bring to the surface the relation between problems of patients at the grass-roots level and those among the leadership.

Yet it is always possible that serious psychopathology in the leader is, indeed, responsible for the problems of morale, breakdown of task groups, and development of regressive group processes. It then becomes necessary to differentiate the symptomatic activation of emotional regression in the leader that reflects problems in the institution, from the deterioration of organizational functioning that reflects psychopathology in the leader.

Traditional analysis of institutional management focuses on the leader's personality, particularly her inborn characteristics (such as charisma) and her authoritarian qualities. Psychoanalytic thinking has focused on the distorted perception that staff may have of the administrator or leader as a function of the irrational relations with authority that stem from infantile conflicts, particularly the oedipal situation. More recent sociological thinking stresses the role aspects of leadership; that is, the activation of socially sanctioned and recognized functions in which leader and follower have mutually reinforcing perceptions and behavior. This sociological analysis focuses on the confusion that often develops in organizations between the leader's personality, her behavior when performing certain roles, and the perception of that behavior by staff who cannot easily differentiate role from personality (particularly, of course, when perception of the leader is distorted by unconscious conflicts).

But the application of psychoanalytic methods to the study of small-group processes reveals the activation in nonstructured and informal groups of primitive emotional contents and defensive operations that are ordinarily latent in all individuals and become manifest only in patients with severe regression, such as borderline conditions and the nonorganic psychoses. These findings further complicate the study of the interactions that involve the personality of the leader, her behavior, the perception of that behavior by the staff, and the mutual induction of regressive behavior by staff and leader under the influence of regressive group processes. It is at this point that a systems approach may be helpful not only in clarifying the mutual influences of the leader's personality, group processes, organizational structure, and organizational tasks but also in pointing to the major origins of the distortions affecting them. A systems approach to organizations considers the institution as an overall system that is dynamically and hierarchically integrating various subsystems (such as the personality of leader and the nature of group processes, in addition to the ordinary task systems and administrative structures of the organization); it defines the environment of the organization as composed of suprasystems that affect the institution in dynamically and hierarchically organized ways (Dolgoff, 1973; Levinson and Klerman, 1967; Rice, 1963, 1969).

In addition to being a theoretically satisfying model, a systems approach can have significant diagnostic and corrective impact on the work in psychiatric institutions. Such an approach is in contrast to linear and mechanical models, which attribute the sources of organizational disturbances to a single member of the sub- or suprasystems mentioned. Systems analysis, for example, contrasts with a model that perceives the fluctuation of group processes (from task-oriented to regressive) as the origin of all institutional conflicts; if the leader appears to be authoritarian or demagogic, it is the group that is making him behave that way; if patients become regressed, it is because the group is putting its illness into them, and so forth. Or else—another example of a nonsystems approach—the leader is to blame for everything; the staff feels powerless and paralyzed because of the irrational, authoritarian leader. The attribution of blame to the leadership often not only reflects the staff's effort to deny serious conflicts between staff and patients and to project them onto the leader (the director of the unit, service, or the institution) but also serves to protect the staff from awareness of its own responsibility in protecting and perpetuating the authoritarian structure.

At times the nature of the task is overwhelming, as when an ideology that conceives of psychiatric treatment as so powerful that all patients should be able to improve is confronted with the illusionary nature of this conviction (as demonstrated by treatment outcomes over an extended period). Then, too, there are poor leaders. It is important to be able to differentiate this situation from the much more frequent case in which the leadership represents a symptom of the problem rather than its cause. Otherwise, most of the energy in an institution may be expended on "curing" the leader; perhaps the surprising capacity of so many people in so many places to tolerate such a situation over an extended period indicates how gratifying it is to attribute the cause of all problems to the administrator, rather than to focus on the painful and complex interaction of the various systems involved in bringing about his behavior.

So far, I have not mentioned the political dimension of these conflicting interests among groups that influence their relation to the task as well as to the leader and management at large. If we conceive of political strivings as the conscious or unconscious efforts of individuals or groups to defend their interests and expand their influence over individuals and groups at their boundaries, political action becomes a normal aspect of institutional interactions. Insofar as group interests stem from group members' identifications with social, cultural, or professional values, conflicts develop between belonging to task or nontask determined groups, which are called sentience groups (Miller and Rice, 1967). "Sentience" here refers to the emotional bonds that influence group formation and cohesiveness; such bonds may derive from the task performance itself or from past or present, real or fantasied commonalities that link individuals in groups. ("We shall therefore talk of *sentient system* and *sentient group* to refer to that system or group that demands and receives loyalty from its members; and we shall talk of *sentient boundary* to refer to the boundary around a sentient group or sentient system" [Miller and Rice, 1967, p. xiin].) Political strivings may reflect the efforts to bring about an optimal equilibrium between these conflicting identifications.

However, when political strivings evolve into an ideological commitment to establish an optimal equilibrium between politically opposite groups regardless of task requirements, a new complication for organizational functioning has arisen. The fundamental purpose of psychiatric institutions is a professional and technical one, rather than a political one, and serious distortions in the task and in group processes, administrative structures, and leadership may evolve when political objectives replace task-oriented or functional goals. For example, "democratization" of an administrative structure may be perceived as an ideal solution to organizational conflicts, but it can also lead to the deterioration of task groups, specialized skills, and individual functions and responsibilities. It is an illusion that authoritarianism in institutions can be successfully overcome by democratization of them, rather than by a functional analysis of task requirements and the functional administrative structures that correspond to them. There are dictatorships of groups as well as of individuals, and these can result as much from paralysis as from capriciousness at the top.

Let me offer a few clinical examples of these theoretical formulations.

CASE 1

In a department of psychiatry, a chronic problem with morale and the chaotic functioning of the nursing service led hospital administrators to hire a strong director of nursing who would be given full authority to reorganize the department. The assumption had been that the department had discouraged strong nursing in the past and that to bring in a strong nurse at the top represented a commitment to nursing. The new director of nursing did indeed establish a powerful personal leadership, increasing the power and prestige of the nursing service in the process. However, she developed a new organizational structure, "team nursing," without considering the recent introduction of interdisciplinary teamwork that was being developed throughout the hospital at the same time. The two concepts of teamwork resulted in new conflicts between the nursing staff and the other professions, as well as in resentment among the nursing staff over the interference by the administrations of the other disciplines.

The new director of nursing had difficulties in explaining the department's emphasis on interdisciplinary work to her staff, and in communicating the new nursing plans and developments to the department. In other words, she had trouble carrying out the "boundary functions" that were an essential part of her leadership. After a period of growing conflict between the department's administration and the nursing staff, in the course in which the battle of mutual distortion, accusation, and incomprehension escalated rapidly, the director of nursing resigned and left. Once she was gone, however, the myth developed among the nursing staff that she had been forced to leave because she was too strong a leader. This myth was dispelled only when a new director of nursing, who was, if anything, even stronger than her predecessor, was hired. The new director was able to diagnose and successfully carry out the basic tasks of the nursing service in consonance with the task definition of the entire department. Eventually, the department perceived the second director of nursing as highly effective rather than as overly strong, and the nursing staff itself gradually recognized her as a much better leader. This case illustrates problems in task definition and boundary control. Technical failures in the leadership induced regressive group processes across the boundaries between nursing staff and the rest of the department; the personality problems of the individual leader were not the issue.

CASE 2

The activities department of a psychiatric hospital perceived its leader as inefficient, weak, and wavering; an organizational analysis of the functions of the department revealed that during the leader's tenure the hospital had been reorganized along a compartmental basis. This led to a contradiction between having independent hospital units on the one hand and trying to integrate the various units of the activities department, on the other. This contradiction had brought about innumerable complications in scheduling meetings, in communication, and in interdisciplinary work. The administrative structure and functions of the activities department were consequently changed by a joint effort of the department and the medical director to accommodate the developments in the hospital, with the result that the activities staffing and functions became flexibly integrated into the new units, while certain activities specialists were still available for the hospital. The activities department personnel fundamentally altered their perception of the departmental leadership. The director and his associates were now seen as strong and reliable. We see here how the perception of weak leadership was a symptom of problems in the organizational structure of the department rather than a reflection of the personalities involved.

CASE 3

In one hospital service, an acute conflict concerning a particular difficult patient erupted among the service director, several senior consultants, the psychiatric resident in charge of the treatment, and various other staff members, who took positions in one of two feuding fields. An in-group, led by the service director, considered that the patient had been treated too leniently, that insufficient hospital-milieu structure had been provided, and that acting out of rebelliousness against authority figures by the resident had complicated the treatment situation: the patient was seen as acting out the resident's rebellion. An "out-group," consisting of various staff members, the psychiatric resident, and his supervisor, all felt that the patient's ego weakness had been underestimated, that more time and patience were needed rather than consistent confrontation. This group perceived the service director as ruthless and domineering in his handling of the clinical conferences in which the case was discussed.

Analysis of the situation showed that specific intrafamilial dynamics of the patient had been activated and projected onto the staff relationships, intensifying the potential conflicts around authority and power of all those involved in the patient's treatment. Once this was clarified and the split among the staff was healed, better understanding of the patient's dynamics could be used in his psychotherapeutic and hospital-milieu treatment (Kernberg, 1975a). This illustrates the regressive effects of the patient's pathology on the nature of the interactions among staff and on the perception of the leadership of the service as authoritarian.

CASE 4

Conflicts developed in a psychiatric hospital between the departments of rehabilitation, occupational therapy, and recreational therapy. These conflicts were first perceived as personal power struggles between the leaders of two of the three groups; it later emerged that the leader of one of the groups had indeed been given some authority over the other two, but without a clear mandate over who controlled the joint boundaries of the three departments. Insofar as the three departments continued to function autonomously and clear coordination or integration of their activities was impossible, the leader who had been tentatively selected to direct the entire area projected an image of uncertainty and doubt.

The question arose: Where does the problem lie? In the personality of the leader who was unable to assert his authority over the entire area? In the nature of the administrative structure of the three departments, which were confusingly intermingled? In the nature of the task, which had become unclear as changes in the hospital philosophy and use of occupational, recreational, and rehabilitative services clashed with the departments' traditional experience?

This example illustrates the diagnostic process required to answer the question of where the source of the problem resides. In order to arrive at an answer, we must start by defining, first, the nature of the task and its constraints; second, the optimal administrative structure required for it; third, the nature and amount of the authority required by the leader; fourth, the leader's technical and conceptual skills and liabilities; and, finally, the leader's personality characteristics, which could be involved in the problem.

For practical purposes, it is sometimes helpful to simply hire a new leader, selecting a person with known and proven conceptual, technical, and personal skills (Katz, 1955) to diagnose both the nature of the task and the administrative structure necessary to do it. Selection of the leader thus precedes diagnosis of the other factors in the hope that a solution will become available before the problem is fully diagnosed. An alternative method exists, namely, to first diagnose the nature of the task and the administrative structure necessary for it and only then to search for the best leader to fit into that structure. This second method is slower and requires more input from the organization at large before a leader can be chosen, but it may be less risky than the first method. It is much easier to hire the right person when the nature of the task and its constraints have been clarified. However, time considerations or political organizational constraints may make the first method preferable. In either case, the analysis of task priorities and respective administrative requirements should provide a safety margin against problems that may reemerge (rightly or wrongly) under the mask of personality difficulties in the new leader. Hidden contradictions between organizations' apparent, expressed goals and their real, underlying goals sometimes reveal themselves in the symptomatic act of selecting one incompetent or naive leader after another for an impossible task.

From the administrator's viewpoint, unresolved problems in her personality and unresolved problems in the nature of the specific tasks of the organization and its administrative structures are not the only sources of regressive pressures on her ability to function. The executive administrator of a psychiatric institution occupies various boundaries. First, she occupies the boundary between the organization and its social environment, and contradictions in and pressures from the social environment, as well as those stemming from within the institution, may affect her psychological functioning. Second, she is at the boundary between her professional background or convictions (her sentience) and the nature of the task. Third, she is at the boundary between her personal value systems and ethical commitments and the task requirements of relating to a human, social organization. Conflicts of loyalty regarding moral convictions and other difficult choices may predominate at times, creating regressive pressures on her functioning. In summary, from a practical standpoint, the major forces determining the effectiveness of leadership stem from: (a) the leader's personality; (b) the nature of her technical and conceptual skills; (c) the adequacy of task definitions, availability of human and material resources, and priority settings of the institution; and (d) the adequacy of the administrative structure to the task requirements.

A major tool in evaluating the optimal functioning of an administrator's system is the exploration of group processes within his unit, ward, service, hospital, department, or institution. The technical use of his knowledge of group processes will permit him to evaluate the extent to which task groups function as "work groups" or are being influenced by basic group assumptions (Bion, 1961). Analysis of the content of any regressive group processes can reveal the nature of the institution's hidden agenda and thus provide a test of the adequacy of task performance and of the administrative structure. At the same time, and insofar as patients are treated as individuals or as groups within the institution, analysis of such regressive group processes will facilitate important diagnostic work regarding the conflicts within the internal world of the object relations of patients. Both kinds of regressive pressures, that is, the organization's hidden agendas and the distortions of the social processes induced by regressed patients, will highlight the distorted way in which the administrator is viewed or the transferential reactions to him as he carries out his professional and administrative roles. The analysis of regressive group processes, in short, may reveal the effects of organizational and patient conflicts and thus help in the evaluation by elimination of the extent that the administrator's personality is complicating the situation and creating stress and regression in the group processes in the organization.

FRUSTRATION OF BASIC HUMAN NEEDS
IN THE LEADERSHIP FUNCTION

Various aspects of administration or management place powerful regressive pressures on the administrator's psychological functioning. Among these are the loneliness of his position, the loss of spontaneous and unconstrained feedback from peers, and the uncertainty that accompanies significant decision making. Oedipal fears of failure or defeat, the frustration of dependent needs, and the general activation of conflicts over aggression in the administrator as a leader of and participant in various group processes all contribute to inducing this regressive pull. Nor is this all. There is the general "invasive" nature of administrative concerns: the constant invasion of the privacy of his thinking by pressing organizational issues for which no immediate solution can be found; the invasion of his private life as his public work impinges on it, reducing his time for careless leisure and freedom; the threat to the freedom of his fantasy life as his internal relations to people and nature, to art and leisure become contaminated by the stress that is related to responsibilities that always remain with him.

Aggressive Needs

Although creative administration may permit the expression of aggressive needs in sublimated form, there are also temptations to resolve such tensions by the sudden exertion of authority. Groups too readily tempt their leaders into impulsive action, but the leader must resist these temptations: he is usually aware that loss of control over his angry impulses may have devastating effects far beyond those occurring in other, ordinary situations. The role aspects of his functioning—the formal organizational authority he enacts—and the unavoidable transferential distortion of the perception of his behavior by staff may amplify his expression of aggression dangerously and may bring about paranoid distortions in the minds of his staff.

The activation of primitive aggressive needs in the administrator ordinarily depends more upon the regressive pull of group processes in the organization than upon his personality characteristics. There certainly are leaders with strong sadistic trends, and given the amplification of the leader's aggressive behavior by the staff's transferential perceptions and reactions, even relatively minor outbursts become major issues in the organization, but the influence of group processes in triggering and amplifying such reactions in the leader cannot be underestimated. For example, when a regressive group process corresponding to Bion's fight-flight assumption occurs, the leader of this basic assumption in the group—often representing the opposition—may provoke the administrative leader into a personal fight.

Often the most extreme, paranoid, oppositional member of the staff takes over group leadership at such a juncture and appears to control both the group and the administrative leader himself, a development that may induce paranoid, regressive processes in the administrator, who may now fear that the most vehement and irrational of his opponents has taken control of the group. The administrator may react with exaggerated fear, anger, and authoritarianism against the challenger, and thereby miss the internal conflicts in the staff group, that is, the silent support for the challenge that exists in the group. He might also miss the criticism of the violence among themselves by other staff. The administrator's awareness of group processes and of his own reactions to them may be helpful in transforming this potentially dangerous situation into a creative one.

The leader of any group or organization is constantly faced with the expression of aggression of various sources by those under him. From the viewpoint of individual psychology, the aggression directed at the parental images and its expression or projection onto the leader is an important aspect of group life: disappointment, rage, and rebellious hatred are the counterparts of idealization of and submission to the leader that stem from oedipal and preoedipal relations to the parents. Bion (1961) suggests that the inordinate expectations of the dependent group bring about hatred of the task leader who frustrates the group's need for complete gratification and its longings for unlimited dependency. The fight-flight group struggles with aggression against the task leader, who is perceived in distorted, paranoid ways as a vengeful, dangerous authority. In more global terms, the task leaders' consistently explaining the realistic parameters of the task, and thus destroying the hopes and longings of basic assumptions, evokes frustration and aggression.

Because the leader or executive head of an organization does have limitations and make mistakes, there are always grounds for the staff's feelings of frustration and anger, for staff members' rationalizing the deeper levels of their irrational hatred of him in terms of his human limitations. Therefore, hatred of authority usually seems logical enough, and this compounds the actual distortions of leadership functions.

The various origins of the hatred of a particular leader are usually condensed, however, and it is frequently hard to judge whether the leader is hated because the administrative structure is authoritarian, because he is incompetent, because he frustrates his followers' needs for idealization and unrealistic expectations, or because of individual psychopathologies of everyone involved. Ideally, one should be able to determine the origin of the hatred of the leader from an analysis of the primary task of the organization, the adequacy of the administrative structure and functional leadership to the task, and the like.

Only after determining that other factors are not responsible can one raise the question of whether the personalities of key leaders are injecting pathological levels of aggression into the system, or whether pathological regressions within groups are temporarily activating basic group assumptions, and thus excessive aggression.

One must examine the general morale problems within the organization and the task orientedness of the relations among various groups within it before one can conclude that regressive group phenomena are not the primary factor and that the psychopathologies of various individuals, particularly the leader, are involved. Distortions of organizations can be caused by individual psychopathology within crucial administrative points of the organizational structure, but this diagnosis can be made only after all other possible causes of emotional regression within the organization have been eliminated. This viewpoint is in contrast to the analysis of organizational conflicts exclusively in terms of individual psychopathology, or of group processes, organizational structure, or political factors.

If the leader appears reasonably adequate to her task and shows no significant personality disturbance, and if there are no major organizational problems evident—that is, the administrative structure is adequate to task performance and the external environment is relatively stable—the question of "inappropriate" aggression of staff toward the leader can often be resolved in terms of the need for the leader to tolerate a certain amount of aggression without undue concern over it. In practice, when the leader is loved without reserve, and nobody is ever angry with her, something must be wrong. Meaningful decisions always cause somebody pain. Naturally, those painfully affected blame the person on top, and she or he must be able to tolerate this. Tolerance of aggressive outbursts among the staff without overreacting is part of the definition of a good leader: this is one reason why severely narcissistic and paranoid personalities make poor task leaders. Often the administrator's tolerance of temporary irrational staff outbursts may in itself decrease the fears that underlie the expression of such anger and thus create an emotionally corrective experience for all concerned.

Sexual Needs

An increase of oedipal sexual temptations in the leader is the counterpart of the activation of oedipal aggressive rivalries around the issues of power and control within the hierarchy of the institution. Although one genetic aspect of the drive for power is that of taking the place of father and becoming the domineering male of the social group, the staff's unconscious perception of the male leader as the owner of all the women in the institution, and the oedipal orientation of female staff toward him as a complement to this shared myth are potential additional sources of sexual temptations in leader and staff to act out such oedipal conflicts. The reverse situation develops when a woman is the leader of the organization. In either situation, the prevalent social conventions and taboos regulating public and private interactions between the sexes exert a strong influence on these dynamics. The sexual politics of institutions, that is, the political equilibrium reached in the power struggle and the sexual tensions involving men and women as complementary or opposite sentience groups, are often played out at the top of the institution, as in the proverbial relation between boss and secretary, chief doctor and head nurse. Less frequently, homosexual tensions involving organizational leaders' conflicts may complicate the political dynamics of the organization.

Most psychiatric institutions are male dominated; they reproduce the culturally dominant (apparent) control of sadistic-controlling men over masochistic-subservient women. Therefore, the political struggles between the sexes expressed in regressive group phenomena often take the form of men (apparently) dominating the public decision-making process, and of women, in (apparent) admiration of and subservience to male-made decisions, carrying out orders even as they passively protest against such submission by inducing guilt in the men over their mistreatment of women. The conflicts between male physicians and female nurses concerning who makes the final decisions concerning any psychiatric service is one illustration of this problem. The mutual sexual teasing among staff members, and the unconscious efforts of each sex to make the other cross the forbidden boundary from professional to sexual relations so that the "victim" can retaliate by inducing guilt in the offender, is another aspect of the same problem. Behind the temptations and fears of crossing sexual boundaries are those of crossing hierarchical boundaries, where acting out of oedipal rebellion is implicit. Above all, because psychiatric institutions deal with patients who have not been able to satisfactorily resolve their oedipal problems outside the hospital, strong pressures deriving from the task of treating such patients may exacerbate all these potential conflicts between staff members.

The danger that the senior administrator's unresolved oedipal conflicts may trigger a sharp increase in oedipal conflicts throughout the entire institution is often present. This situation becomes complicated by the frequent sexualization of conflicts actually related to the leader's frustrated dependency needs. Oedipal and preoedipal regressive pressures may combine to activate the administrator's sexualized dependent relationships. Typically, "the great man" is "babied" by "mothering" women in his immediate "entourage," who are often admiring and subservient and yet dominant.

In general, groups that operate under the basic assumption of pairing experience intimacy and sexual developments as a potential protection against the dangers and conflicts surrounding dependency and aggression. Sexual pairing may also represent a real or fantasied escape from the dangerous or controlling group pressures in the organization, and it can symbolize a condensation of oedipal rebelliousness against the "established order" with the defensive sexualization of more primitive conflicts surrounding aggression and dependency.

Thus, there may be sexually excited and romanticized pressure surrounding the administrator that fosters a sexualized bond between him and a leading female administrator. Under optimal circumstances, this bond is expressed in a working relationship that has overtones of sublimated erotized trends. Actually, a certain erotization of work relationships may enhance the work group. But when regressive pressures lead workers to cross sexual boundaries, a couple's sexual intimacy may not only bring about an exaggerated condensation of the work group with sexualized sentience (and the consequent distortions in ordinary work boundaries and relationships) but also induce a freeing of the aggressive components related to oedipal conflicts in such sexualized relations, with a general breakdown of interpersonal relations in the system. In organizational terms, it can be said that the sexualization of the relations between staff members increases their level of aspiration to such an extent that ordinary gratifications at work will (sooner or later) fall short of such increased expectations, and a general breakdown of morale will ensue.

For the administrator, it is vital that his sexual gratifications occur outside the boundaries of his administrative functions. This might seem too trivial to mention were not the regressive pressures for sexualized relations within the administrative boundaries so strong. At the same time, when a functional, mutually respectful, and open work relationship between the sexes develops in an organization, erotized perhaps but still within work boundaries, the exhilarating experience of men and women working together as friends without having to become sexually engaged can be most creative and indirectly foster a sexually mature and tolerant atmosphere that in psychiatric institutions will help in the treatment of patients.

From a broader viewpoint, general conflicts between the sexes within the social, cultural, and economic environment, for example, socially fostered and ritualized sadomasochistic relationships between women and men, sexual exploitation, and teasing are automatically expressed as part of the sexualized tension within organizations and threaten to distort task relationships. This is seen in the masochistic submission of female nurses to male doctors and in the manipulative exploitation of sexual seductiveness to reestablish a (real or fantasied) equilibrium between sadistically behaving men and masochistically behaving women. If political tensions among sentience groups and across task boundaries become sexualized, such sexual aggression, submission, and teasing acquire political significance. Sexual politics, powerfully reinforced by general sexual sentience, may interfere with the task relationships and task structure.

In order to bring sexual politics into the open, the extent to which sexual sentience and task sentience are related must be diagnosed, not to strip away the barriers of privacy but to avoid the misperceptions shared by groups and by both sexes when sexual politics operate within the institution. For example, the shared rebelliousness of young female nurses and male physicians against their respective female and male leadership may need to be understood if general distortions in the relations among nursing staff and medical staff are to be avoided.

All this is not to be construed to mean that satisfactory sexual relationships cannot develop between individual staff members of organizations; on the contrary, people often establish lasting sexual and marital relationships with those they meet at work. When a couple establishes a sexual relationship, the work relationship between them usually changes; one or both might even withdraw from that specific work. Should a married couple or a couple with a stable relationship continue in a work relationship as well, the partners must consolidate the sexual relationship in terms other than that of the work relationship proper; the couple that marries will have to establish a close relationship in areas separate from those of the task. In turn, it will become particularly important for the organizational leaders to oversee the maintenance of the task when a couple functions within a certain task system.

It is often unsatisfactory when husband and wife work together as leader and subordinate in the same task system, for this may have a deleterious effect on task relations with their peers. Couples are frequently perceived as powerful and even threatening by the individuals within the organization, so that even when the couple scrupulously maintains the task relationships, groups do not perceive this and react to the couple with fear, aggression, resentment, and suspicion.

Even under ideal circumstances this may reduce the couple's effectiveness. Under less than optimal circumstances, the couple may be sucked in by the role-inducing, shared fantasies and behavior of groups. Furthermore, the couple may be tempted to act out its own conflicts by projecting aggression onto the environment and by developing an idealized bond that tends to exploit their alliance to the disadvantage of others in the organization. At times, the more powerful member of the couple controls the more subservient or masochistic one for his or her needs; when such a couple occupies a position of leadership, the two may distort their exercise of authority and develop typically authoritarian relationships, which can be destructive. There is wisdom in the administrative principles within institutions that are intended to prevent just such an eventuality. There is also the risk, however, that couples will be discriminated against because of the shared fantasies about them within the institution. It is unfortunate when two creative people are limited in their development and contributions by organizational bias.

If to work and to love are the principal tasks in life, creative developments within organizations should permit eros to be placed at the service of work and work to be placed at the service of (sublimated) love. The main objective of an organization is not to satisfy the human needs of its members but to carry out a task; one objective of intelligent leadership is to permit the gratification of human needs in carrying out that task.

Dependent Needs

The major regressive pressure on the leader usually derives from the frustration of her dependency needs. There are many reasons for this frustration. For one thing, there is always the potential that Bion's (1961) basic assumption of dependency will be activated. Then, too, the administrator carries the burden of responsibility for the entire institution, including responsibility for processes that to some extent are outside her control and boundaries. She also faces a staff whose freedom of expression of the dependency needs is greater than her own. The "carefree" attitude of subordinates and their comparatively greater availability for support, applause, and gratification create additional pressures for the leader. Leaders often reward subordinates who do well, but top administrators usually receive few direct human rewards for effective job performance. The staff tends to takes the leader's performance for granted when things go well; when things go wrong, they hold the leader responsible.

There are, of course, compensations in the work as such. To begin with, there are the financial rewards of the position. In addition, when the administrator knows that she has done her job well, that she has introduced and carried out new ideas and programs, and that she has stimulated her staff to grow and become creative, she receives important gratification of her human needs. In general, creativity in administrative work may simultaneously gratify dependency needs (by projection), narcissistic needs (by success and approval), and oedipal strivings (by administrative victories). As part of the working relation, the administrator's immediate group of coworkers can provide her with gratification of her dependency needs. In this regard, mutual gratification of dependency needs by the senior administrative staff is an important, realistic requirement of work situations, particularly in large institutions.

Another major compensation for the frustration of the administrator's dependency needs is the availability of friendship and support outside her own administrative boundaries. Realistic gratification of the administrator's instinctual needs in her life outside the work situation becomes important in the long run. An excessive search for the gratification of dependency needs from subordinates may distort the administrative structure and burden the staff. There is a delicate balance between the administrator's being so reserved and self-contained that she feeds the staff's dehumanizing and distorted perceptions of her and her relying so much on gratification and support from staff that she overwhelms them and decreases their concentration on the work. This balance also raises the issue of the extent to which the administrator should share concerns and difficulties with staff.

The leader's self-openness may increase the staff's understanding of her own constraints, clarify distortions derived from their perception of her role (that is, from confusing the role with the personality), and increase their morale. But for the leader to burden staff with her management problems may cause anxiety in them about problems they cannot solve; as well, it can increase expectations that reasonableness and openness will solve all problems. In other words, paradoxically, the leader who is "ideal" in her openness, warmth, and non-defensiveness may, by the same token, so increase expectations that disappointments become unavoidable. In short, there is a danger that the "perfect" administrator will foster primitive idealizations related to the dependency assumptions of staff, and such idealizations necessarily lead to disappointment.

The regressive pull of needs involved in aggression, dependency, and sex may derive from the personality of the administrator, from his true situation with regard to his staff, and, particularly, from the regressive group processes among staff members. Regardless of origin, these pressures are ordinarily compensated for by a variety of factors. Major among these is the overcoming of oedipal conflicts in the normal capacity for achieving and experiencing success and the ability to use success creatively. There is a proverb that says that every man should plant a tree, write a book, and sire a child. Translated into the functions of an administrator, planting a tree may represent getting things done or building new things; writing a book, the development of new ideas and knowledge; and siring (or bearing, in the case of female administrators) a child, the creative development of the human resources of the institution and the encouragement of the staff to grow and develop their capacity for good and gratifying human relationships in the process of carrying out significant work.

Chapter 5 Regression in Organizational Leadership

Choosing good leaders is a major task for all organizations. Information regarding the prospective administrator's personality should complement details about her previous experience, her general conceptual skills, her technical knowledge, and her specific skills for the particular job. The growing psychoanalytic understanding of the crucial importance of internal rather than external object relations, as well as of the mutual relations of regression in individuals and in groups, offers an important practical tool for the selection of leaders.

In chapter 4, I described the effects of regressive pressures in psychiatric institutions on their administrators. I pointed out that although crises often appear to be caused by the leader's personality problems, through further analysis one often discovers a more complex situation. Frequently, regressive group processes are first induced by a breakdown in work effectiveness that stems from various internal organizational factors and relations between the organization and the environment; regression in the leader's functioning follows. If these group processes remain undiagnosed, only their end product may be visible, in the form of what appear to be primitive, inadequate leadership and, more specifically, the negative effects of the leader's personality on the organization. Thus, leadership problems are not always the cause of the crisis. I now turn to the regressive pressures that do stem from the administrators. I must reemphasize, however, the importance of distinguishing between regressive organizational components and regression in the leader.

I take a middle way between two theoretical positions: the traditional approach, according to which leadership is inborn—particularly charismatic leadership—and the more recent theoretical thinking, in which leadership is derived largely or exclusively from learned skills and understanding. I base my approach on the findings of various authors (Bion, 1961; Dalton et al., 1968; Emery and Trist, 1973; Hodgson et al., 1965; Levinson, 1968; Main, 1957; Miller and Rice, 1967; Rice, 1963, 1965, 1969; Rioch, 1970a, 1970b; Sanford, 1956; and Stanton and Schwartz, 1954). This approach has three aspects: a psychoanalytic focus on the personality features of the leader; a psychoanalytic focus on the functions of regressive group processes in organizations; and an open-systems-theory approach to organizational management. The three interact dynamically; the origin of the failure or breakdown in the functioning of individuals, groups, or the organization as a whole may lie in any one or all of these areas.

THE CONSULTANT

Consultants are usually called at times of crisis, but the nature of their task is not always clear: an organization may use a consultant to escape from full awareness and need to resolve a problem as much as to diagnose it and realistically consider its potential solutions (Rogers, 1973). The consultant's first task is to clarify the nature of his contract and assure himself that resources are available to carry it out. This means not only that he be given sufficient time and financial support but that he have the authority to examine problems at all levels of the organizational structure.

Support from the leader of the organization is essential. The consultant needs to be sufficiently independent from the organization that he can reach his conclusions without worrying about antagonizing the leader; therefore, he must not be too dependent on any one particular client.

The first thing that must be determined is whether a certain conflict within the organization represents a problem stemming from: personality issues; the nature of the task and its constraints; or morale—that is, group processes within the organization. The problem is often described in such confused and confusing terms that placing it into one or several of these three domains is difficult.

It is helpful to focus first on the nature of the organizational tasks and their constraints, for only after the task has been defined, the respective constraints outlined, and priorities set is it possible to evaluate whether the administrative structure does indeed fit with the nature of the tasks—and if not, how it should be modified. The consultant must therefore clarify the organization's real tasks in contrast to its apparent ones. In one psychiatric hospital, the apparent tasks were to treat patients and to carry out research, but the real task seemed to be to provide the owners of the institution with an adequate return on their investment. The interest in research hid a desire to obtain funding from external sources with which to cover part of staff salaries, and the treatment of patients constituted a constraint on the real task.

Once tasks and constraints have been defined, one can consider the administrative structure. Does the organization have effective control over its boundaries, and if not, what administrative compensating mechanisms can be established to restore boundary control? In one case, a psychiatric organization depended on one institution for its administrative-support funding and another for its staff funding. Chronic fights between administrators and professionals throughout the organization reflected the lack of resolution of boundary control at the top. The consultant's recommendation that all funding be channeled into a central hospital administration that was directed by a professional with administrative expertise provided an organizational solution to the morale problem.

If boundary control is adequate, the nature of the delegation of authority to each task system can be studied. Inadequate, fluctuating, ambiguous, or nonexisting delegation of authority on the one hand and excessive and chaotic delegation on the other are problems that have to be solved in order for the administrative structure to fit task requirements.

Once the overall task and its constraints have been diagnosed, and the respective administrative structures corrected, one can focus on the nature of the leadership and, more concretely, on the qualities of the leader himself. The consultant should attempt to diagnose those personal qualities of the administrator that influence organizational functioning, the regressive pulls the leader is subjected to from group processes in the organization, and his own contributions to such regressive group processes. What kind of intermediate management has the leader assembled? How much understanding does he have of people, their assets and liabilities? How much tolerance of criticism, strength, warmth, flexibility combined with firmness, and clarity does he show in his communications to and relationships with the staff? The accuracy and quality of the leader's judgment of those around him is a crucial indicator not only of his administrative skills but of his personality as a whole. What are his reactions under stress? In which direction does his personality regress under critical conditions? The strength of his convictions, his envy of staff or lack of it, his moral integrity and courage—these are usually well known throughout the organization.

The psychoanalytic exploration of group processes in the organization may become a crucial instrument for the evaluation of problems in both the administrative structure and the personality of the leader. The regressive nature of group processes in psychiatric organizations—morale—may reflect conflicts in the organizational structure, the impact of the leader's personality, the regressive pull directly induced by the pressure of patients' conflicts, or a combination of these factors. And the closer the observed group processes are to the actual work with patients, the more the patients' conflicts will directly influence the development of regressive group processes among the staff and within the staff-patient community generally. The closer the observed staff groups are to the final decision-making authority, the more the conflicts of the leadership and of the organizational structure will dominate. Yet it is impressive to see how the conflicts affecting the entire organization are reflected in actual group processes at all levels. Therefore, the careful observation of group processes at various administrative levels constitutes a kind of organizational projective test battery, which may give the direct information needed to clarify problems at the levels of task definition and constraints, patients, administrative structure, and leadership, all in one stroke.

The accuracy of the consultant's diagnosis can be tested when her suggestions are implemented. For example, the change in the functioning of the administrative leadership after primary tasks and constraints are redefined should improve morale in a relatively short period. The restoration of a functional structure—in contrast to an authoritarian structure brought about by distortions of the hierarchical network of power—may have an almost immediate positive effect.

For practical purposes, the consultant usually obtains the most helpful information from the active participation of senior and intermediate management in an open discussion of issues in an atmosphere that permits exploration of group processes as well as of the actual content of the administrative problems being examined. The consultant's diagnosis of the problems of top leadership and intermediate management should include an evaluation of the human resources in the organization. Because human resources are the primary potential assets of organizations, the extent of intactness of senior leadership has an important prognostic implication. A capable and mutually trusting intermediate leadership group can provide the basis for an effective restructuring.

When the consultant concludes that the leader's personality problems or his general incompetence result from lack of technical knowledge, conceptual limitations, or administrative inadequacies, the question arises of whether he can be helped to change or whether he should be helped to leave his job. There are no obvious answers to this question. Leaders may sometimes be helped to improve their ability to function by reducing the regressive pulls on them that stem from group processes in the organization. Improvement in task definition, task performance, boundary controls, and the administrative structure as a whole may all bring out the leader's positive assets and reduce the negative impact of his personality. Increase in gratification of his emotional needs (in the areas of aggression, sex, or dependency) outside the organizational structure may sometimes help. At other times, the best solution seems to be to help him step down by either changing his professional functions or moving him geographically within the organization, if such alternatives are available.

Although the recommendation that he resign is always a serious narcissistic blow, it often happens that the administrator really knows that he has not been able to do his job well; he may feel relieved when an outsider confronts him with that fact. On the other hand, when the consultant concludes that the organization has a bad leader at the top, she might discreetly withdraw (or be discreetly asked to withdraw).

The situation is different, of course, when the problem involves an administrator at a lower hierarchical level. In this case, the top leaders must recognize that firmness in eliminating bad situations is indispensable for the health of the organization. To help a person who cannot do her or his job leave may seem aggressive or even sadistic, but it is usually worse to leave a bad leader in charge of an organizational structure. The suffering visited on the staff by a bad leader should be a primary concern of the top leader. Optimal leadership means hard decisions, and at times the top leader must be firm and decisive in dealing with someone who may be a close personal friend.

There are times when the problem can be diagnosed but for some reason cannot be resolved. Some organizations seem geared to self-destruction, unable and unwilling to accept positive change. This is a dramatic situation for a consultant—and even more dramatic for the staff of the organization. Understanding the organizational structure and its conflict may help the staff, particularly senior staff who have an overview of the situation, to reach realistic conclusions about how and whether these conflicts can be resolved, which will have a strong effect on their own future.

There are certain situations that are so bad that the only solution for self-respecting staff members is to leave; in other words, there is such a thing as a poisonous organizational environment. It is noteworthy how often staff members who work in such a destructive environment deny to themselves the insoluble nature of the problems of the organization, indeed, gratify their pathological dependency needs by such denial, and fail to admit the need to move on. Understanding organizations in depth can be painful; at times, such awareness does not improve the effectiveness of staff members; but understanding always makes it possible to gain a more realistic grasp of what the organization's future is likely to be. The parallel to the painful learning about aspects of one's unconscious in a psychoanalytic situation is implicit here: there are pathological defenses against becoming aware of the true situation at the place where one works. At some point, the individual has a responsibility to him- or herself that transcends the responsibility to the organization; and knowledge of organizational conflicts can help him or her realize more quickly when that point has been reached.

Under less extreme circumstances, there is much that an educated, task-oriented staff can do to help its leadership correct or undo distorted administrative structures and reduce the effects of the pathology of top leadership. The intermediate management may be of particular help in preserving functional administrative relationships by an open sharing of communication and analysis of the situation. In this regard, I cannot overemphasize the responsibility of followers not to perpetuate and exacerbate the problems of the leader.

Disruption of functional administration always brings about regression to basic group assumptions. I refer here to Bion's (1961) basic-assumptions groups: dependency, fight-flight, and pairing, which become activated when groups— and organizations—do not function adequately. Such regressive phenomena in groups involving intermediate leadership and staff at large may reinforce the personality difficulties of individual staff members and reduce their awareness of the need for change or their willingness to fight for it. If individual staff members acknowledge the situation, their action may have a positive therapeutic effect in increasing rational behavior throughout the organization; in such instances, they help not by taking an attitude of criticism based on fight-flight assumptions but by showing a genuine interest in helping the leader and staff generally to improve their understanding and functioning in the organization. Open communication among the intermediate management group members may also help reduce their mutual suspicion and distrust and their fear of speaking up. An alliance for the sake of the functional needs of the organization is a good example of political struggle in terms of the task, rather than in terms of perpetuating the distortions in the distribution of authority and power.

For the top administrator, particularly at a time of crisis, when uncertainty is increased for her and everyone else, the availability of senior staff who are willing to speak openly and responsibly, without excessive distortion by fear or anger, can be reassuring. A mutual reinforcement between staff members who are able and willing to provide new information to the leader and a leader who encourages such staff openness may strengthen the task group throughout.

"Participatory management" as a general principle is an important protection against regressive effects on the administrative structure caused by the leader's personality. A variety of factors affect the general issue of what level of participatory management or what level of centralized decision making is required. When the administrative structure has been distorted under the impact of regressive pulls on top leadership, from whatever source, increasing participative management is indicated. Such an emphasis on participatory decision making does not mean that the functional structure is replaced by a "democratic" one. The organization must be flexible about how much it will shift back and forth from centralized to participatory management; at periods of rapid environmental change, of crisis or turbulence in the external environment, there may be a need for increased centralized decision making. At times of external stability, increased decentralization and participatory management may be helpful. Internal change often requires participatory management, especially in the preparatory or early stages. A centralized, simplified administrative structure can become functional in times of internal consolidation or stability.

AUTHORITARIAN PERSONALITIES AND AUTHORITARIAN ORGANIZATIONAL STRUCTURES

Adorno and his coworkers (1950) describe the "authoritarian personality" as follows: he tends to be overconventional, rigidly adherent to middle-class values, and oversensitive to external social pressures; he is inappropriately submissive to conventional authority and, at the same time, harsh toward those who oppose such authority and toward people under him; he is generally opposed to feelings, fantasies, and introspection, and tends to shift responsibility from the individual onto outside forces; his thinking is stereotyped, rigid, and simplistic; he tends to exercise power for its own sake and admires power in others; he is destructive and cynical, rationalizing his aggression toward others; he tends to project onto others—particularly outgroups—his own unacceptable impulses; and finally, he is rigid about sexual morality.

Although Adorno and his coworkers applied psychoanalytic concepts to study the metapsychological determinants of such a personality structure, in their methods and clinical analyses they combined both personality and sociological criteria. Their authoritarian personality structure seems to be a composite formation, which reflects various types of character pathology exacerbated by the authoritarian pressures that are exerted by social, political, and cultural systems. Within the restricted frame of reference of a study of the leadership of psychiatric institutions, the social, cultural, and political issues may become less important than the mutual reinforcement of authoritarian pressures derived from the institutional structure and from various types of character pathology that contribute to the authoritarian behavior. In what follows, I explore the pathological contributions of the specific personality characteristics of the leader to the development of authoritarian pressures throughout the organizational structure. I emphasize again, however, that a leader's authoritarian behavior may stem from features of the organizational structure and not from his own personality.

Sanford (1956) pointed out the necessity to distinguish between authoritarian behavior in leadership roles and authoritarianism in the personality; the two do not necessarily go together. An authoritarian administrative structure is one that is invested with more power than is necessary to carry out its functions, whereas a functional structure is one where people and groups in positions of authority are invested with adequate—but not excessive—power.

The adequate power invested in the leadership in a functional structure usually receives reinforcement from social and legal sanctions. Authoritarian behavior that exceeds functional needs must be differentiated from authoritative behavior that represents a functionally adequate or necessary exercise of authority. In practice, authority—the right and capacity to carry out task leadership—stems from various sources (Rogers, 1973). Managerial authority refers to that part of the leader's authority that has been delegated to him by the institution he works in. Leadership authority refers to that aspect of his authority derived from his followers' recognition of his capacity to carry out the task. Managerial and leadership authority reinforce each other; both are, in turn, dependent upon other sources of authority, such as the leader's technical knowledge, his personality, his human skills, and the social tasks and responsibilities he assumes outside the institution. The administrator is responsible not only to his institution but also to his staff, to his professional and ethical values, to the community, and to society at large: responsibility and accountability represent the reciprocal obligation of the administrator to the sources of his authority. In addition, because of his personality, or because he belongs to special groups or to political structures that invest him with a power that is unrelated to his technical functions, the leader may accumulate power beyond that required by his functional authority—the excessive power that constitutes the basis for an authoritarian structure.

In contrasting an authoritarian administrative structure with a functional administrative structure, I am emphasizing the opposition between authoritarian and functional structure, not the one between authoritarian and democratic structure. This point is important from both theoretical and practical viewpoints. A tendency exists in some professional institutions—and psychiatric institutions are no exception—to attempt to modify, correct, or resolve by means of democratic political processes problems that were created by an authoritarian structure. Attempts are made to arrive at corrective decisions in a participatory or representative decision-making process. Insofar as the people involved in actual tasks ought to participate in decision making, such democratization is helpful; but where decision making is determined on a political rather than a task-oriented basis, the task structure and in fact the entire administrative structure may become distorted. These distortions are extremely detrimental to the work being carried out, and they eventually may even reinforce the authoritarian structure they are intended to correct. In addition, the attempt to correct authoritarian distortions by political means leads to the neglect of a functional analysis of the problem. This is certainly a temptation for top leaders: by means of political management or manipulation, they may be able to dominate the negotiations across task boundaries. If so, they may come to rely more on the exercise of political power, eventually focusing almost exclusively on the increment or protection of their own power base and neglecting the functional interests of the institution.

FREQUENT PATHOLOGICAL CHARACTER STRUCTURES OF THE ADMINISTRATOR

Schizoid Personality Features

Schizoid personality features may, in themselves, protect the leader against excessive regression—his emotional isolation makes him less pervious to regressive group processes. But the proliferation of distorted fantasies about him among the staff is hard to correct because of his distance and unavailability. An excessively schizoid leader may also frustrate the appropriate dependency needs of his staff; usually, however, schizoid leaders at the top tend to be compensated for by the warmth and extroversion of managerial figures at the intermediate level.

A schizoid head of a department of psychiatry conveyed the impression that no one was in charge; most of the authority for daily operations had been delegated to the director of clinical services, who was seen as the actual leader of staff and who, because of his capacity for carrying out the boundary functions between the department head and the staff, did indeed fulfill important leadership functions. Yet the needs of the senior staff for mutual support, warmth, and understanding were not met, and the feeling each had of being on his own was transmitted throughout the entire institution. Although this department was considered a place with ample room for the independent, autonomous growth of staff who had what it took, many staff members were unable to work in such isolation and left.

In another institution, a markedly schizoid hospital director was insufficiently explicit and direct in the decision-making process, and this vagueness created ambiguity in the delegation of authority. No one was certain how much authority was vested in any particular person, and no one cared to commit him- or herself on any issue without repeated consultations with the director. This produced excessive cautiousness, hypersensitivity, and politicization of decision making throughout the organization. Eventually, the message was conveyed that a person had to be a skilled and tactful manipulator to get ahead in the department and that direct emotional expression was risky. Thus, the leader's personality characteristics filtered down through group interactions and became characteristic of the entire organization.

Obsessive Personality Features

Obsessive personality features in top leaders are frequent. On the positive side, the focus on orderliness, precision, clarity, and control may foster good, stable delegation of authority and lead to clarity in the decision-making process. Contrary to what one would expect, obsessive personalities in leadership positions exhibit little doubtfulness; severely obsessive personalities do not usually reach top positions when doubt and hesitation are their predominant characteristics. Chronic indecisiveness in the administrator may have obsessive origins; however, chronic indecisiveness at the top is usually a consequence of the leader's narcissistic problems. Obsessive personalities, then, usually function rather efficiently from an organizational viewpoint. Their clear stand on issues and their commitment to their values have important creative functions for the institution at large.

On the negative side, some dangers are the leader's excessive need for order and precision, her need to be in control, and the expression of the sadistic characteristics that often accompany an obsessive personality. An inordinate need for orderliness and control may reinforce the bureaucratic components of the organization—that is, encourage decision making on the basis of rules and regulations and mechanized practices, all of which may interfere with the creativeness of the staff and with the autonomy of the decision-making process at times of rapid change or crisis. Excessive bureaucratization may at times protect the organization from political struggle, but it reinforces passive resistance in negotiations across boundaries and misuses resources.

Because pathological defensive mechanisms and, particularly, pathological character traits of the leader tend to be activated in times of stress, an increase in obsessive perfectionism and pedantic style may characterize the obsessive leader at critical moments. This may create additional stress for the organization at a time when rapid and effective decision making is required. The staff must be aware that under such conditions it is necessary to protect the security system of the leader—the character defenses—in order to get the work done. This, of course, is true whenever a leader has pathological character features; knowing how to help the leader in times of crisis is a basic skill demanded of intermediate management.

Some obsessive personalities in leadership positions may also exercise their severe, unresolved sadism, and their need to sadistically control subordinates may have devastating effects on the functional structure of the organization. Whenever there is strong opposition among the staff to an administrator's move, she may become obstinate and controlling, revengefully rubbing the message in, and continually forcing her "opponents" to submit. Such behavior reinforces irrational fears of authority and the distortion of role-perception in the staff; it also fosters a submissiveness to hierarchical superiors, which reduces effective feedback and creative participation from the entire staff.

The result may be the development of chronic passivity, a pseudodependency that derives from fear of authority rather than from an authentic dependent group. Authoritarian, dictatorial ways of dealing with staff and patients may be transmitted to the institution. In one department of psychiatry, the appointment of an obsessive and sadistic chair drove the most creative members of the senior professional leadership away from the institution within a year. In consequence, the leader surrounded himself with a group of weak, inhibited, or mediocre professionals, who were willing to sacrifice their autonomous professional development for the security and stability they received by submission. The repetition of these conflicts approximately a year later at the next level of organizational hierarchy, however, created such a combination of general fight-flight grouping and overall breakdown in carrying out organizational tasks that the administrator was finally removed by the combined efforts of the staff at large.

Paranoid Personality Features

Paranoid personalities always present a serious potential danger for the functional relationships that administrators must establish with their staff. The development of fight-flight conditions in the group processes throughout the organization—a development that may occur from time to time even in the most efficiently functioning institution—can propel a leader of the opposition into the foreground. With the silent tolerance or unconscious collusion of the majority of the staff, an attack on the administration by this opposition leader may induce the top leader to regress into paranoid attitudes, even though he does not have any particularly paranoid traits. In other words, there is always the potential—especially in large organizations with several levels of hierarchy—that the administrator will become suspicious, that he will be tempted to exert sadistic control, and that he will project his rage onto the staff. When the administrator also has strong paranoid character features, the danger of paranoid reactions to fight-flight conditions is intensified; he may perceive even ordinary discussions or minor opposition as dangerous rebelliousness or a potential, disguised attack. The need to suppress and control the opposition, which we saw in the obsessive leader with sadistic trends, becomes paramount in the paranoid leader. Because of the ease with which the leader may interpret what "they say" as lack of respect, mistreatment, and hidden hostility toward him, the staff may become afraid of speaking out. The staff's fearfulness, in turn, may increase the administrator's suspiciousness, creating a vicious circle.

Because paranoid personalities are particularly suitable to take on the leadership of basic-assumptions groups in a fight-flight position, the leader of the opposition is often a person with strong paranoid tendencies. This does not mean that all leaders of revolutions are paranoid personalities; rather, because of the nature of their psychopathology, paranoid personalities can function well under revolutionary conditions. They perceive the in-group they represent as all good and the external groups or the general environment against which they fight as all bad. The successful projection of all of his aggression onto an object outside the boundaries of his group permits the paranoid oppositional leader to function more effectively within its boundaries, though only by means of a great deal of perceptual distortion of external reality. But when the paranoid leader succeeds in seizing power and takes control of the organization, the very characteristics that helped him gain leadership of the fight-flight group may lead to his damaging the institution. The tendency to project all hostility outward—that is, to see the institution as good and the environment as bad— may temporarily protect the good relations between the leader and his followers; in the long run, however, the price paid for this is institutionalization of paranoid distortions of perceptions of external reality, distortions in the boundary negotiations between the institution and its environment, and the possibility that the leader's capacity to carry out his organizational tasks will break down. Within the organization, the revengeful persecution of those the paranoid leader suspects of being potential enemies can limit creative criticism to a greater degree than in the case of obsessive personalities with sadistic features.

The director of one psychiatric institution that worked in close conjunction with several other psychiatric institutions felt chronically endangered by what he saw as the power plays of the directors of the other institutions against him. At first he appealed to his own staff for help and support, and morale improved temporarily as they all united against the external enemy. Eventually, however, by constantly antagonizing the leaders and representatives of the other institutions, the director became less able to carry out his functions in representing his own institution and started to blame his own subordinates for the difficulties he encountered in obtaining space, staff, funding, and community influence. He began to suspect some of the members of the intermediate management of his own institution of having ,betrayed him, thus further reducing the effectiveness of his institution within its professional environment. The situation was resolved when the boundaries of the institution were transformed into a true barrier, behind which it isolated itself from the local community and redefined its task in terms of a regional chain of institutions to which it belonged. This isolation, however, led to a strong negative community reaction and, eventually, the dismissal of the director.

The following example, in contrast, illustrates the resolution of paranoid regression that was induced in an organizational leader without paranoid personality characteristics by fight-flight conditions. The director of a hospital was suspicious and upset over a senior member of his staff, Dr. B., who seemed to challenge him at all professional meetings. The director saw Dr. B. as a severely paranoid character whose group behavior was splitting the staff and potentially damaging the organization. He wondered whether Dr. B. should remain on the staff. He nevertheless accepted other staff members' judgment that Dr. B. was a good clinician and was providing valuable services to the hospital. A consultant recommended to the director that he meet privately with Dr. B. and discuss his group behavior. The director did so and discovered that Dr. B. was much more open and flexible in individual meetings than in group situations. But Dr. B. did not change his challenging behavior in groups, and the director now concluded that regardless of Dr. B.'s personality characteristics, a group process must be fostering his contentious behavior and that a study of this particular organizational area was indicated. In the course of the study, it became apparent that there were serious conflicts within the institution that had reduced the effectiveness of the professional group to which Dr. B. belonged, so that fight-flight assumptions chronically predominated and pushed Dr. B. into the role of leader. The director's analysis of the organizational problem led to resolution of the conflicts for the entire professional group; Dr. B., finding himself no longer supported by the silent consensus and actively discouraged by the group itself, stopped dominating group discussions.

Narcissistic Personality Features

Of all the character pathologies of leaders that endanger institutions, narcissistic personality features are perhaps the most serious. I must stress that I am using the concept of narcissistic personality here in a restrictive sense, referring to persons whose interpersonal relations are characterized by excessive self-reference and self-centeredness; whose grandiosity and overvaluation of themselves exist together with feelings of inferiority; who are overdependent on external admiration, emotionally shallow, intensely envious, and both disparaging and exploitative in their relations with others (Kernberg 1970, 1974).

The inordinate self-centeredness and grandiosity of narcissistic people is in dramatic contrast to their chronic potential for envy. Their inability to evaluate themselves and others in depth makes them incapable of empathy with and sophisticated discrimination of others, all of which may become damaging when they occupy leadership positions. In addition, when they do not receive expected external gratifications, or when they experience severe frustration or failure, they may develop paranoid trends in place of the more usual depression and sense of personal failure. Such paranoid tendencies exacerbate the leader's narcissistic character traits and the damage they can do to the organization.

Because narcissistic personalities are often driven by intense needs for power and prestige to assume positions of authority, individuals with such characteristics are frequently found in top leadership positions. They are often men and women of high intelligence, hard working, and extremely talented or capable in their field, but their narcissistic needs neutralize or destroy their creative potential in the organization.

Pathologically narcissistic people aspire to positions of leadership more as a source of admiration and narcissistic gratification from staff members and from the external environment than because they are committed to a certain task or ideal represented by the institution. As a consequence, they may neglect the functional requirements of leadership, the human needs and constraints involved in the work, and the value systems that constitute one of the important measures against which to judge administrative and technical responsibilities. Leaders with narcissistic personalities are unaware of the variety of pathological human relationships they foster, both around themselves and throughout the entire organization, as their personalities affect administrative structures and functions at large.

In contrast to leaders with pathological obsessive and paranoid features, the narcissistic leader not only requires submission from staff; he also demands their love. He artificially intensifies the staff's normal tendency to depend on and idealize the leader: as the staff becomes aware of how important it is for the administrator to receive perpetual demonstrations of their unconditional love and admiration, adulation and flattery become constant features of their communications with him.

The negative influence of pathological narcissism must be differentiated from the normal narcissistic manifestations that are part of the gratifications of any position of responsibility and leadership, gratifications that may be the source of the leader's increased effectiveness as well as a compensation for his administrative frustrations. In earlier work (Kernberg, 1970, 1974), I examined the differences between normal and pathological narcissism. I shall limit myself here to outlining some of these differences as they apply to the person in the leadership position.

Administrative and leadership positions in general provide many sources for gratification of narcissistic needs. Under optimal circumstances these needs have been integrated into mature ego goals and the need to live up to a mature ego ideal and superego standards. Normal narcissistic gratification have mature qualities; for example, normal self-love is enlightened and deep, in contrast to childlike and shallow self-aggrandizement; normal self-love goes hand in hand with commitments to ideals and values and the capacity to love and invest oneself in others.

The leader of a psychiatric institution may obtain normal narcissistic gratification from her ability to develop an ideal department or hospital, from the opportunities for professional growth and development of staff, from the scientific progress the institution fosters, from enhancing organizational and administrative effectiveness, and, above all, from being able to offer the best possible treatment for the patients. Narcissistic gratifications also come from the administrator's awareness that she can help provide job satisfaction to coworkers and subordinates, a gratification that enhances their self-respect and can contribute to broader social and cultural goals. In other words, striving for a position of leadership may involve idealism and altruism, which are intimately linked with normal narcissism.

With pathological narcissism, in contrast, the narcissistic leader's aspirations center around primitive power over others, the desire for admiration, even awe, and the wish to be admired for personal attractiveness, charm, and brilliance, rather than for mature human qualities, moral integrity, or creative leadership. Under conditions of pathological narcissism, the leader's tolerance for the normal, unavoidable frustrations that go with his position is low, and a number of pathological developments take place within him in his interactions with the staff and in his leadership of the entire organizational structure.

Above all, the preeminence of unconscious and conscious envy has detrimental consequences for his relationships with his staff. Because he cannot tolerate others' obtaining success and gratification and cannot accept the professional success of others that he sees as overshadowing or threatening his own, the narcissistic administrator may become resentful of the most creative members of his staff. Narcissistic personalities may often be helpful to trainees or junior members of the staff, whose development they foster because the junior members unconsciously represent extensions of the leader's own grandiose self. When these younger colleagues reach a point in their development in which they become autonomous and independent, however, the leader's previous support may be transformed into devaluation and relentless undermining of their work.

A narcissistic mental health professional who assumes administrative functions that interfere with his clinical or research interests may envy his colleagues who continue their clinical work. One solution in such instances—which are fairly common—is for the senior administrator to obtain his narcissistic gratification from developing administration as his theoretical or practical specialized expertise, or for him to find a professional area other than his administrative work where he can continue doing creative work on his own.

It is part of normal narcissism to be able to enjoy the happiness and triumph of those one has helped to develop; enjoyment of the work and success of others—a general characteristic of the normal overcoming of infantile envy and jealousy—is an important function that is missing in the narcissistic personality. The narcissistic administrator may also envy some on his staff for the strength of their professional convictions; it is one of the tragedies of narcissistic personalities that their very lack of deep human values helps destroy those value systems and convictions they do have.

Another consequence of pathological narcissism stems from the encouragement of submissiveness in the staff. Since narcissistic leaders tend to surround themselves with yes men and shrewd manipulators who exploit their narcissistic needs, more honest and therefore critical members of the staff are pushed aside. Eventually, these staff members may constitute a relatively silent but dissatisfied and critical opposition. The dependent group of admirers further corrodes the administrator's self-awareness and fosters in him additional narcissistic deterioration.

The narcissistic leader might depreciate those he perceives as adulating him, but he cannot do without them; and his respect for the integrity of those who criticize him gradually erodes into paranoid fears. In terms of internalized object relations, it is as though the narcissistic leader induces in the human network of the organization a replication of his internal world of objects that is populated only by devalued, shadowy images of others and by images of dangerous potential enemies.

The narcissistic leader's inability to judge people in depth is a consequence of his pathology of internalized object relations. It stems both from the narcissistic personality's tendencies to achieve part object rather than total object relations (Kernberg, 1967, 1970) and from his lack of commitment to professional values and to value systems in general. The narcissistic administrator therefore tends to judge people on the basis of superficial impressions of their behavior, in terms of their past prestige or out of political considerations, rather than by a mature judgment of the nature of the task, the nature of the personality required to carry it out, and the personality and knowledge of the performer. This inability to form mature judgments about people and the reliance on sycophants reinforce each other and can lead to a situation in which the narcissistic leader is surrounded only by people similar to himself, people suffering from other serious behavior disorders or cynically exploiting their awareness of his psychological needs.

Paradoxically, in large institutions, the worse the distortion of the administrative structure by the leader's narcissistic pathology, the more compensating mechanisms may develop in the form of breakdown of boundary control and boundary negotiations, so that some institutional functions may actually go underground or, in more general terms, become split off from the rest of the organization. The situation appears parallel to what happens in some cases of severe psychopathology, when generalized splitting or primitive dissociation of the ego permits the patient to maintain a semblance of adaptation to external reality at the price of fragmentation of his ego identity. But the overall creativity of the organization suffers severely under such excessively narcissistic leadership. Although in the short run the grandiosity and expansiveness of the narcissistic leader may transmit itself throughout the organization as a pressure to work hard or as charismatic excitement and in so doing bring on a spurt of productivity, in the long run the deteriorating effects of pathological narcissism predominate. Creativity disappears in sweeping dependency or in the cynicism that develops among those in the organization with the greatest knowledge and strongest convictions.

When the institution directed by a narcissistic leader is small, the negative effects may be overwhelming from the beginning, for everyone is directly affected by the leader's problems. The development of his understanding is hampered by the leader's constant doubts and uncertainty—doubts derived from unconscious envy, devaluation, and lack of conviction—and by his need to constantly change his interests as he loses enthusiasm for what is no longer new and exciting. The narcissistic leader's incapacity to provide gratification of realistic dependency needs of the staff—in the simplest terms, his incapacity to listen—frustrates the staff's basic emotional needs and at the same time strengthens the negative consequences of the distortions in group processes: the creation of a submissive and dependent in-group and a depressed and angry out-group.

Severely narcissistic leaders whose ambition is frustrated by the external reality of the organization may require so much additional support from their staff that most of the institutional energy is spent in attempts to restore the leader's emotional equilibrium. In a department of psychiatry, the chairman had reached his position at an early stage of his career, when he seemingly was one of the promising members of his generation; however, he had progressively lost his ability to lead and had become embittered and depressed. After a number of years, those senior staff members who remained saw it as their principal organizational task to protect the leader from unnecessary stress and narcissistic lesions and to stimulate his capacities by offering ongoing applause and rewards. As a result, the general productivity of the department decreased noticeably.

It is encouraging to note that staff members of institutions directed by a narcissistic leader can maintain their personal integrity, autonomy, and independence in spite of the corrupting influence of their immediate environment. These isolated members can provide an outside consultant with the most meaningful information about the organization's hidden agendas, and they can give their coworkers hope for change in the midst of general despondency. It is as though the social situation of the institution were reflecting the intrapsychic life of narcissistic personalities—with fragments of healthy ego floating in a sea of deteriorated internalized object relations.

Although narcissistic leaders often emit an aura of extreme self-confidence and can stimulate the group's identification with that self-confidence, not all narcissistic leaders are charismatic and not all charismatic leaders are narcissistic. Personal charisma may stem from a combination of various personality traits and may be embedded in strong technical excellence, moral convictions, and human depth. Sometimes staff members accuse a strong and committed leader of being "narcissistic" when in reality they are projecting onto her their frustrated narcissistic aims and expressing envy of a successful person. The consensus leader—whom Zaleznik (1974) has contrasted with the charismatic one—may also present either severe narcissistic or normal personality characteristics. We must differentiate the mature consensus leader, who has the capacity to explore the thinking of her staff and creatively exploit the understanding and skills of her administrative group, from the power-oriented, smoothly functioning, politically opportunistic, narcissistic consensus leader, who shrewdly exploits groups phenomena for her own narcissistic aims.

There is a special kind of narcissistic leader whose gratifications come mostly from making himself the center of everyone's love, and at the same time the center of the decision-making process, while coolly sacrificing any considerations of value systems or the organization's functional needs to whatever is politically expedient. The typical example is the leader who is a "nice guy" with no enemies, who seems slightly insecure and easily changeable, and who at the same time is extremely expert in turning all conflicts among his staff into fights that do not involve himself. The general narcissistic qualities of shallowness, inability to judge sensitively, and inability to commit oneself to values are evident in his case, but what seems to be missing is the direct expression of grandiosity and the need to obtain immediate gratification from other people's admiration. At times this kind of leader obtains the gratification from using his position as a source of power and prestige beyond the organization itself. He may let the organization run its own course, trying to keep things smooth but more concerned that his power base be stable.

A somewhat similar outcome may occur when a different type of personality structure is in charge—namely, individuals with strong reaction formations against primitive sadistic trends. In this case, the direct friendliness of the leader to her immediate subordinates contrasts to the violent conflicts she precipitates at the level below that of her immediate administrative group. Still another type of consensus leader has achieved her position of the basis of her technical or professional skills and has accepted the position without ever fully assuming the responsibilities it entails. This is one of the conditions that creates an essentially leaderless organization: the person at the top is more interested in her own specialty than in developing authentic leadership, and for that reason avoids the painful process of making hard decisions. In summary, both charismatic and consensus leadership may stem from various normal and pathological sources.

One major issue that can be affected by pathological narcissism is the perennial one of when to compromise and when to stick to one's convictions in a particular conflict. At one extreme, the rigid, self-righteous person who insists on his own way and cannot accept compromise may reflect pathological narcissism; at the other extreme, the man willing to betray his convictions—and his staff—as self-interest dictates may equally reflect severe pathological narcissism. Somewhere in between these two positions are the realistic compromises by which the leader's essential convictions are respected and effective boundary negotiation is carried out in achieving a creative balance among conflicting priorities, tasks, and constraints. In other words, intelligent political maneuvering may protect the task and clarify what is essential and what is not. Sometimes it takes long-range vision to separate the immediate political implications of a certain move from its value in terms of the overall, long-range organizational tasks and goals. Pathological narcissism strongly interferes with the leader's ability to differentiate the expedient from the constructive.

THE CHOICE OF A NEW LEADER

When choosing a leader for an organization, it is necessary to explore intensively the broad area of human or interpersonal skills so that those skills are not inferred from what may be only surface adaptability and social charm. As we have seen, skill in judging immediate situations, skill in negotiating conflicts on a short-term basis, never creating enemies, and driving ambition are not necessarily good indicators of good leaders. The following are some questions that should be answered when selecting a leader.

How much creativity has the candidate shown in his field in the past? How much investment does he have in a professional source of gratification, and would it continue to be available to him once he assumed his administrative functions? How much gratification will he obtain from his own creativity as an administrator, rather than from external applause and admiration? Implied here is the depth of the prospective administrator's identification with professional values and with value systems in administrative theory and his capacity to identify with the goals of the organization. As a general rule, if the future administrator is judged capable of giving up his new administrative functions without a major loss in professional self-esteem, he has an important source of security that would be an asset in his position.

A major issue is the extent to which the administrator is aware of and invested in basic professional values, as opposed to issues that are fashionable and that offer short-term returns. Particularly during times of rapid change, a number of uncreative and even mediocre professionals rise to the top of their organization because they quickly shift to areas of popular interest.

Another question is to what extent the candidate has shown the courage to fight openly for her convictions, rather than manipulating conflicts with regard to power and prestige. The courage to stand up for her beliefs, to fight for her staff, to challenge the established powers—in terms of the task, rather than through immature emotional rebelliousness—is an important asset. One has to differentiate here courage stemming from strength of conviction from that representing paranoid querulousness, obsessive stubbornness, or narcissistic ruthlessness, but in practice it is not too difficult to do so. Strength and decisiveness are crucial to the decision making that is the main task of the administrator.

The extent to which the candidate obtains authentic enjoyment from the growth and development of other people is one more important consideration in the selection of a leader. The creativity and success of those who will work under her should not be threatened by excessive conflicts owing to envy in the leader.

Those in charge of evaluating potential leaders are usually aware of the importance of the leader's moral integrity, in addition to purely professional skills and assets; my stress has been on the additional importance of the leader's adherence to values—including professional values—and his relations with internal as well as external objects.

I mentioned earlier that there are normal narcissistic gratifications in leadership functions that ought to help prevent pathological regressions in the administrator's personality and compensate him for the regressive pulls coming from group processes throughout the organization. In addition, an adequate resolution of his oedipal conflicts may permit the leader to protect himself from regressive group processes and may contribute to his ability to take the position of leadership, to enjoy success, to triumph over rivals, and to combine assertiveness with tolerance and humanity—all important aspects of administrative work. Similarly, sufficient gratification of his sexual and dependent needs outside the organizational structure will also help the leader to resist regressive group pressures. Still, I am not saying that these issues are practical considerations that should enter into the selection process. Regardless of its important role in his ability to function, the administrator's personal and intrapsychic life, in contrast to his behavior, should be protected by boundaries of privacy. His character and moral integrity are part of his public domain.

Finally, under the best of circumstances, there will be built-in organizational constraints related to the human condition of social organizations, to the limitations of the personalities of the individuals involved; some battles need to be fought over and over again, endlessly so. The ideal administrator, like the ideal organization or the ideal group, reflects the regressive fantasies of groups and individuals.

Chapter 6 The Couch at Sea:
The Psychoanalysis of
Organizations

Psychoanalytic contributions to the theory of group and organizational psychology have a puzzling quality. A few of the key theoretical contributions in this area occupy a territory that is somewhat peripheral to the mainstream of psychoanalysis, and most psychoanalysts tend to shy away from them. These contributions have nevertheless had a significant impact on the intellectual, scientific, and even political scenes. Their impact, however, has been limited in the field of organizational intervention, and there are good reasons for that. More about this later.

In what follows I present a brief overview of this field, with an emphasis on an area that seems to have received less attention than it merits—that of leaders of groups and organizations. The title of my chapter is intended to convey the sense of uncertainty and even danger that I have come to associate with attempts to apply psychoanalytically gained knowledge to large groups and organizations.

FREUD AND LEADERSHIP

As mentioned before, Freud (1921) initiated the psychoanalytic study of group processes, explaining them in terms of his then newly developed ego psychology. In illustrating his theories of group psychology, Freud used the organization of the Church and the army as examples of the relation of the group or, rather, of the whole organization, to its leader. But, as François Roustang reminds us in *Dire Mastery* (1982), Freud was never actually in the army, nor was he a member of any church. His personal experience of leadership came from the psychoanalytic movement. Roustang notes the paradox that Freud, who critically described the irrational relations between leaders and followers in organized institutions, should have been the author of "On the History of the Psychoanalytic Movement," written in 1914. Freud's paper clearly indicates, according to Roustang, his conviction that a truly scientific commitment to psychoanalysis must coincide with loyalty to his (Freud's) ideas, whereas any questioning of key psychoanalytic concepts represented an unconsciously determined resistance to truth. The ad hominem nature of Freud's arguments against Jung and Adler is painful reading for any admirer of Freud's genius. One could dismiss Freud's relationships with his immediate followers as an irrelevant historical curiosity, were it not so intimately linked with subsequent psychoanalytic history. Roustang, in his study of the relation between master and disciple, calls attention to a contradiction inherent in all psychoanalytic societies. The goal of psychoanalysis is to resolve the transference. But psychoanalytic education attempts to maintain the transference that psychoanalysis tries to resolve. If fidelity to Freud, the charismatic founder of psychoanalysis, were required, the members of the societies could not become scientifically independent. This tradition has persisted, as Roustang makes clear in his discussion of Lacan.

Was Freud describing his psychoanalytic movement or unconsciously using it as a model while writing "Group Psychology and the Analysis of the Ego" (1921)? And how can one explain his lack of interest in examining the personality of the organizational leader? Freud seems to consider the nature of the leader mostly in terms of his symbolic function as the youngest son of the symbolically murdered father. Freud simply attributes to the leader characteristics of self-assuredness and narcissistic self-investment, in contrast to the libido the group invests in him.

BION AND LEADERSHIP

Bion's findings concerning small-group processes, summarized in his *Experiences in Groups* (1961), are the most important single contribution psychoanalysis has made to small-group psychology. But whereas Bion's method of exploring primitive defenses, object relations, and anxieties in small, unstructured groups may be of great value in learning about small-group psychology and group processes, or even about large organizations and large unstructured groups, the therapeutic value of his technique is questionable.

In fact, inherent in Bion's method is the refusal of the leader to participate in the group. The leader observes and interprets all transactions, even those directed toward himself, in terms of group processes as though he were a cipher. This strategy reduces the ordinary role relation between the members and the leader. The attempt to eliminate the leader as a distinct personality not only prevents the ordinary structuring of the group situation by means of socially accepted and reassuring roles and interactions, it creates—when applied to group psychotherapy—an artificiality in the posture of the leader. It results in making a mockery of the psychoanalyst seated unobserved behind the couch.

Confusing the psychoanalyst's technical neutrality with "disgruntled indifference," to which Freud himself (1927) objected, is a problem that is still prevalent. Some analysts think that to be technically neutral one not only must not share one's inner life with the patient (which is entirely appropriate) but must create the illusion that the analyst has *no* personality at all, which is hardly realistic. I doubt whether it could have been said of Freud that he appeared to his patients as a "man without qualities."

This issue is related to the current analytic controversy regarding the extent to which the transference is based on the reality of what the patient observes in the analyst or belongs to the patient's past. This discussion neglects the fact that the transference usually crystallizes around realistic aspects of the analyst's personality, which are exaggerated and distorted as a consequence of the patient's unconscious transfer from experiences in the past. To differentiate the reality of the stimulus for the transference from the transference per se as a distortion or an exaggeration of that stimulus has always been a primary technical task. My point is that the fantasy or wish to erase *any* reality stimulus derived from the analyst only serves the patient's unconscious need for idealization.

There are advantages and dangers in Bion's technique. Among the advantages are the sharp highlighting of primitive modes of mental operations and the possibility of examining unconscious processes that influence group behavior. On the negative side, questions have been raised (Scheidlinger, 1960; Malan et al., 1976) concerning the extent to which the artificial distancing of the group leader, the elimination of ordinary supportive features of group interactions, and the failure to provide cognitive instruments for self-understanding to individual patients regarding their particular psychopathology may be too demanding on the individual patient and thus be therapeutically counterproductive. Bion's technique may also artificially foster the idealization of the therapist.

Bion stresses that the basic-assumptions–group leaders are sucked into their leadership role by the very nature of the regression in the group. Hence, Bion's leader is really a prisoner of the group atmosphere, or, rather, the group uses his personality characteristics for its own purposes. In contrast, the leader of the work group has a rational approach to reality and an awareness of the boundaries of the group. This rational leader has a capacity for reality testing, an awareness of time, and the ability to stand up to the hatred of rationality activated under basic-assumptions conditions. The distinctions Bion draws between the two types of leaders offer seminal concepts for the understanding of the ascendancy of narcissistic and paranoid personalities under basic-assumptions–group conditions; but they also convey a strange failure to consider the reality of the person who is the work group leader. Did Bion assume that his own extremely powerful personality (which was apparent to everyone who met him) was submerged by his refusal to fulfill the ordinary role expectations in the group?

Again, this might appear to be a trivial issue, were it not that, after many years of silence regarding group issues, Bion again introduces the theme of the group and its leadership in *Attention and Interpretation* (1970). Here he refers to the "exceptional individual" who may be a genius, a messiah, a mystic, or a scientist. Bion offers Isaac Newton as an outstanding example, pointing to Newton's mystical and religious preoccupations as the matrix from which his mathematical formulations evolved. It is hard to avoid the impression that Bion is referring here not only to the work-group leader and his creativity, but also to a special type of leader whose convictions have a religious core, and whose behavior, as indicated by the collective term *mystic* (with which Bion frames this category), implies the secrecy of the initiated, an obscure or occult character, someone mysterious or enigmatic.

Bion here, I believe, is referring to himself, and the question of whether he was aware of that resonates with the question of whether Freud was aware of the nature of the model of the unmentioned leaders of the army or the Church. Be that as it may, Bion conveys a sense of the impotence of rationality, the fragility of the creative mystic, who is endangered by the envious, paranoid, pedestrian, conventional, and limited nature of what Bion calls the establishment. Bion describes three types of interactions between mystic and establishment; a mutually enriching, or "symbiotic," one, a mutually destructive, or "parasitic," one, and a mutual ignoring or "commensal" one. His emphasis is on the risk that the mystic who cannot be "contained" by the establishment will be destroyed by it, or vice versa, on the risk that the disruptive creativity of the mystic will destroy the establishment.

KENNETH RICE'S SCHOOL

Kenneth Rice's systems theory of organizations treats the individual, the group, and the social organization as each being a continuum of open systems. Rice (1965) integrates Bion's theories of small-group functioning with his own and with Turquet's (1975) understanding of large-group functioning and an open-systems theory of social organizations.

Within this model, psychopathology may be conceptualized as a breakdown of the control function, a failure to carry out the primary task, and a threat to the survival of the system. In the individual, we see breakdown of the ego and emotional regression; in the group, breakdown of leadership and paralysis in basic assumptions; and in the institution, breakdown of the administration, failure to carry out the institutional tasks, and loss of morale. Breakdown of boundary control is the principal manifestation of breakdown in the control function.

In my experience with both large and small groups, including group-relations conferences, the following phenomena emerge rapidly with impressive regularity and intensity: first, the activation of intense anxieties and primitive fantasies in the small study groups, and second, the activation of a primitive quality to both group functioning and potential individual aggression in the large group. The rapid development of ad hoc myths about the leadership or about the conference, and the search for a comprehensive and simplistic ideology in contrast to discriminating reasoning, illustrate in one stroke what happens during breakdown of organizational functioning. The crucial function of boundary control and of the role of task-oriented leadership in task performance emerges in contrast to the temptation, at points of regressions, to elevate the most dysfunctional members of subgroups to basic-assumptions–group leadership and to blur all boundaries in the emotional turmoil that pervades the group.

One important drawback to group-relations conferences is the relative failure on the part of the corresponding theory to consider the effects of their temporary nature. Katz and Kahn (1966), pointed out that when the staffs of social and industrial organizations try to learn new attitudes in the context of exploring the irrational aspects of group processes in an experiential setting, they frequently fail. This failure comes from their neglecting to analyze the stable features of the organizational structure and the relation between that structure and the real (in contrast to fantasied or irrational) conflicts of interests that such organizational structures mediate.

Short-term learning experiences in groups do not give the group members time to study the impact of personality structures on members of organizations, particularly the personality of key leaders.

Here we are touching again, now at the level of the relation between large-groups and organizational structures, on the same barely perceptible neglect of the impact of the personality of the leader on organizational conflicts. Rice has the enormous merit of having fully developed a theory of organizational functioning that permits the diagnosis of both organizational regression—"loss of morale"—and the administrative distortions that facilitate such regressive group processes, in a theoretically elegant and eminently practical approach to organizational dynamics. But, once again, the effects of the distorted personality on stable social organizations are missing here. It is almost as though the optimal, rational leader were a person without qualities or perhaps *should be* a person without qualities?

The more severe the leader's personality pathology and the tighter the organizational structure, the greater the destructive effects of the leader on the organization. It may be that under extreme circumstances, the paranoid regression of an entire society maintains the sanity of the tyrant and that when his control over that society breaks down he becomes psychotic: Hitler's final months point to this possibility.

Under less extreme circumstances, the effort to correct organizational distortions by changing the behavior of the leader may have disastrous consequences for her as well as for those at the next level. If the organization has to live with a characterologically dysfunctional leader, it may become preferable to adapt the administrative structure to an optimal balance between task requirements and the leader's needs—a solution that is the opposite of Rice's.

But how is one to know where to draw the line between restructuring the organization to protect it from the leader's pathology and acknowledging that the organization requires a different leader?

The application of a combined psychoanalytic and open-systems–theory model of institutional functioning to therapeutic community models (see Main, 1946) illustrates the limits of the therapeutic use of large-group analysis. (For a critique of therapeutic community models, see chapter 11.)

There is an enormous danger within a therapeutic community setting. The open exploration of the entire social field, wherein patients and staff interact by analyzing the content of the communications that emerge in the community meeting, may be transformed into a messianic denial of reality should the group come under the sway of a leader with a narcissistic and paranoid personality. It is exciting and potentially helpful to view the content of large-group meetings as a reflection of the unconscious of the organization and to trace the origin of distortions in the social system to its administrative structure, the psychopathology of individual patients, or conflicts at the boundary between patients and staff. By the same token, the transformation of trust and openness into the messianic spirit of the dependent or pairing group or, rather, the large group that has found a narcissistic leader and a soothing, simplistic ideology is a great and constant temptation for group and leader alike. The threat to rational evaluation of task boundaries and constraints and to the ordinary political negotiation around boundaries is enormous. The proverbial disillusionment and burning out of the staff involved in this process, who overextend themselves in a messianic overevaluation of what can and should be accomplished, needs no illustration.

Here we find a paradoxical effect of the psychoanalytic illumination of the unconscious in institutions: the deepest, hidden agendas of the institution appear at the surface in verbal communication at large-group meetings. But this is an illusion. The immediate availability of understanding of basic issues is no guarantee that they will be resolved. Unlike individual psychoanalysis, there is no direct link between emotional reality in groups and conflict resolution by actual institutional mechanisms of change. The neglect of the personality of the leader in the psychoanalytic contributions to group and organizational functioning mentioned before is compounded by the underestimation of the risk that all rational functioning will be disrupted by the snowballing effects of expanding small-group and large-group regressions in the process of self-exploration. The diagnostic instrument self-destructs, the collective patient becomes psychotic.

RATIONAL LEADERSHIP

Combining psychoanalytic observations of mobs, large groups, and small groups, I proposed in chapter 1 that group processes pose a basic threat to personal identity, a threat that is linked to a proclivity in group situations for the activation of primitive object relations, primitive defensive operations, and primitive aggression with predominantly pregenital features. For me, Turquet's description of what happens in large groups constitutes the basic situation against which (1) the idealization of the leader in the horde, described by Freud; (2) the idealization of the group ideology and of leadership that promotes narcissistic self-aggrandizement of the group, described by Anzieu (1981) and Chasseguet-Smirgel (1975); and (3) the small-group processes described by Bion (1961) are all defending.

Large-group processes also highlight the intimate connection between threats to one's identity and the participants' fear that primitive aggression and aggressively infiltrated sexuality will emerge (see chapter 3). I made the point earlier that an important part of nonintegrated and unsublimated aggression is expressed in vicarious ways throughout group and organizational processes. The exercise of power in organizational and institutional life constitutes an important channel for the expression in group processes of an aggression that would ordinarily be under control in dyadic or triadic relations.

I shall now modify and expand these formulations. I still maintain that large-group processes threaten individual identity and therefore activate defenses against identity diffusion and a defensive idealization of the leader. But this formulation underestimates the primary gratification to be found in dissolving in fantasy the boundaries between the self and the primitive forerunners of the ego ideal, in what Freud (1921)—referring to falling in love—called the fusion of ego and ego ideal in mania, in hypnosis, and in the excitement of identifying with others in the group. Anzieu and Chasseguet-Smirgel clarified this illusion of merger when they noted its preoedipal nature, which is in contrast to the illusion of merger with a cruel but morally sophisticated superego that characterizes Freud's group member. To put it differently, the messianic characteristic of small- and large-group regression, with its pregenital features and its denial of intragroup aggression, must be differentiated from the spirit of the mob, which satisfies every member's need to overcome a sense of separateness by participating in a common, powerfully self-righteous, emotionally laden movement forward, a movement that becomes the destructive expansion of a rioting mob (Canetti, 1960).

But these two levels of regressive temptation (of the small and large group as opposed to that of the crowd) also call for two layers of regressive leadership. At one extreme we find the self-indulgent narcissist who can lead the small, dependent, assumption group or pacify the large group with a simplistic ideology that soothes while preventing envy of the leader, or, in a more sophisticated combination, the sexually liberated narcissist who preaches sexual liberation in the group's (symbolic or actual) bathtub and condenses polymorphous, pre-oedipal sexuality with messianic merger. At the other extreme, and more disturbingly, we find the sadistic psychopath, who with a well-rationalized cruelty energizes the mob into destructive action against a common enemy and frees it from responsibility for murder.

In the previous chapter, I described the effects on organizational regression of various personality characteristics of the leader, with particular reference to schizoid, obsessive, paranoid, and narcissistic personalities. I limited my observations to small organizations, such as psychiatric hospitals and university departments, however, where there are usually no more than three hierarchical levels and where it is still likely that the leader and the followers know one another.

The question now is the extent to which such small, self-contained types of social organization surround the leader's position with a structure of rationality that would avoid the takeover by a sadistic or narcissistic leader or neutralize his regressive effects over an extended period. The possibility that the leader will be personally acquainted with everyone in the organization protects the realistic nature of the leadership of the institution. But larger organizations, such as national bureaucracies or international corporations, where four to seven hierarchic levels of leadership are the rule, may no longer offer the possibility of ordinary social control. In such large organizations, any direct contact between the different levels of staff becomes impossible or unrealistic, and the replacement of reality by projective mechanisms increases.

Jaques (1976) made a systematic study of bureaucracy. He found that well-functioning bureaucracies have merit. They provide the social system with rationally determined hierarchies, public delineation of responsibility and accountability, stable delegation of authority, and an overall accountability of the organization to its social environment by both legal and political means and through a parallel organization of employees or labor unions. Bureaucracies may thus provide an optimal balance between the potentially regressive consequences of hierarchically determined relations between individuals, on the one hand, and the redress of grievances and protection from arbitrariness, on the other.

Jaques's assumption is that the leaders of large social institutions are accountable to or controlled by the state. The implicit counterpart to this assumption is that when such social controls do not exist, the distortions at the top will go unchecked and will spread throughout the entire organization. A well-functioning bureaucracy in a democratic system may be an ideal model of organizational structure. In contrast, a tightly organized bureaucracy, controlled by a totalitarian state with a paranoid psychotic or a sadistic psychopath at its head, would represent a social nightmare into which the regression of all included groups would easily fit, without any possibility of rational correction. The totalitarian bureaucracies of Nazi Germany and the Soviet Union were able to murder millions of people without causing internal convulsions. These examples suggest that the authoritarian power generated within organizations, which stems from both individual psychopathology and organizational regression, not to mention the ordinary discharge into the organization of the unacknowledged narcissistic and aggressive needs of all its individuals, may rapidly increase, given certain social and political conditions, and transform into socially sanctioned cruelty and dehumanization. The distinction between an ordinary dictatorship in which the right to privacy is preserved as long as no direct action is taken against the regime and a totalitarian system in which all social interactions are regulated by an imposed ideology may be one of the painful discoveries of our time.

Canetti, in *Masse und Macht* (Crowds and power, 1960), describes the universal temptation to become part of a crowd and to ensure personal survival and immortality by killing others as a basic unconscious motive for desiring the leadership of the crowd. The psychoanalytic study of a particular subgroup of narcissistic patients with aggressive infiltration of their pathological grandiose self elaborated by Rosenfeld (1971) provides a counterpart to Canetti's description.

Psychoanalytically oriented consultants for institutional problems, whether they follow the model of Rice, Jaques, Levinson (1972), or Zaleznik (1979), assume that regressive manifestations in group processes indicate institutional malfunctioning and that these group processes potentially point to the nature of the conflicts affecting the system. The consultant's usual procedure is to study the primary tasks of the organization, its administrative structure, how authority is distributed and delegated, whether its system has checks and balances, and whether it provides for redress of grievances. With the possible exception of Levinson's, all these approaches focus on the leadership only after other factors have been explored, arriving there by the process, as it were, of elimination. Personality problems always appear at first in the foreground, but they can be diagnosed as causal features only after all the other institutional issues have been analyzed and discarded.

Jaques's (1976, 1982) findings regarding an individual's capacity for work as measured by his capacity to estimate the time it will take to accomplish certain tasks and his ability to organize and carry out such tasks (the maximum time span of decision making in his work) offer an important contribution to organizational psychology and to selection criteria for leadership. Yet the psychoanalytically oriented consultant may be averse or reluctant to take this factor into consideration and would more likely think in terms of psychopathology than of the leader's unequal capacity to perform various tasks. In fact, it may be more difficult to assess this quality than to assess or even identify the aspects of personality that produce optimal leadership functioning. The leader of an organization, as well as the consultant, must be constantly alert to the danger of giving rein to his own narcissism and aggression and therefore may have difficulty acknowledging that managerial leaders do differ in administrative capabilities. The leader (and the consultant) must also resist any tendency to allow himself to be influenced by fears of arousing unconscious envy by exposing these differences. The leader's task is to judge. Perhaps the best he can do is remain alert to the implications of standing in judgment on others.

On the basis of my experience as a psychoanalyst, leader of groups (including therapeutic communities), medical director of psychiatric hospitals, and consultant to mental health institutions, I offer a list of the personality characteristics most conducive to rational task leadership. Intelligence, which is necessary for strategic conceptual thinking, is the most important, followed by honesty and uncorruptibility, the capacity to establish and maintain object relations in depth (which is essential for evaluating others realistically), a healthy narcissism (in the sense of being self-assertive rather than self-effacing), and, finally, a sense of caution and alertness to the world—what someone I once knew called justifiable anticipatory paranoia.

The importance of intelligence that is expressed in the capacity for strategic conceptual thinking and probably also in creative imagination is self-evident. The value of honesty and uncorruptibility is also self-evident, but these qualities must be tested under conditions of stress and political constraints. In practice, many leaders can be fair and just to people they know personally; but to be fair and just to unknown subordinates is the test of disinterested integrity. The leader's fairness to the entire staff will necessarily appear as rigidity to the few in her immediate entourage; her incorruptibility in the face of the temptations of leadership will be experienced as sadistic rejection by the tempters, as may her maintenance of fair rules for all. Here the narcissistic investment in moral righteousness, together with paranoid distrust of temptation, may protect rational leadership. These functions require a well-integrated and mature superego, which assumes the sublimatory nature of ideals and value systems and signifies the preconditions for normal (in contrast to pathological) narcissism.

Under optimal conditions, the leader's narcissistic and paranoid features may each neutralize the other's potentially negative effects on the organization and on the leader herself. The paranoid implications of suspiciousness toward subordinate kowtowing may prevent the disastrous consequences of a narcissistic leader's needs to be obeyed *and* loved at the same time. The narcissistic enjoyment of success in leadership may prevent the erosion of self-confidence that derives from paranoid fears about potential attack or criticism from others. In contrast to these optimal combinations, a severe character pathology in the leader in the form of pathological narcissism complicated by paranoid features may prove disastrous (see Kernberg, 1980b, chap. 13).

What is the "correct" balance of normal narcissism and paranoia required for rational leadership? Is it firmness without sadism, incorruptibility without rigidity, warmth without manipulativeness, or emotional depth without the loss of distance required to focus on the gestalt of the group, and on the task rather than its human constraints? The ideal leader of an organization may have to ignore the impact of his own personality on the organization if he is to address the needs of the group, but he must not thereby lose his capacity to exploit his personality in the leadership role.

A small amount of narcissism and paranoia may reinforce the power of rationality and honesty, and a small amount of sadism may protect the task systems from regression. Yet an excess of these traits can trigger regression in leaders: a sense of justice and fairness may become self-righteousness and sadistic control. Regression in the leader can in turn trigger regression in the organization.

In the psychoanalytic situation, the psychoanalyst has sufficient boundary control to help a patient discover his unconscious and permit the development and potential resolution of the patient's unconscious conflicts over sexuality and aggression in the transference. In transferring the psychoanalytic investigation to group processes, an easy activation of primitive processes may occur, which would immediately exceed the boundary control of the exploring psychoanalyst. By the same token, the psychoanalytic consultant, in exploring organizational issues that deal with the personality of the leader, may trigger a violent reaction that would destroy not only the consultative process but the capacity of the organization to tolerate this confrontation. The complexities of communicating organizational dynamics may be one factor limiting the consultant's task. But it is not the dominant one. The discrepancy between the analytic instrument that is used to evaluate group-shared unconscious fantasies and basic-assumptions groups and apply a system theory of organizations, on the one hand, and the capacity for containment by the institution, on the other, may be a more important, perhaps intimidating barrier to advances in this field.

Ambiguity pervades the subject of leadership in Freud, Bion, and others. My metaphoric title, "The Couch at Sea," should communicate some of the excitement I find in exploring the social unconscious, even if the uncertainties still facing us mean that we must navigate in troubled waters—and on the couch rather than behind it.

Chapter 7 The Moral Dimension of Leadership

In this chapter, I focus on the psychological pressures that may induce or reinforce corruption in organizational leadership. This corruption is manifest in practices that violate the ethical principles of leadership by tolerating contradictions between public and confidential actions and thus doing injustice to organization members or to those who depend on the organization. Corruption can lead to deterioration of the task-oriented function of groups, task systems, and the entire organization. I shall focus on the forces that tend to undermine the moral character of leaders in organizations and on the counterforces, including the leader's personality, that can control and reverse this process.

Even in the absence of gross corrupting factors, that is, when a relatively normal, mature, intelligent, and capable leader assumes a position that he could leave without undue threat to his self-esteem, or when the job offers no inherent occasions or temptations for financial or power abuses, or when the prestige the leader obtains from the position does not exceed that available to him in other areas—even under these circumstances, there is a risk of moral deterioration that derives from the two major dimensions of narcissism and paranoia.

Psychoanalytic theorizing about group functioning, starting with Freud (1921), has explored the psychology of the followers rather than the leader. Bion's (1961) basic-assumptions groups—the dependency, fight-flight, and pairing assumptions—focused on the characteristics of small groups of followers.

Bion pointed to the potential for the leader to be seduced into assuming a role that fit with the regressed groups' momentary desire rather than their long-term needs, but he did not describe the group leader's personality as a cause of this situation. But he implies that narcissistic personalities can be easily "seduced" into leadership functions when faced with the regression of the dependency group and that paranoid personalities can be "seduced" into leadership functions under prevailing conditions of fight-flight assumptions.

Rice (1969) and Turquet (1975) complemented the basic psychoanalytic studies of mass phenomena by Freud and of small-group processes by Bion with their analysis of large-group processes and, particularly, of regression in large groups. Once again, the function of the leader's personality was ignored. In fact, as Katz and Kahn (1966) first pointed out, the functional analysis of group processes, organizational structure, and their interaction derived from psychoanalytic models typically omit the influence of the leader's personality as a crucial codeterminant of the organizational structure.

It was only natural that once the basic psychoanalytic theory of group processes stemming from these fundamental contributions became integrated into actual research on organizational functioning, the previously ignored (or denied) role of the personality of the leader was brought back into focus. Thus, Levinson (1972), Zaleznik (1979), Chasseguet-Smirgel (1975), and Anzieu (1981) focused on personality aspects of the leader that foster or may control the regression in groups within organizational functioning. Zaleznik concentrated on the respective impacts of the consensus and the charismatic leader, Levinson on the mutual relation between transference regression in followership and the personality of the leader, and Anzieu and Chasseguet-Smirgel on the "merchant of illusions," the narcissistic, self-indulgent leader of regressed groups who gratifies the group's search for an all-giving, grandiose yet nonthreatening, pseudopaternal leader and who protects them from reality and the higher level of oedipal conflicts.

Rangell (1974), in describing the syndrome of the compromise of integrity, pointed to the corruption of superego functioning induced by unbridled narcissism, noting as well the facilitating function of regressive group processes in bringing about such superego deterioration in leaders. He stressed that the superego was more open to environmental influence than the other psychic structures and that group processes affecting the leader would typically pressure him into adopting moral stances that were mutually contradictory.

Earlier, I stressed the specific effects of obsessive, schizoid, paranoid, and narcissistic aspects of the personality of the leader on social organizations and groups within them, pointing to the importance of analyzing how the channels of gratification of the leader's narcissistic, dependent, sexual, and aggressive needs run within and outside the organization. In exploring the respective interactions between paranoid leaders and fight-flight groups, narcissistic leaders and dependency groups, and seductive-hysterical leaders and pairing groups, I concluded that the essential ingredients of the leader's personality that determine its impact on organizational functioning are her level of narcissistic integration, the extent of her paranoid tendencies, her intelligence, and her moral integrity. I shall now explore the factors that can lead to the leader's corruption, particularly those that derive from regression in the leader's group.

COLLECTIVE TRANSFERENCES

Even in the best-run organization, where task groups are organized efficiently and the administrative structure is attuned to the organizational tasks so that a minimum of group regression develops, regressive pressures surround the leader. These derive from the universal transference dispositions of all the members of the organization, transference dispositions that might be classified—perhaps too simplistically but comprehensively—as preoedipal and oedipal longings. The preoedipal longings for dependency and nurturance are accompanied by preoedipal types of idealization on the one hand and preoedipal types of envious resentment, and paranoid projections of this envy onto the leader, on the other. The effect of these trends is that the leader's image is changed in the followers' mind into that of a person who fulfills (and consequently frustrates) magical expectations for protection, guidance, nurturance, and personal affection and love. Preoedipal idealization also defends followers from negative preoedipal transferences and may foster or reinforce the leader's narcissistic tendencies while potentially frustrating his own dependency needs.

Unconscious—and conscious—envy of the leader tends to blend with oedipal conflicts in relation to him. At the level of oedipal transferences, the leader-follower relationship may vary for male and female members of the organization. For men in organizations with a male leader, oedipal idealization of the father as an omnipotent and omniscient protector blends with the preoedipal need for dependency and an implicit desire for unconscious homosexual submission. These needs are balanced by oedipal competitiveness (expressed as rivalry) and the wish to rebel against and triumph over the oedipal father, with its corollary of projection of aggression onto the leader and corresponding paranoid fears of him. Insofar as leadership implies the exercise of authority over followers, the realistic aspects of leadership strengthen these trends. Oedipal rivalry and submissiveness strengthen the paranoid features of the transference reaction toward the leader. Dissociative tendencies in followers may emerge: there may be an alternation between paranoid fearfulness and idealizing, submissive playing out of the homosexual dynamics of the negative Oedipus complex.

The relationship of female staff members to the male leader may carry the transference implications of oedipal sexualization with its complement of seductive submissiveness, direct erotization of the relationship, and the temptation to masochistic behaviors as an expression of unconscious guilt owing to the oedipal aspects involved. In women, the idealization of the oedipal father usually predominates over the aggressive conflicts related to the negative Oedipus complex, to envy and resentment of men, and to the desire for pseudoaggressive interactions derived from masochistic tendencies.

These oedipal relationships tend to be inverted in organizations with female leaders, with the additional complication that, insofar as female leadership runs counter to ingrained, traditional patterns, complex compromise formations between culturally stereotyped behavior and deeper transference dispositions tend to develop. (This is an important subject, but it is outside the scope of this chapter.)

The cumulative effect of all these transference dispositions is pressure to idealize the leader that stimulates his narcissistic tendencies as well as paranoid fearfulness in relating to him. Even the cautious expression of paranoid developments by followers tends to evoke counterparanoid tendencies in the leader. Projective identification is probably the mechanism most responsible for inducing behavior related to repressed or dissociated object relations between leaders and their followers. Thus, even under optimal organizational circumstances, there are powerful trends leading to narcissistic and paranoid stimulation of the leader. The net effect of these transference dispositions is to stimulate the leader's narcissistic self-aggrandizement and his paranoid disposition, frustrate his dependency needs, amplify his aggressive responses as perceived by the staff under the influence of the followers' paranoid dispositions, and lend a subtle sexuality to his relationships with members of the organization, which may add an erotic quality to institutional life but which may also destroy administrative relationships by leading to sexual conflicts.

Under less than ideal conditions (which, given human nature, is the rule rather than the exception), the regressive potential is magnified. This increase of the narcissistic, paranoid, or sexual dimension of organizational regression may simply be a response to an organizational structure that is less than functional and is moving in the direction of either authoritarianism or chaos. I am still talking only about the consequences of transference dispositions for the administrative structure; I am not yet addressing the complications that derive from the development of regressive group processes.

THE EFFECTS OF NONFUNCTIONAL ADMINISTRATIVE STRUCTURES

The administrative structure can be considered functional when the distribution and delegation of authority, task definition, task performance, and task monitoring are matched by appropriate—that is, sufficient and stable but not excessive—investment of authority in managerial leaders at all levels. I shall not explore in detail the characteristics and the "check-points" of this here. What interests me is that when excessive authority is vested in the leader of the organization or in any level of leadership within it, it tends to distort administrative relationships throughout the entire organization. When I speak of authoritarian administration, I mean administration invested with power beyond what is functionally required for carrying out organizational tasks.

One immediate consequence of authoritarian leadership is a reduction in the flow of information, the reduction of feedback from followers to leaders, and an intensification of the dependent-idealizing-narcissistic dimension of the leader-followers relationship and of its rebellious-submissive-paranoid dimension as well. If the leader seems to take on the functions of the fantasied oedipal father whose will is almighty, who cannot be questioned, and yet who tempts the son to rebel against him, the dynamics of transference regression are exacerbated. Under these conditions, the erotization of immediate relationships around the leader may defensively protect the organization from excessive regression into the narcissistic or paranoid dimensions by involving him in an isolating erotic network. This development, however, is the exception rather than the rule. An authoritarian leader is usually strengthened in his authoritarian tendencies by the intense idealization, admiration, and submission he evokes, as well as by the subtle or not-so-subtle hatred and rebelliousness he also evokes. An authoritarian administrative structure, in short, fosters narcissistic and paranoid regression in the authoritarian leader at the same time it induces transference regression along the same lines among the members of the organization.

If the level of authority vested in the leader is reduced rather than increased in comparison to functional requirements—in other words, if there is insufficient or inadequate authority vested in the leader to allow him to define and establish priorities for organizational tasks, to direct them, to monitor them, and to maintain viable organizational boundaries among them, a similar regressive process occurs. The reduction in the authority of functional leadership reduces the clarity of task systems, weakens leadership functions throughout the organization, blurs the boundaries of functional, task-related groups, and tends to bring about an immediate regression in the group processes of the organization. The result is an activation of the unstructured small- and large-group processes referred to earlier. Typically, small-group regression occurs as fight-flight— and dependency-group assumptions, a process that affects the task systems (which are typically small groups), while large-group regression (including a loss of morale) occurs throughout the organization.

THE EFFECTS OF SMALL- AND
LARGE-GROUP REGRESSION

In practice, the development of fight-flight–group regression is characterized by organizational splits in which subgroups strongly defend the leadership while other subgroups attack it, a development that can coincide with a tendency in other groups to regress into dependency, which shows in a generalized sense of passivity, helplessness, and "deskilling" even as they hope for magic solutions from above. If primitive idealization of the leader, punctured by frustrated, angry helplessness because he is failing in his leadership functions, characterizes the dependency group, rage, attacks on, and desperate fears of retaliation from the leader characterize the fight-flight group. The reduction in functional leadership activates the paranoid and narcissistic dimensions of leader-followers relationships that are characteristic of authoritarian developments. In addition, the loss of functional group structure that gradually evolves under authoritarianism also brings about group regression, particularly small-group regression of the fight-flight type, as staff splits into subgroups whose members assume a passive, submissive, defensively idealizing attitude toward the leadership on the one hand and an angry, fearful, and suspicious position on the other.

Simultaneously, under authoritarian extremism or chaotic loss of authority, large-group processes tend to become activated. Signs that these processes are at work are a sense of disorientation regarding external reality, the loss of a clear sense of identity, a pervasive fear that aggression will be activated, and a search for some soothing, nonthreatening, self-indulgent authority figure—in other words, narcissistic regression (Kernberg, 1987). If the organization is naturally split into opposing camps—management and labor, for example, or doctors and nurses or teachers and students—the large group may be transformed into the dynamic mass described by Freud (1921) that seeks a powerful, aggressive leader who will organize it and the organization in the context of a fight against external enemies. Here the search for a paranoid leader to conduct organizational warfare replaces the search made by the static large group for a narcissistic leader.

In summary, any breakdown in the administrative structure, particularly when it triggers regressive group processes throughout the organization as well, will generate powerful tendencies of a persecutory-paranoid as well as an idealizing-narcissistic type in the organization, putting enormous pressure on the leader to become either paranoid, autocratic, and aggressive or self-indulgent, self-idealizing, and soothingly narcissistic. A sexualized "privatization" of the leader's immediate environment is an infrequent and usually inadequate defense against these powerful processes. Jaques (1955, 1976) coined the term *paranoiagenesis* to refer to paranoid regressions as a constant potential in organizations, and I might add that such paranoiagenesis usually runs parallel to primitive idealization, processes being kept separate by a generalized splitting of object relations in the context of organizational regression (see chapter 8).

There are, however, corrective forces that may be activated in what I have described as the potential for regression in social organizations. These corrective forces constitute potential devices to protect the leader from regression and, particularly, from the deterioration of the moral dimension of leadership. If the leader can continue to analyze the main tasks of the organization and their constraints, the relation between developments in the environment and the mission and capabilities of the organization, and the monitoring and protection of organizational boundaries, he may have time to analyze the organization's internal constraints and conflicts and resolve them. In addition, his use of certain basic principles of organizational management may counteract group regression. These principles include reinforcing the functional aspects of the administration, strengthening the formal channels of communication, and emphasizing the means of grievance redress. Such principles can protect against excessive paranoid tendencies and provide opportunities for analyzing the organizational conflicts in the context of clearly structured meetings. Executive conferences can be set up, for example, in which information is shared, as opposed to executive meetings at which decisions are made; the three-level system of administrative checks and balances and redress of grievances (a staff member, her supervisor, and the supervisor's supervisor) can be emphasized; and rational relations may be fostered among such internal and external control agencies as legal structures, professional organizations, the board of trustees, and labor unions, all of which offer forums for rational analysis that can counteract the rumors, institutional demoralization, and sense of diffusion of decision making.

THE LEADER'S PERSONALITY

Earlier, I concluded that from the point of view of optimal resistance to the regressive pressures operating on the leadership, the leader's personality should include a moderate quota of narcissistic tendencies, some paranoid potential, intelligence, and a well-developed sense of morality. In what follows I expand on this proposal and bring it into the context of the temptations for regression in the organizational leader.

In briefly summarizing some generally accepted conditions for effective leadership I shall refer to what Klerman and Levinson (1967) call the leader's technical, human, and conceptual skills. Technical skills refer to his knowledge of the particular field his organization is involved in. The leader's technical skills tend to be important in inverse proportion to the number of hierarchical levels in the organization and the job level he achieves. In fact, one might say that while conceptual skills become increasingly important at the higher levels of hierarchically complex organizations, technical skills are more important at the lower levels of hierarchy or in less hierarchical organizations. Again, I am stressing the functional level of hierarchies that correspond to significant discontinuities in the span of administrative authority, an issue discussed by Jaques (1976, 1982).

The leader's conceptual skills correspond to his intelligence, and Jaques has convincingly proposed that the leader's conceptual skill is reflected in his capacity for an extended "time span of decision making," which means, in practice, the capacity to develop realistic long-range plans, in which are implicit many levels of information and relative independence from short-term constraints on the decision-making process.

Technical and conceptual skills refer to knowledge and intelligence; human skills refer to the leader's personality. There are infinite individual personality traits that are commensurate with leadership functions and a limited number of known, severe personality disorders that for various reasons may limit or severely cripple leadership capacities. Here I shall focus on the positive aspect of certain personality traits, particularly narcissistic and paranoid structures.

A strong sense of personal security that is relatively independent of immediate social feedback—in other words, a modicum of normal (infantile or adult) narcissism embedded in a somewhat neurotic yet basically adaptive personality structure—can provide healthy insulation for the leader. All neurotic character pathology serves narcissistic functions; if an excessive level of self-assurance, ambition, and need to be admired are part of a character structure that does not reflect the pathological narcissism of a narcissistic personality disorder, such narcissistic traits may protect the leader from narcissistic lesions (insecurity) as well as from excessive paranoid reactions to not being loved all the time by everyone. The danger is that the leader's narcissistic tendency might be reinforced by adulation. Such adulation may bring about a circular process wherein artificially inflated self-esteem derived from idealization and admiration gradually diminishes the leader's capacity for self-criticism and leads to a chronic narcissistic regression that may become unfitted to leadership. This narcissistic regression can corrupt the leader's abilities, because his emotional needs may now run counter to the demands of the organizational tasks. The protection of the leader's self-esteem and the reinforcement of his narcissistic gratifications take precedence over painful decision making, and favoritism may replace justice in dealing with colleagues and subordinates.

Here an integrated, autonomous superego may intervene as a protective structure that provides the leader with a capacity for self-evaluation and fairness, thus counteracting the danger of narcissistic deterioration. But it is difficult for the leader with narcissistic tendencies, however benign, not to feel reassured by the friendly responses of those who know how to cater to his narcissism. It is difficult for him not to come to resent those who refuse to give him those responses. The leader's narcissism will convey his need to be loved, which will tempt some of his followers to ingratiate themselves with him. An element of corruption inevitably enters into this interaction.

In contrast, the tolerance for other people's criticism, the mature narcissistic gratification at being able to tolerate criticism and to learn from it, is an important corrective. Sometimes a leader's narcissism permits him to listen to criticism privately though not publicly; here begins the responsibility of a realistic assessment by followers: What are the limits of the leader's capacity to listen? Only the consistently responsible behavior of followers defines the objective boundaries of the leader's capacity to respond positively to critical feedback.

Also related to narcissism is the leader's potential envy of those of his followers whom, because of his envy of their capacities, he perceives as more gratified by their functions than he is—in particular, as more gratified in their dependency needs or their needs to be positively rewarded for their work. And there is his envy of those whom he perceives as more successful or more creative than he, or those whom he perceives as a potential threat to his authority. The latter also relates to the paranoid aspects of the leader's personality, but the conscious and unconscious envy of followers (and projective defenses against such envy) are important concomitants of narcissistic leadership. It cannot be stressed too strongly that when leaders retain an independent area in which to develop their own technical, professional, or conceptual expertise, their tolerance of the creativity of coworkers is much greater, and this tolerance helps creativity within the entire organization. The leader, however, whose main motivational goal is not the same as that of the rest of the leadership, who becomes an absent leader, and who views the organization as a constraint to his own interests will have a negative impact on the organization and its staff.

The other major dimension that may protect—and also threaten—leadership functions is paranoid alertness. There is an enormous difference between a "normal" paranoid capability and a paranoid personality: the leader with the paranoid personality feels constantly hurt and potentially persecuted; he perceives all critical feedback as insubordination; and at times he may transform his organization into a fortress against the external environment, behind whose boundaries he must deal with the ever-present danger of a fifth column. At the opposite pole, a complete absence of concerned alertness and suspiciousness implies naïveté, that is, a denial of the ubiquity of aggression, of the ambivalence that is normal in all human relations and that is certainly typical of organizations.

The leader cannot afford to be naive, because there will be objective aggression in the ambivalence toward him from all the members of the organization of whose collective transferences he is the target. We have already examined these transferences, and here it remains only to say that they may express themselves in ambivalent behaviors that reduce the efficiency of the organization and that, unconsciously, also express indirect aggression toward the leader. The leader of the organization needs to be aware that he is the target of such aggression, as well as of idealization, and that he is the focus of both narcissistic and paranoid temptations. His alertness may help him to diagnose early or even to prevent potentially damaging actions against him and the organization, but at the same time, his paranoid capability may also activate his own counteraggression and increase his suspiciousness beyond the reality of the situation.

In fact, one of the sources of authoritarian behavior in the leader is precisely the acting out of counteraggression that is spurred by paranoid sensitivity to staff ambivalence. The leader who needs to exercise absolute control in order to feel secure from aggression may by the same token corrupt the organization because his authoritarian behavior will foster submissiveness and opportunism as it splits the staff into a narcissistic-submissive and a paranoid-withdrawn group. The "paranoid urge to betray" (Jacobson, 1971a) is typically expressed in the leader's righteous indignation over real or imagined slights, with a subsequent, revengeful misuse of his authority in order to punish the culprits of the attack. Here it is the paranoid dimension of leadership that triggers organizational corruption, as the leader's revenge induces the followers' shared gleefulness, colluding indifference, or attitudes of innocence. The extent to which the leader's paranoid tendencies permit him to absorb the aggression of his followers rather than to return it in the form of authoritarian self-assertion marks the difference between the positive and negative effects of paranoid personality features in the leader. Thus, both narcissistic and paranoid trends in the leader may either protect his leadership function or bring about its deterioration. The deterioration of leadership in turn reinforces narcissistic and paranoid regression in the organization and fosters organizational corruption as part of the defensive processes triggered by such regression.

The narcissistic and the paranoid aspects of the leader and the followers influence their relationships in complex ways. There may be a hidden grandiosity of the leader that is fostered by the idealizing and submissive tendencies of the followers, especially in relatively isolated organizations with long-term leadership. By the same token, the hidden aggression of the followers expressed in chronic "passive" ambivalence may first bring about the leader's hypersensitive and eventually authoritarian reaction and then intensify and be successfully projected onto the leader himself, eventually tempting him into a paranoid response.

The leader's narcissistic and paranoid tendencies may balance each other, so that his narcissistic stability protects him from reacting with excessive aggression to challenges within the organization, and his paranoid tendencies offer a relatively harmless channel for balancing angry responses to narcissistic lesions.

But with more severe character pathology, narcissistic and paranoid tendencies may reinforce each other. Under extreme conditions, leaders with severely narcissistic and paranoid tendencies may exert a sadistic control over the organization, with devastating consequences for themselves and everybody else in it.

I described elsewhere (1984a) the syndrome of malignant narcissism, constituted by the combination of a narcissistic personality disorder, severe paranoid tendencies, ego-syntonic aggression, and antisocial features. In fact, the deterioration of superego functioning under the impact of narcissistic and paranoid regression is one of its most dangerous consequences. Revolutionary mass movements often boast leaders with such a narcissistic and paranoid personality structure: the paranoid dimension provides the leadership needed for an aggressive challenge to the status quo while the narcissistic dimension provides the certainty of a utopian future once the revolutionary group has triumphed. Both Hitler and Stalin presented a personality structure with features of malignant narcissism, which may be a characteristic common to revolutionary leaders who end up as sadistic tyrants.

The consensus leader, under optimal circumstances, has a healthy narcissism that permits him to work with a group, to obtain and tolerate feedback, to experience narcissistic gratification in the shared decision-making process, and to transform his group into a functional task system. A consensus leader may, however, also evolve into the narcissistic "good guy" leader who tries to avoid conflicts and painful decisions, whose leadership function becomes overly politicized and opportunistic, and who eventually corrupts the system. Similarly, the charismatic leader's self-assertiveness may make him firm in the exercise of his leadership functions. On the negative side, it may lead to excessive idealization of and submission to him by followers, fear about their own rebelliousness and a paranoid projection of that fear onto him. It can thus reinforce the paranoid dimension of the leadership and cause an authoritarian regression in the organization. What really counts is the underlying nature of the narcissistic and paranoid equilibrium. Particular leadership styles do not necessarily protect the organization from regression.

THE LEADER'S VALUE SYSTEMS AND
ORGANIZATIONAL CORRUPTION

Three dimensions of organizational functioning are intimately connected with carrying out leadership roles. These dimensions present us with the paradox that what is most useful for the organization is also threatening to its functioning, particularly to the moral aspect of leadership. I refer to (1) the political dimension of negotiation across task-system and organizational boundaries; (2) the exercise of power as part of legitimate authority; and (3) the activation of an ideological superstructure on the basis of the task sentience of the members of the organization.

The political dimension of leadership refers to the leader's capacity to create allies dedicated to task performance. Given the contradictory aims and motivations of competing parts of the organization and the different constraints within it, conflicts of interest are to be expected. To convince those who have conflicting loyalties and interests that it is necessary to compromise in order to achieve broad institutional goals cannot be done simply on the basis of rational argument but requires what might best be called tactful lobbying.

The danger is that expediency may run counter to the overall organizational interest; that in order to gain the goodwill of one group, for example, the leader will have to sacrifice basic task requirements. Here either the strength of the leader's commitment to overall institutional goals will protect him from making counterproductive deals (though there is a risk that should he remain rigid in his decision making, it will alienate the people who have to carry out the task), or he will compromise at the expense of overall organizational interests. An obsessive leader faced with such a situation may create unnecessary constraints and even paralyze organizational decision making. At the other extreme, flexibility may become deal making that can eventually corrupt the leader's work for the organization.

The use of financial incentives illustrates the conflict. Offering leading figures in the organization bonuses can tempt them to demand "deals"—or tempt the institution into offering them—that will be distributed unfairly and lead to a general sense of injustice. At the other extreme, a bureaucratic system of rewards that protects the organization against arbitrariness can damage the organization's capacity to compete effectively for leading staff with other institutions.

There is another aspect of the leader's reward system that can also lead to either corruption or self-defeating rigidity. It is almost unavoidable for strong pressures to build up around the leader to offer rewards preferentially to those with whom he has a personal relationship, as well as to those he must engage in political discussion regarding organizational interests. But there are also important workers several levels removed from him who merit or expect rewards. The leader's narcissism might tempt him to reward only the former; this could foster opportunism and corruption.

The exercise of power is an essential, unavoidable part of leadership, and it requires a leader to draw comfortably on the aggressive aspects of her own personality. Power, defined as the capacity to carry out organizational work and, in the case of leaders, to lead staff in this process, stems from many sources: the authority vested in the leader by the institution; the authority derived from her personality characteristics and her technical and intellectual skills; the authority delegated to her by professional or other sentience groups; the projection onto her of aggression as part of the paranoid dimension of organizational functioning; and the idealization of her as part of the narcissistic-dependent dimension of organizational functioning.

As I mentioned earlier, the effective exercise of authority occupies a middle range between excessive exercise of power, which transforms authority into authoritarianism, and inadequate exercise of power, which is a cause of deterioration and failure in leadership and leads to organizational chaos and immediate regression in the group processes. My position differs from the traditionally opposing views that power either resides in the personality of the leader or in the organizational structure.

The concentration of power in the leader and his exercise of it tend to vary, or, rather, there are varying conditions that tempt the leader to increase the exercise of power and that increase or inhibit his capacity to do so. The successful functioning of the organization offers a sense of satisfaction to everyone involved, and it tends to give a sense of power to these individuals and groups as well. Organizational success increases the capital of credibility invested in the leader and thereby increases his power and authority. But this may reinforce the narcissistic dimension of leadership by fostering an unrealistic self-aggrandizement in the leader and tempting him to exercise his power in authoritarian ways.

By the same token, organizational failure tends to reduce the authority of the leader and to activate regressive group processes—the activation of fight-flight conditions and aggression secondary to the frustrated dependency that comes with a sense of failure. These regressive developments in turn tend to generate a search for paranoid leaders as part of fight-flight conditions and random aggression as part of large-group processes that reflect organizational failure and loss of morale.

Typically, organizations whose top leadership fails develop powerful currents of conflicts among subsystems, and new leaders emerge who enact the paranoid demands of regressive groups. These are organizational preconditions that may allow leaders with inordinately strong paranoid and narcissistic personality characteristics to gain power. Or, in response to general group regression and loss of morale, the paranoid and narcissistic dimension of leadership is activated to an extent that fosters a secondary paranoid regression in the leader. This is the time, he feels, to search for the culprits responsible for organizational dysfunctioning; he is tempted to replace rational analysis with an attack on scapegoats or a radical bureaucratization or ritualization of organizational functioning in an effort to control the diffused aggression that seems to permeate it.

Unconscious or conscious guilt over the aggression triggered in the organizational life, however, may be expressed in the temptation to protect an incompetent leader at any organizational level. A person who in the opinion of every responsible organizational manager is incompetent, is "chosen" to expiate the guilt over the organizational aggression, and the whole organization joins in attempting to save this failing member. At times strong and authoritarian, even sadistic, leaders have shown a weakness for an incompetent subordinate even while acknowledging his failings. There may even be an undertone of satisfaction (or moral self-congratulation) in the tolerance of this person in the face of complaints about his incompetence. Paradoxically, the aggression against which the protection of the incompetent is an unconscious expiatory maneuver may reemerge in the injustice done to everyone who suffers under the incompetent leader. Personal morality and unconscious guilt may thus also be subverted by institutional processes.

What is corrupting in such regressive activation of power struggles is that everyone begins to feel the need to protect him- or herself under conditions of organizational failure, authoritarian threats, and paranoid and narcissistic regressions. Task sentience deteriorates, and concern for self-interest takes precedence over organizational goals. Leaders who are uncertain in their functions and in the security of their jobs may become prone to decision making that is no longer based on organizational interests but on self-preservation, a shift in attitude that indicates the corruption of their task.

In addition to the political dimension of leadership, and the varying levels of concentration of power in the leader, the development of an organizational ideology (or of competing ideologies) tends to affect the leader's decision making. By ideology I mean a system of beliefs, convictions, fantasies, and myths that is shared by members of a social group. Many organizations are subject to competing ideological currents, some of which can realistically be put at the service of the task, while others pay only lip service to it and may actually constitute a constraint on it.

The interests of teachers as a professional group, for example, may actually run counter to the educational goals of their institutions: Should teachers be paid according to the institution's educational effectiveness? Teachers' unions would be apt to oppose such a idea; but individual school systems might find it an excellent way to achieve its overall goals. In hospitals, the interests of, say, medical faculty and mental health workers may clash in significant ways even as both groups claim to be committed to the hospital's clinical goals.

Rational leadership should encourage and identify with a task-oriented ideology that corresponds to organizational goals. This is another way of talking about the leader's responsibility for maintaining morale. The danger here is that this task-oriented ideology may run counter to other human needs and value systems, which may be irrelevant to the specific goals of the organization but which are crucial to the members' sense of well-being and dignity. If the needs of individuals and groups in an organization are a basic constraint to optimal organizational functioning—in other words, if human factors limit the efficiency of an organization, then it is important for the leader to be able to identify with ideologies or socially accepted value systems that are tangential to the organization's interest. It is the leader's job to protect individuals from poor working conditions, from arbitrariness in job assignment, from risks connected with the work, regardless of the impact of these measures on work efficiency.

Under ideal conditions, such ideological contradictions may be minimal, but under less ideal conditions, the leader's identification with a complex system of values may actually protect his decision-making process from the expediency of exclusive identification with rarified organizational or other goals. For example, there may be systems of treating patients in hospitals that are financially highly efficient but that run counter to the human needs of the patients. Menzies (1967) described a social system of nursing in a general hospital that protected the nursing staff from excessive anxiety but that was detrimental to the emotional needs of severely ill or dying patients. For practical purposes, the director of a university hospital must identify with the value systems of the medical school, which is interested in clinical and academic work, but he must also identify with the legal system and its corresponding ideology—the legally required preconditions for the hospital's functioning and accreditation purposes—and with physicians' professional ideology, and with his own personal value system, which is activated under conditions where personal ethics influence decision making (for example, regarding when to resuscitate a patient).

All organizations, in order to function, must develop bureaucratic structures that protect task systems from arbitrariness and solidify lines of authority and boundaries of subsystems while protecting the organization from regression into unstructured large- and small-group processes. These bureaucratic requirements, as we have seen, also protect individuals from arbitrariness and may counteract organizational paranoiagenesis. But these same protective structures may express dissociated organizational sadism in senseless rigidities. The sea of bureaucrats may consciously or unconsciously obstruct creative developments by sadistic insistence on procedures, and it is a function of the leaders to counteract such subtle yet persistent expressions of aggression. With an authoritarian leader in control of an inflexible bureaucracy, the danger exists of a deadening of functioning throughout the entire system, of the kind that, for example, damaged and paralyzed the economic life of the Soviet Union (Zinoviev, 1984).

One corrective against such bureaucratization is the flexibility of informal arrangements that circumvent bureaucratic requirements, although they do so at the cost of corruption (personal deals) infiltrating the system. In fact, bureaucratic rigidity combined with a compensating corruption of the system characterizes many dictatorial and totalitarian states.

This brings us to the crucial importance of the extent to which the leader's value system reflects a mature rather than a primitive superego—in other words, the extent to which he can critically explore the contradictory value systems, ideological crosscurrents, and task requirements of the organization. If it is accepted that a moderate level of narcissism and a paranoid potential are essential ingredients of an effective leader, it also needs to be underlined that these very personality characteristics tend to undermine individual morality and commitment to value systems. The leader's favoritism toward opportunistic followers who stimulate the his narcissism and his rejection of honest criticism by those who seem to threaten that narcissism carry with them the danger of moral corruption. The need to defend against potential enemies has the same effect: survival becomes a major "moral" goal. The need to punish those who dare to rebel may not mean that the leader consciously behaves unfairly; but the effect of his inappropriate aggression, amplified in the paranoid atmosphere of organizational regression, is in itself corruptive. The leader's capacity for ideological commitment in the expression of his individual value system may protect him against organizational corruption, but it may also tempt him to make compromises that are counter to organizational goals or to his commitment to human interpersonal interaction.

As Zinoviev (1984) has pointed out, in large groups, where authority is projected outward or upward onto hierarchical superiors, the leadership shows a tendency toward corrupt behavior that its individual members would shun in their private lives. Like Zinoviev, I believe that an authoritarian structure in an organization fosters the projection of superego functioning onto external or hierarchically superior authorities; group regression in the narcissistic-dependent or paranoid direction follows; and corrupt behavior increases. As Zinoviev says, such conditions promote careerism, selfishness, neglect of tasks, the enjoyment of other people's failures, hostility to those who advance, a search for propitiatory victims, a tendency to abandon moral values and individual differentiation and resent those who seem autonomous or courageous, and, finally a tendency toward blind egalitarianism and a paradoxical reinforcement of the authority of authoritarian leaders as a defense against mutual envy. These conclusions dovetail with Chasseguet-Smirgel's (1975) and Anzieu's (1981) ideas concerning regressive group processes.

It might be said that what I have described here is the human condition in general. That the same individuals who behave morally under more differentiated circumstances present such behavior patterns under conditions of organizational regression can have consequences for organizational management. The leader must not be seduced by conventional demands for a primitive sense of justice and punishment but should stand by his individual moral judgment.

The moral integrity of the leader as it appeared before he took on leadership functions is the organization's best protection against the consequences of narcissistic and paranoid regression. A social system that invests a leader with accountability to the organization as well as to supraordinate social, economic, and political institutions within which it operates provides external guarantees for an adequate structure to protect leadership functioning. The leader's professional sentience to the profession within which he was trained, his human sentience to the staff who will work for him, and his general sense of social responsibility regardless of the particular task of the organization should go a long way to protect his moral integrity.

The careful analysis and setting down of organizational guidelines in all areas of conflicts that affect leadership functions can protect the leader against times of acute regression when the narcissistic and paranoid dimensions are activated and his internal freedom for guidance by his own ethical systems becomes challenged.

Chapter 8 Paranoiagenesis in Organizations

Jaques (1976) distinguished two types of social organizations, requisite and paranoiagenic. Requisite organizations are structurally sound—that is, authority and accountability are matched, and it is possible to get the right number of people for the right task at the right time; they are organizations with a functional administrative structure. Such organizations, Jaques writes, also enable "people to relate to one another with confidence and to rule out suspicion and mistrust." Paranoiagenic organizations, notes Jaques, "make it . . . impossible for individuals to have normal relationships of confidence and trust. They force social interactions into a mould calling for forms of behavior which arouse suspicion, envy, hostile rivalry, and anxiety, and put brakes on social relationships, regardless of how much individual good will there might be" (p. 6).

The open-systems theory of organizations Jaques adopts was originally proposed by Kenneth Rice (1963, 1965, 1969; Miller and Rice, 1967). According to this theory, the regression in group processes in organizations (with the paranoid behaviors in individual members and groups and the parallel pathological idealizations) is a consequence of the lack of a sound administrative structure. Open-systems theory views institutional paranoid group reactions as symptoms of institutional malfunctioning. The malfunctioning induces regression in both individual members and groups and is not simply the consequence of the sum total of the psychopathologies of the members.

EXAMPLES AND SYMPTOMS
OF PARANOIAGENESIS

Examples

At an international gathering of a professional organization, a distinguished member of one of various factions that were competing for scientific prominence disparaged the representatives of another country in a private, informal meeting. An hour later, at a luncheon meeting with those representatives, he spoke warmly about their important contributions to the field and the need to increase their presence in it, talking in an adulatory fashion. From all available evidence, the man was otherwise honest and ethical, and his flagrant dishonesty in the organizational context was contrary to his habitual behavior.

The director of an educational institution sharply criticized one of the teachers. The director, whose aggressive style was known and feared, went on for twenty minutes while the other senior teachers were silent. At the end of the meeting, a few of those present approached the person who had been attacked to express to him, privately, their sympathy and their view that the attack was unfair. Among them were several teachers who were notorious for their submissive and even sycophantic attitude toward the director.

A senior professional in a state bureaucracy made special efforts to support her younger colleagues, providing them with guidance in the organizational and political intricacies of the institution. Hearing that the work of one of her protégés had been questioned in an administrative meeting by his supervisor's boss, she alerted her protégé, who immediately went to his critic to ask for an explanation. The man was surprised, because he had raised questions in response to what he considered relatively minor issues. The senior professional had wanted to help her young protégé; the young protégé, in good faith, wanted to correct what he perceived as an unfair bias against him; the boss, in good faith, perceived the senior professional as generating distrust and distorting the functional administrative structure of the organization.

A leading researcher with an international reputation decided to leave his research institute after a series of incidents that made him feel unwanted: in the course of a few months, intramural funding for a major project of his had been denied; the resignation of two senior secretaries had left openings that were filled by two other senior secretaries who, he found out later, had been dismissed from other programs in the institute; the director had been sharply critical of him at a scientific gathering. The senior researcher became depressed, showed strong self-critical and self-demeaning behaviors, hoped to start again in another organization, and was surprised when on the point of resigning, he made his decision to leave public, and everybody expressed deep concern over his leaving, and the organization made a strenuous effort to retain him.

These examples are not extraordinary. I do not suggest that they are indicative of major failures in organizational functioning. They do illustrate several central aspects of institutional paranoiagenesis: a variety of individual behaviors running from the blatantly dishonest through ordinary suspiciousness, distrust, and fear to a self-deprecating, demoralized, and depressive reaction; members in organizations being dishonest, deceptive, and antisocial—qualities they may not evince in their private lives; and members of an organization acting in good faith and still creating confusion and turmoil.

Symptoms

In general, the symptoms of paranoiagenesis in organizations range along a broad spectrum from the psychopathic to the depressive. Under conditions of paranoiagenic regression in nonrequisite functioning organizations, the psychopathic end of the spectrum is characterized by members who manifest patently deceptive, dishonest, antisocial behaviors that they would not evince in their private lives. And members who show antisocial tendencies throughout all their social interactions and who also manifest those tendencies in their organizational life are not only accepted with such behaviors but also admired for getting away with them when conditions favoring paranoiagenesis prevail: An admired and beloved leader in an organization was known to carry out ruthless financial operations that bordered on the unethical as a way of improving his position within that organization. In a university center a leader who was loved for his warm, soft, even cuddly manners was widely known to privately spread venomous rumors about his political opponents while publicly acting with utmost social friendliness toward them. A leading figure in a social-service institute was admired for a flamboyant manner that contrasted with his intellectual brilliance. His chronic mendacity, which was close to being *pseudologia fantastica,* was privately celebrated as a courageous flouting of reality.

The rank and file of the organizations led by such people evinced, in contrast, markedly paranoid features in their institutional dealings that contrasted with their personality characteristics outside the organization. Paranoid behaviors constitute a middle range of the spectrum of paranoiagenic regression and are the most prevalent manifestations of the nonrequisite nature of the organization. Typically, the relationship of the staff or the employees to the supervisors and the leaders is characterized by fear, suspicion and resentment, a sense of hyperalertness and cautiousness, a search for subtle and hidden meanings and messages, and an effort to establish alliances with peers to defend against the common dangers. The staff members frequently have the frightening experience that allies in their hidden opposition to authoritarian leadership have suddenly become turncoats and have adopted sycophantic attitudes toward the leaders. The pervasive atmosphere of mistrust brings to mind the proverbial story of the small village in which, one day, everybody received a telegram from a practical joker saying, "Fly, everything is discovered!" Thereupon 50 percent of the villagers left precipitously. The counterpart of the staff members' reactions is the leaders' sense that paranoid members of the organization have begun to challenge legitimate leadership in a hostile, defiant, depreciatory way while a silent majority implicitly condones the attacks.

At the depressive end of the spectrum of paranoiagenic regression, individual members typically feel lonely, isolated, unappreciated, and hypercritical of their own faults and shortcomings. They overreact to criticism, experiencing it as a threat to their professional future. Their exaggerated self-criticism inhibits their work functions, thus creating self-perpetuating cycles that interfere with work performance and work satisfaction and lead to efforts to escape from the organization. Not surprisingly, the most mature or integrated members of the organization (those with the most integrated superegos) predominate among those with a depressive reaction. Normal people in paranoiagenic institutions become the most alienated from it. Schizoid withdrawal also protects the person from the painful deterioration of the institution's human condition.

ETIOLOGY

In the simplest terms, the cause of organizational paranoiagenesis resides in the breakdown of the task systems of organizations when their primary tasks become irrelevant or overwhelming or are paralyzed by unforeseen, undiagnosed, or mishandled constraints; the activation of regressive group processes under conditions of institutional malfunctioning; and the latent predisposition to paranoid regression that is a universal characteristic of individual psychology. Faulty organizational leadership may be a major cause of the breakdown of task performance, even when external reality would foster the successful carrying out of the organization's primary tasks, and even when no major external constraints to such primary tasks exist. Faulty leadership is expressed in the inadequate diagnosis of primary tasks and their constraints, the failure to devise optimal compromises between tasks and constraints, and the faulty organizational structuring that runs counter to the functional demands of task performance.

Faulty leadership may derive from the personality characteristics of leaders in key administrative positions. All breakdown in organizational functioning, however, with its consequent regression in the group processes throughout the organization, initially appears to be owing to the troublesome personalities of key leaders. Only a careful organizational analysis may differentiate those cases in which the leader's personality pathology is actually the cause of the organizational breakdown from those cases in which the leader's personality pathology is only a presenting symptom, reflecting regression in leadership that is secondary to organizational breakdown, rather than its cause.

Jaques (1976) summarized the relations between the structural characteristics of social institutions and individual psychology and psychopathology in the following way: "The constant threat . . . is that the social institutions become so anti-requisite and so seriously alienating as to create a descending spiral: anti-requisite institutions arousing objective suspicion with its resonating persecutory anxiety; the anxiety in its turn disrupting individual functioning . . . making the social institution's functioning worse" (pp. 8–9).

Scarce Resources

The most frequent cause of paranoiagenesis in social organizations is the limitation and, particularly, a reduction in the resources available for carrying out the organizational tasks. At times of budgetary constraints—for example, when expenses must be reduced significantly—waves of apprehension and objective anxiety are compounded by individual staff members' regression to primitive anxieties of being abandoned, rejected, discriminated against, and exploited.

Insofar as promotions also imply competition for positions whose numbers diminish as individual members ascend the administrative ladder, these members begin a struggle for limited resources. When a competition between people involves search committees, comparative judgments about the value of individual members for the organization, and a political process influencing such appointments, it is no longer simply a matter of distributing resources but of adding a fundamentally new dimension, politics, to the conditions favoring paranoiagenesis.

Politics

Political processes that influence decision making are probably the next most important factor promoting paranoiagenesis in organizations. Masters (1989) described politics as "behavior that simultaneously partakes of the attributes of bonding, dominance, and submission. . . . Political behavior, properly so-called, comprises actions in which the rivalry form and perpetuation of social dominance and loyalty impinges on the legal or customary rules governing a group" (p. 140).

From the viewpoint of organizational functioning, the definition of politics may be narrowed further to the behavior carried out by individual persons or groups that is designed to influence other people or groups across institutional boundaries in the pursuit of individual interests or goals. In that regard, institutional politics may be considered "a form of rivalry to determine which humans are permitted to transmit 'authoritative' messages or commands to the rest of the society" (Masters, 1989, p. 140).

Insofar as political action derives from goals linked to an organization's primary tasks, such action may be considered essentially functional and rationally related to organizational functioning. For example, political action may determine whether a school of social work orients itself predominantly toward community action or toward psychotherapeutic interventions; a political process is linked to reasonable priorities within the overall objectives of training social workers.

Yet when political action is tangential or unrelated to functional institutional goals, it has negative effects on institutional task systems and task boundaries and may lead not only to significant distortions in institutional functioning but also to an increase in paranoiagenesis. When the choice of competing value systems is no longer decided rationally in terms of optimal institutional goals, a disruptive regression in group processes may quickly follow the discrepancy between political aspirations and organizational objectives. The competition among diverse groups that is totally unrelated to the task—for example, in an educational institution dealing with the arts—could prove disruptive.

If authority is defined as the functional exercise of power within an institutional setting, the exercise of power as part of a political process that has no links to institutional tasks cannot be called functional. And if the exercise of power is not functional, a spectrum of institutional dysfunctioning results. That spectrum ranges from chaos to petrification—chaos when insufficient power is located at points of functional authority; petrification when excessive power is located with institutional leaders, transforming authority into authoritarianism.

In terms of group processes within an institution, politicizing always implies an increased dependence of all members on all others; the anonymous members of the organization all carry potential political, decision-making power, a situation maximized under conditions of democratic decision making. To have to depend on everyone under conditions that are not objectively regulated by organizational structures immediately activates large-group functioning. Large-group functioning implies an unstructured interaction of members of a group who can listen to one another and interact with one another without confirming a stable status-role relationship in the process; all interpersonal relationships remain uncertain, and defensive operations that would stabilize conflicts under small-group conditions or in dyadic and triadic relationships do not work (Kernberg, 1992).

The political process immediately activates the psychology of large-group regression, with a consequent sense of loss of personal identity by all involved, a feeling that aggression and violence threaten, a sense of impotence, a need to form subgroups so that aggression can be projected onto other groups, an effort to assert personal and individual group power, the fear of being victimized by the same process, the wish to escape from the situation, and a sense of paralysis and impotence as one disengages from the group.

Those whose positions in an organization depend on an electoral process experience a sense of disorientation and fear, the temporal disruption of ordinary work and personal relationships, the need to identify with a public role that they feel is artificial, and a devastating dependence on other people's opinion of them; the situation is similar to the psychopathology of the narcissistic personality who is overdependent on other people's judgments. Even mature and well-integrated people tend to experience an electoral defeat as a severe narcissistic lesion.

Faulty Structures

Whereas a scarcity of resources and politicizing—particularly nonfunctional and nonrequisite politicizing—can easily be seen as providing fertile ground for paranoiagenesis, a lack of correspondence between an organization's objectives and its actual administrative structure is an important but much less evident source of paranoiagenesis. For example, the objectives of psychoanalytic education combine the goals of a university college and an art school (psychoanalysis as a science and an art), but the actual structure of psychoanalytic education often resembles the models of a trade school and a religious seminary (psychoanalysis as a technique and a profession of faith). Although the causes of those discrepancies were found in the historical origins of psychoanalytic education and in the nature of the primary task—that is, psychoanalytic treatment carried out in the context of institutional boundaries—the actual mechanisms by which those causes operated were precisely the contradiction between professed objectives and implicit organizational structure. The effect of that discrepancy between professed goals and institutional structure is a marked level of paranoiagenesis, with splits between idealization and persecutory fears in those institutions.

The most typical examples of those unrecognized discrepancies are institutions that officially exist to perform a social function for the common good, whereas their actual primary function is to provide jobs and satisfaction for their constituent bureaucracies; another example is the hospital whose avowed mission is to provide health care, whereas its actual mission is to make money. Whereas an organization whose objective is to produce financial gain and whose structure maximizes that goal should be considered an optimally functioning institution.

Within the general category of institutional distortions or inadequacies are many restricted problems, often affecting only sections of the institution: lack of clear boundary control by managerial leadership; lack of stability of boundary control; inadequate, ambiguous, or overlapping delegation of authority; and discrepancy between the extent of authority invested in particular leaders and the actual power the leaders have; the last problem constitutes a boundary between organizational problems and a failure in individual leaders throughout the organization.

Incompetent Leaders

Incompetence in leaders not only has a devastating effect on organizational functioning but is enormously paranoiagenic. Incompetent leaders, in protecting themselves against competent subordinates, become highly distrustful, defensive, and deceptive; they become authoritarian toward subordinates and subservient toward superiors. Those qualities activate paranoiagenic regression, particularly at the level of its paranoid and frankly psychopathic characteristics. The corrupting effect of dishonesty in leaders provides the breeding ground for general psychopathic responses throughout the organization, and the underlying paranoid potential may be masked by the surface equilibrium of general corruption.

In chapter 3, I proposed five desirable personality characteristics for rational leaders: (1) intelligence; (2) personal honesty and incorruptibility; (3) a capacity for establishing and maintaining object relations in depth; (4) a healthy narcissism; and (5) a healthy, justifiable anticipatory paranoid attitude, in contrast to naïveté. The last two characteristics are perhaps the most surprising and yet the most important requirements for task leadership. As pointed out in chapter 6, a healthy narcissism protects the leader from overdependence on approval from others and fortifies his capacity for autonomous functioning. A mildly paranoid attitude keeps the leader alert to the dangers of corruption and paranoiagenic regression, to the acting out of diffuse aggression unconsciously activated in all organizational processes, and protects the leader from a naïveté that prevents the careful analysis of the motivational aspects of conflicts that surface in the institution.

The danger is that under the effects of organizational regression, the narcissistic and paranoid features of leaders become accentuated and in themselves come to constitute powerful regressive forces that mobilize regression further along the narcissistic-dependent and paranoid-sadistic lines. Here a major paradox in institutional leadership emerges: the same personality characteristics that, if moderate in degree, may strengthen a leader's backbone may also foster regression and have devastatingly paranoiagenic effects on the entire organization. The moral dimension of leadership is also threatened by narcissistic and paranoid regression in the leader and the institution, which leads us to the mechanism that links paranoiagenesis to its psychopathic consequences.

Projective Identification

By means of projective identification, the aggression triggered in institutional conflicts is projected onto adversaries in the administration. But the regression to large-group processes renders projective identification inoperant (Turquet, 1975). The behavioral aspect of projective identification—that is, the effort to control the object onto whom the aggression is projected while unconsciously enacting that very aggression—fails. If aggression cannot be firmly projected and anchored onto any one person, and if those onto whom aggression is projected cannot be controlled, the fear of presumed enemies increases, resulting in an increase in the diffusely projected aggression.

Betrayal

When fear of retaliation reaches a certain level of intensity, the mechanism of the "paranoid urge to betray" (Jacobson, 1971a) comes into play. What happens is that moral restraints are dropped in an all-out struggle for survival. There are no limits to what one will do to protect oneself from the dangers of attack—the direction, form, and intensity of which one can only vaguely intuit. Sociologists have examined the phenomenon under the heading of the prisoner's dilemma: two prisoners with personal ties but in separate cells who have regressed sufficiently to suspect everybody, even the unreachable comrade, are prone to betray each other. At a widespread, national level, the complete corruption of a political system became evident even to the leadership of East Germany shortly before the collapse of the regime (see, for example, Schabowski, 1991).

Malignant Narcissism

The most extreme form of paranoiagenic leadership is represented by leaders whose personality is characterized by malignant narcissism—that is, a narcissistic personality combined with ego-syntonic sadism, paranoid tendencies, and antisocial features. That syndrome is characteristic of totalitarian leaders, with Hitler and Stalin as classic examples.

Projective Processes

The activation of primitive aggression in members' functioning within social groups reflects the latent disposition for regression to preoedipal levels of intrapsychic organization. At those levels the projection of aggression onto parental figures, the reintrojection of such parental figures under the distorted consequences of projected aggression, and the consequent circular reaction of projection and introjection of aggression are dealt with by massive splitting mechanisms, leading to idealization, on the one hand, and to paranoid, persecutory tendencies, on the other. Those psychic operations, having their origin in the dyadic relationship with the mother, resonate with subsequent triangular problems reflecting the oedipal situation and transform the disposition toward multiple preoedipal transferences into the typical triangular oedipal ones that become dominant in the member's relation to authority.

The distortion of rational authority resulting from those projective processes leads to defensive activation of narcissistic affirmation and to regressive relationships with feared or idealized parental leaders. As we have seen (chapter 3), the process is completed by a general tendency to reproject the advanced aspects of superego functioning onto the institution. Under those conditions there is not only a threat of emotional and characterological regression but also of regression in the moral dimension of individual functioning. The paranoid urge to betray is a logical consequence of that regression. When a leader presents the syndrome of malignant narcissism, massive paranoid and psychopathic regression spreads rapidly throughout the organization.

CORRECTIVE MECHANISMS
AND THEIR LIMITATIONS

Bureaucracy

The most important means by which organizations can protect themselves against paranoiagenesis is to establish a bureaucratic system. A well-functioning bureaucracy in a democratic system has the potential for being an ideal model of organizational structure. Masters (1989) summarized the principal characteristics of the bureaucracy: First, a bureaucracy provides an element of coercion, which is necessary if large groups of people with conflicting interests are to function for the benefit of all. Second, the bureaucratic system, by creating new ways of cooperation between the constituent groups, has the potential for increasing efficiency. Third, bureaucracies provide benefits for their members, thus ensuring their self-perpetuation.

Within a bureaucratic organization, internal conflicts can be diagnosed, controlled, and rationally resolved by standard mechanisms of bureaucratic functioning. For example, the three-level system allows subordinates to complain to their supervisor's superior about dissatisfactions with their supervisor, with a proviso that the supervisor is informed of the complaint; simultaneously, employees' organizations that are collectively defending the interests of employees within the bureaucratic organization may back up the individual subordinate's legal rights.

Bureaucratic structure and functions reduce the regression into large-group processes and, under ordinary circumstances, keep paranoiagenic regression at a low level. Effective bureaucratic functioning may make for optimal task performance, maintain normal social interchanges, and impose firm compliance with what is generally assumed to be the common good. Bureaucracies may use resources effectively, and the participants may find their work gratifying.

Limitations

There are important limitations to the ameliorating effects of bureaucratic functioning. Those limitations arise from the unavoidable infiltration of dissociated sadism into all group processes. That infiltration affects all institutional functioning, including the performance of functional tasks.

All members of an organization experience narcissistic challenges, oedipal rivalries, and frustrations of the preoedipal need for dependence and for autonomous control—all of which generate aggression. Insofar as such aggression cannot be expressed in immediate social interactions or sublimated in task performance, it is projected either onto the institution's group formations—typically leading to splitting, idealization, and persecution—or onto the leadership, and it is expressed as combined oedipal-preoedipal conflicts that are also dealt with by idealization of the leadership and fear of persecution by them. Inadequate leaders of a bureaucratic structure, particularly a leader with severely narcissistic and paranoid tendencies, may transform a regressed bureaucratic system into a social nightmare. Such leaders expect and foster subservient behaviors by their subordinates, reward the idealization of the leadership, and are prone to persecute those whom they sense to be critical of them.

The terrible consequences of the effective functioning of bureaucracies in Hitler's Germany and Stalin's Soviet Union on the ordinary lives of large segments of the population requires no spelling out. To a limited extent, similar types of regressive leadership of well-functioning bureaucracies may be encountered within democratic states.

A state secretary of health who became convinced that the medical profession was not fulfilling its tasks and needed to be made aware of them developed a punitive system under which a shortcoming or failure in one institution had disastrous effects throughout the state. Each incident not falling clearly within the law was followed by the imposition of additional rules and regulations that added enormous burdens to both the bureaucratic system itself and all the state health-delivery systems. The spiraling effect of that increased bureaucratization was a general increase in costs, delays in task performance, a swamping of the state bureaucracy, and an increase in bureaucratic staffing; at the same time, a paranoid atmosphere pervaded all contacts between the health-delivery systems and the state inspectors and between the the people responsible for the control systems within the health-delivery systems and the remaining staff members of those institutions. Narcissistic self-enhancement and paranoid developments at the top increased paranoiagenesis and reduced resources in all the organizations involved.

Mechanisms at the periphery of bureaucratic systems tend to increase the systems' size and scope of operations beyond what is functionally warranted, and the systems gradually deteriorate. As Masters (1989) pointed out, equal justice for all implies that any particular person may feel that he or she has been treated in impersonal, dehumanized, neglectful ways by bureaucracies. In fact, that negative aspect of bureaucratic systems is the first effect they may make on the lives of the people who enter into contact with them. That impersonal effect leads many people to try to beat the system and to escape from its rigidities and, in turn, leads to a paranoid reaction of bureaucracies to catch the cheaters. However, efforts to humanize the system and to do an individual a favor may lead to favoritism—particularly to nepotism—and may bring about the corruption of the system.

The gradual expansion of a bureaucratic system to protect itself further against actual or potential cheaters may lead to a bureaucratic overgrowth that affects not individuals alone but entire institutions that are bureaucratically regulated. Functional administrative leaders may have to find ways to cut through intolerable bureaucratic rigidities for optimal task performance. In short, the dangers of rigidification, on the one hand, and chaotic breakdown on the other (as corruption gains the upper hand) constitute the major limits to the potentially corrective effects that bureaucratic systems may have in preventing paranoiagenesis.

When bureaucratic systems grow to such an extent that they dominate their society, their self-serving functions become manifest: the bureaucrats become a privileged class who use the payoff to placate the underprivileged citizens surrounding them. The bureaucracy is no longer functional; its petrified and chaotic features serve its own interests. Here paranoiagenesis seems a justified response by everybody concerned both inside and outside the bureaucracy. National bureaucratic systems in some countries seem to have reached their level of equilibrium, with a consequent high level of paranoiagenesis in their societies. The economic breakdown of the Soviet Union, ultimately determined by a wholly centralized system of economic management, found its most dramatic expression in the development of a parasitic bureaucracy that combined extreme rigidity with widespread corruption and contributed to the high level of paranoiagenesis in that society even when political terror decreased (Roberts and LaFollette, 1990; Todd, 1990; Boukovski, 1990).

A less apparent, subtle, and yet prevalent deterioration in bureaucratic organization stems from the assignment of particular members as gatekeepers to protect the common good against potentially unjustified demands, expectations, appointments, or privileges. The chairs of committees deciding on the selection of personnel, on the adequacy of the documentation of various requests, on the distribution of resources of any kind, and on the evaluation of people inside and outside the bureaucratic structure are unconsciously invested with the dissociated sadism that is prevalent throughout the organization. In other words, the sum total of the narcissistic and paranoid tendencies that are controlled in ordinary social interactions by means of the bureaucratic structure are perversely placed onto the guardians of the gate. Those guardians, under the guise of objective justice, are frequently victims of that role and become grandiose (narcissistic), sadistic, and suspicious (paranoid) arbiters of human destiny. The impotence of people who are restricted in their scope of autonomous decision making by an immense bureaucratic system may foster in them an explosion of narcissistic needs when opportunities for power become available; the arbitrariness and the sadism with which individual bureaucrats—particularly those in subordinate positions—may treat the public is proverbial.

Humanism

Another mechanism intended to protect against paranoiagenesis in institutions is the activation of a humanistic ideology, which has at its center the aspiration of justice, equal opportunity, and equality before the law for all. Such an ideology, embedded in a democratic system of government, may support the social controls that protect the requisiteness of organizational structure. And such control systems may protect the organizations against the corruption of leaders and against the paranoiagenic deterioration derived from the misuse of power.

Yet the concepts of equality before the law and equal opportunity may be subverted by the regressive atmosphere created in the context of large-group processes. The activation of the syndrome of identity diffusion and of primitive aggression in the context of large-group processes takes the form of unconscious collective envy of people who escape the regression and of their creativity. Unconscious envy, generalized under the rationale of an egalitarian ideology, may be destructive to functional leadership; it may foster the selection of grandiose leaders with narcissistic personalities whose proclamations of conventional clichés assure everybody that they do not need to be envied. The selection of a "merchant of illusions" (Chasseguet-Smirgel, 1975; Anzieu, 1981) as the leader is largely determined by the enactment of collective unconscious envy of realistic authority, values, and creativity.

Social ideologies that are tangential to institutional functioning may also have a destructive effect on it, particularly through their skillful misuse by individual members of the institution—a painful side effect of well-intentioned efforts for the socially mandated and protected redress of grievances.

In a hospital in the United States during an effort to correct social injustice and bias against minorities, a black male psychologist invited a white female nurse to a social get-together; she refused. He felt that she had turned him down because he was black, and he complained to the hospital's human-rights committee. What began as a personal interaction, dominated by the psychologist's personality characteristics, resulted in a general strike by all the blacks at the hospital. The dispute, which moved out into the surrounding black community, came close to leading to the destruction and closing of the hospital.

Within the context of social concern to correct social biases against women in organizations, a female staff member accused, over a period of time, several male supervisors of particularly harsh behavior against her because she would not respond to their sexual advances. Male supervisors cautiously withdrew from her, and a general reluctance to become involved with her evolved, although nobody dared to bring up the issue in large administrative settings. Everybody seemed afraid that ventilation of the problem would lead to divisive organizational conflicts. A particularly serious allegation on her part triggered a broad investigation, which determined that sexual harassment had not taken place. However, the investigation also showed that her colleagues had failed to give the woman help with her organizational difficulties, which included problems with female, as well as male, supervisors and staff.

Democracy

Still another major mechanism to control paranoiagenesis is a democratic process of decision making. Such a process includes the open discussion of issues that affect everyone; the assurance of equal rights for open communication at all levels of the hierarchy; the public, stable, and socially sanctioned distribution of authority on a functional basis; and the full participation of all followers in the selection of their leaders.

Here, unfortunately, paranoiagenic effects may derive from two major causes: the nature of political processes and the confusion between the democratic and functional mechanisms of decision making. Democracy is a political system of government that, in essence, is optimally geared to social regulation in open societies or, in systems terms, in open systems with an infinite number of boundaries. In contrast, limited social organizations—that is, open systems with a limited number of boundaries and specific primary tasks—require functional leadership that corresponds to the primary task systems.

A department chair of a state university in a Latin American country was selected by democratic means during a time of political turmoil in the late 1960s. Everybody—from porters to full professors—voted. The rationale for the process included the assumption that anyone who worked in the department could judge who was the best person for the job. In actuality, the democratic process was controlled by the struggle between political factions. The candidate who won did so on the basis of his political allegiance, and he was generally considered a mediocrity.

Another illustration is a conception of the therapeutic community within which decisions about patient privileges are taken by vote at the community meeting. In one institution, for example, the community voted democratically on whether a potentially suicidal patient should be given a weekend pass. Functional decision making, in contrast, would entrust the decision to the person with most expertise and legal responsibility in assessing suicidal risks.

In some psychoanalytic societies in Europe and Latin America, full membership coincides with appointment as a training analyst, an essentially educational function. The custom of using secret ballots for electing full members seems a justifiable democratic way for a society to invite new members to join its institution, but the procedure is highly questionable from the viewpoint of selecting those most qualified to carry out its educational functions. One consequence of the procedure is a tendency to develop a high level of paranoiagenesis in certain psychoanalytic societies that are otherwise split into groups competing for power in the institution. There is a justified generalized fear that election has to do more with belonging to a certain power structure than with educational merits.

Functional decision making, however, involves participatory management—that is, the possibility of group discussions and joint decision making among leaders at a determinate hierarchical level. If participatory management coincides with the clear and stable delegation of authority to each group involved, and if the individual authority of leaders is commensurate with their responsibilities—authority may be delegated but the responsibility cannot— such a functional organization may appear to be democratic, but it corresponds, in effect, to the functional principles of social organization.

Altruism

An apparently simple, sometimes highly effective, but easily subvertible mechanism of reducing paranoiagenesis is represented by well-motivated people with integrity, concern for the organization, and concern for its human values who reach across organizational boundaries and task systems to help someone in trouble. Bringing together two enemies to straighten out their conflicts; talking extensively with a person caught up in a paranoid, self-perpetuating web of misconceptions; gathering a significant group of peers to present to their superiors the problems that these superiors are ignoring or mismanaging—under the right circumstances, all these actions can be helpful. Individual courage, the normal sense of commitment to values, and altruistic drive can move individual members to transcend paranoiagenic regression.

Such an approach to institutional management can broaden the awareness of paranoiagenesis, of its universal nature, and of the importance of activating corrective measures to deal with it. However, that corrective process, undertaken with the best intentions, may also be subverted. The qualities of individual decency and high moral values can be corrupted by their combination with naïveté, that is, with an unconscious denial of the aggressive and sadistic temptations in members and group functioning. My earlier example of the senior professional who was attempting to help her younger male colleagues while, unconsciously, increasing paranoid developments within her administrative setting illustrates that fact.

In open institutions where feedback is encouraged and a functional organization prevails, people with severely antisocial tendencies are easily able to circulate false information that acquires weight precisely because of the mutual respect of all involved.

A man with serious paranoid and antisocial pathology, who had been appointed representative of his group under conditions of institutional conflict, raised a question about the honesty of the tellers appointed by the institutional management as part of a political process regulating the election of staff representatives to deal with the administration. In a public meeting the man accused a leading member of management of having a personal friendship with one of the tellers that, the man went on, raised questions about the outcome of the elections. Both the teller and the member of management felt attacked and paralyzed by what they experienced as unwarranted questioning of their honesty; within the group situation, numerous members who had already privately heard accusations of dishonesty expressed by the same man experienced his behavior as being the courageous revelation of a generally known rumor. The accusations further poisoned the already highly paranoiagenic atmosphere of the institution. The chronic mendacity of the man who had made the accusation was only discovered many months later.

The elevation to leadership positions of people with strong paranoid, narcissistic, or antisocial features may in itself indicate the extent of regression of the group processes in the organization: the level of prominence of paranoid persons in the group process at any one particular time may be considered an indirect indicator of the extent to which paranoiagenesis prevails.

Chapter 9 Leadership Styles

In chapter 8, I noted the paranoiagenic effects of the elevation to leadership positions of people with strong paranoid, narcissistic, or antisocial characteristics but suggested that such ascendance may sometimes be secondary to the level of regression of the group processes in the organization. I proposed that the level of prominence of paranoid individuals in the group process at any particular time may be considered an indirect indicator of the extent to which paranoiagenesis prevails in the organization.

This brief statement provides the background and context for a further exploration of the effects of the leader's personality on increasing or decreasing paranoiagenesis in the institution. I have been impressed in recent years by the extent to which, regardless of the challenges posed to institutions by external reality or even by crises affecting their very existence, good leaders can crucially help the organizations survive and function without a severe paranoiagenic regression. Indeed, an institution that may appear to have clear and viable tasks and a task-oriented organizational structure may suffer from severe paranoiagenesis derived from the characteristics of its leaders. Earlier, I discussed the negative consequences of excessively narcissistic, paranoid, obsessive, and schizoid traits in the personality of the leader, with particular emphasis on the negative effects of pathological narcissism on the leader's immediate entourage and on the organization as a whole. Here I shall elaborate, focusing on certain pathological leadership styles and their effects on the organization.

Although positive bonds among the members of an organization depend on their mutual identification with a common task (task systems) and on their identification with a particular professional group (sentient system [Rice, 1965]), such libidinal ties also depend upon the members' reliance on and admiration of their leader (Freud, 1921). At the same time, inasmuch as all human relationships are ambivalent, and members of an organization are particularly susceptible to rivalries because of professional advancement and administrative hierarchies, the potential for aggression also becomes important in the organization's social life. In addition, together with idealizing and depending on their leaders, the individual members exhibit preoedipal and oedipal conflicts with parental authority. These conflicts, ordinarily submerged and controlled by the reality of the common task (the work group [Bion, 1961]), become activated in institutional life.

These subtle undercurrents of libidinal and aggressive strivings of the members are intensified by the activation of regressive group processes, that is, the activation of the basic group assumptions of fight-flight and dependency described by Bion (1961), and the generalized fear of aggression characteristic of large-group processes described by Turquet (1975). The aggression mobilized by these regressive group processes is controlled by defensive operations, including their general unconscious displacement of aggression onto the organizational gatekeepers, namely, those who control entrance to the organization, adherence to rules and regulations, and hiring, firing, and promotion procedures. Thus, aggression is displaced and projected onto the organizational leadership at all levels, and, as part of this aggression, so is repressed or dissociated sadism.

A jointly generated ideology reflecting the idealization of the institutional tasks and what often amounts to a mythology of such institutional tasks (a commonly shared fantasy about the institution's purpose and importance) also becomes charged with aggressive as well as libidinal investment. Institutionally vested authority in the organization's leadership is reinforced by the power stemming from the authority delegated to them by members and by the strivings for power residing in the leaders' own personalities. Thus real and projected aggression crystallize in the administrative structures and are conducted upward to the top leadership.

When socially determined excess of power is vested in the leadership, or a historically determined excessive power vested in the leadership transforms functional authority into authoritarian power, the conditions are ripe for misuse of such power in the discharge of surplus aggression, which can have a paranoiagenic effect. Now the personality of the leader becomes crucial in managing that excessive, potentially dangerous and explosive but also potentially creative and work-protective use of power, as well as in handling the discharge of its implicit aggression.

The power vested in the institution's leadership is not stable. It may be incremented or decreased on the basis of fluctuating delegations of authority from outside the institution to top leadership, the adequacy or inadequacy of the organizational structure to the task, the delegated authority from all the members of the institution in terms of their confidence and idealization (versus distrust and devaluation) of their leaders, the rigidity or chaos of the institution's bureaucratic arrangements, and the leader's management of his power and authority.

The organizational leader stands at the center of powerful aggressive forces impinging on her ability to function. They include her internal aggressive strivings, her ability to sublimate her aggression in her leadership tasks, the effort to resist the aggression being projected onto her, and her ability to make decisions under conditions of uncertainty. At the same time, the loneliness of leadership, the necessary frustration of the leader's dependency needs, the unconscious oedipal, sexualized temptations offered by the organization, the seduction into "justified indignation" that gives vent to a dissociated sadism of her own—all operate upon the leader to stimulate the activation and discharge of aggression onto the institution. Unresolved unconscious conflicts and personality structures of various kinds collude with these temptations.

In a complementary fashion, the expression of aggression by the leader is immediately amplified by her authority, by the influence she exerts over group processes in the organization, and by the direct control she may exercise over task systems, groups, and individuals. Such direct control over others can activate primitive defensive operations in the leader, particularly of projective identification. Paradoxically, the leader is in a position vis-à-vis her subordinates that is comparable to that of the patient toward his psychotherapist. The subordinates' task is to understand the messages from the leader and to utilize them for task performance, just as the psychotherapist is open to messages from the patient to help him carry out his psychotherapeutic task. The patient's projective identification powerfully influences the therapist's counter-transference; the leader's projective identification has a strong influence on the attitudes of her subordinates.

Under optimal circumstances, these projective processes are controlled by the leader's orientation to the task; her intelligence, security, and moral integrity; her respect for her subordinates; and her libidinal investment in them as part of the joint dedication to the task. The leader's sense of security helps her tolerate the unavoidable ambivalence of her subordinates in their organizational functioning.

Under pathological circumstances, projective mechanisms are exaggerated, amplified in their effects because of the concentration of power invested in the leader's authority; and self-fulfilling prophecies distort the leader's interpersonal relationships as the administrative structure is affected by her actions. The most general dynamic involved here includes the projection of her internal world of object relations on the surrounding organizational environment. Idealized and persecutory object representations, as well as realistic, idealized, and devalued self-representations are projected onto her psychosocial environment, and the intrapsychic relationships to her internalized object world are played out unconsciously in the interpersonal world of the organization. In other words, the leader treats her staff as internal objects or induces in them the attitudes of her repressed and dissociated, projected self- and object representations. The more pathological her internal world of object relations, the more it is played out in the interpersonal world of the organization. Let us consider some typical examples.

THE LEADER WHO CAN'T SAY NO

I begin with this example because although on the surface, this type of leadership would seem diametrically opposed to the kind that ordinarily would increase paranoiagenesis in the institution, the effect of this leadership style is in fact paranoiagenic. Various types of personality style may foster the incapacity to take a firm, determined stance. Narcissistic personalities who need to be loved by everybody and wish to avoid frustrating potential worshipers; or narcissistic personalities with enormous internal pressure to "feed" everyone because of the projection of their dependency needs onto the members of the organization; dependent-infantile personalities who hope that gratifying their coworkers will, in turn, promote these coworkers' efforts to gratify them—all are personality qualities contributing to the inability to take a stand.

At a different level, fear of the consequences of their own aggression may promote such compliant behavior in leaders. A more complex underlying dynamic is presented by leaders whose reaction formation against intense sadistic needs is manifested as friendliness of manner. These leaders try to agree with everybody but, unconsciously, they are thus intensifying interpersonal competition and fostering a paranoid atmosphere among their immediate subordinates. These leaders may seem agreeable, but those who work with them experience them as friendly but disconcerting and are left with a sense of uncertainty about what is expected of them.

The subordinates of such leaders often find themselves in the middle of conflict with others who have parallel functions, while the leader keeps himself carefully at a distance and emerges as well-intentioned (but not very helpful). Sometimes strong paranoid developments may occur two levels below the leader, who has unconsciously engineered the conflict. His attitude of puzzled and fascinated "unhappiness" over the "senseless fights" between his subordinates may betray the underlying repressed and dissociated sadism.

There are, of course, instances in which a person is promoted to a position for which he is simply not qualified. Such a leader expresses his uncertainty by trying to keep in the good graces of his subordinates, and in his incapacity to live up to the role demands of his position, lack of conceptual clarity, tendency to become lost in details or paralyzed by tasks—with a corresponding tendency toward excessive delegation of authority and a lack of clarity about the contradictory nature of his delegation to various members of his team. The incompetent leader who cannot say no, however, induces a sense of chaos and frustration rather than suspicion in those who are depending on him. The leader whose unconscious sadism is expressed in contention among subordinates, by contrast, tends to be protected for a long time from being recognized as the true locus of origin of the conflicts.

The leader who cannot say no responds positively to the last person he talked with, and conflicts between subordinates may derive from the contradictory conclusions drawn by these subordinates. This does not apply to the leader whose support of his subordinates contains the unconscious seeds of conflicts among them, and where a much greater subtlety obscures the contradictory messages being given.

Another, more pathological variant of this constellation is presented by the leader who consciously attempts to manipulate his subordinates by the principle of divide and rule, a sign that narcissistic pathology with antisocial tendencies is in the foreground. The avoidance of open conflicts represents a defense against the expression of direct aggression in organizational interchange, an effort to avoid overtly making enemies while attempting to maintain control. The result is a decrease of mutual trust throughout the entire system, leading to paranoid developments. Major institutional mismanagement and administrative scandals may erupt from the apparently harmonious surface of interaction created by this type of leadership.

THE LEADER WHO HAS TO BE ADMIRED AND LOVED

This pattern reflects the psychopathology of the narcissistic personality in a leadership position. Leaders with narcissistic personality show strong exhibitionistic tendencies, make it clear to their subordinates that they need to be loved and admired, have great difficulty accepting criticism from subordinates, and tend to transform administrative structures into an inner circle of sycophantic favorites complemented by an outer group of disgruntled, disappointed, resentful, and suspect "enemies." This type of leader can be direct and certain and may accept advice from those he feels sure are admiring subordinates, but because of his intolerance of criticism he may not be given necessary feedback regarding institutional problems.

In the long run, the lack of ability to assess individuals in depth that is typical for the psychopathology of narcissism may bring about a deterioration in the leadership quality throughout middle-management levels and add to the organizational damage. Although narcissistic leaders are often charismatic, it is important not to confuse these two characteristics: a leader with great conceptual skills, plenty of energy and enthusiasm, and an aggressive pursuit of goals who, at the same time, possesses a strong capacity for investment in depth in others may provide charismatic leadership without creating the negative side effects of the narcissistic personality.

Although the leaders who cannot say no and those who need to be admired and loved may look like consensus leaders, consensus leadership may also be provided by a completely different personality style, namely, that of a leader committed to a functional, team-oriented leadership that is strong and decisive.

Indeed, the leader who is self-confident may find it easier to delegate authority, under specific circumstances, to other members of the organization who are more prepared than he to deal with certain problems.

The narcissistic leader's lack of capacity to listen to what is not harmonious with his own views, his need to defend himself against his own intense unconscious envy, make the position of his most creative coworkers difficult. It is not enough to admire him; it is important that conscious envious feelings not be stirred up in him. The unconscious (or conscious) awareness of these dynamics within his inner circle tends to transform the energy of most capable coworkers into passive acquiescence, and a situation is created in which it seems as though original thinking and decision making were located exclusively in the leader. Furthermore, his devaluation of those who are not his admirers and whose productivity he unconsciously envies may inhibit the development of creativity in other areas of the institution. Typically, narcissistic leaders find it easier to hire valuable people from outside the institution rather than to promote their subordinates, thereby inhibiting organizational development. In educational institutions, these leaders are highly admired teachers who may help young students, but not senior faculty, develop.

**THE LEADER WHO NEEDS TO BE
IN COMPLETE CONTROL**

This leadership style corresponds to that of a traditional authoritarian leadership and should be differentiated from an objective need to carry out adequate boundary control of the institution, to set goals and implement them, and to really be in charge. What I am referring to here is a leadership style wherein the exercise of control becomes an objective in itself. It is typically reflected in micromanagement and suspiciousness and resentment when decisions are made without the leader's knowledge or approval. In addition, all processes throughout the organization have to follow nonfunctional "loops" to ensure support from the top, even before a proposal is worked out at a local level.

Various types of personality difficulties may converge to engender this leadership style. Some narcissistic personalities need to be not only admired and loved but also scrupulously obeyed; otherwise, as the leader sees it, enemies can appear. Narcissistic personalities with strong paranoid features tend to develop such a leadership style. Some leaders with strong paranoid tendencies may express their suspicious nature through the need to control, the need they have to constantly protect themselves against manipulation, cheating, and betrayal.

If the underlying pathology of the need for excessive control is predominantly narcissistic, it also may reflect the leader's unconscious fears of being left out, of failure and incompetence if he is not in charge—in other words, the need to defend an idealized self-concept and to avoid the emergence of a devalued one. And, insofar as the narcissistic leader projects his devalued self- and object representations onto his subordinates, his unconscious devaluation of those who work with him may have devastating effects on their creativity and self-esteem, and it may also foster the development of the depressive and excessive self-critical attitude I have described earlier as a typical consequence of paranoiagenesis within the healthier spectrum of the members of the institution.

Some obsessive-compulsive personalities need complete control in order to avoid a feared situation of "chaos," and as a direct expression of striving for sadistic power. In more inhibited obsessive personalities, the need to be in control may exist in association with indecisiveness, so that organizational functioning is dramatically slowed down. Here, however, I am describing a style that is excessively controlling but decisive at the same time.

When the leader's obsessive-compulsive tendencies dominate, he has a strong capacity for establishing object relations in depth—making a realistic assessment of his coworkers. The need to be in control is not accompanied by an inordinate need to be loved and admired, as it is with the narcissistic personality. If the leader has exceptional intellectual, creative, and moral qualities, the tendency toward excessive exercise of control may be compensated by this very efficiency; this may be an ideal leadership style when "turbulence" exists in the external environment, or rapid organizational change, or a crisis situation. For a stable organization, however, the long-term effects of this leadership style may still be significantly paranoiagenic and, in this regard, diminish organizational efficiency.

If the underlying dynamics are predominantly paranoid, the leader who needs to carry out excessive control typically presents projective mechanisms, the need for omnipotent control as a complement to projective identification, the division of the world into friends and enemies, and, particularly, the definition of individuals or areas of the organization as hostile, which provokes in him a corresponding challenging hostility in reaction to those hostile forces and a generalized hyperalertness and suspiciousness in his organizational dealings. Here the mutual reinforcement of paranoid features in the leadership and a consequent group regression and reinforcement of paranoiagenesis in the institution, which in turn further strengthen the paranoid elements in the leadership, is the rule. In the organization's group processes, the leader may typically attack one or several of his subordinates, who submit meekly to these attacks. A silent majority seems to condone the leader's attack, while the reactions among the other members of the management group may be gleeful ("I'm glad I didn't catch it today") or depressed (expressing the unconscious feelings of guilt for abandoning their colleagues).

In the long run, an excessively controlling organizational leadership may have exhausting effects on intermediate levels of management, for an enormous amount of energy must go into reassuring the leader about his control and into negotiating the organization's functional needs in compromises with the leader's demands. Intuitively, leaders at an intermediate level attempt to protect their junior workers from the effects of excessive control at the top, but an atmosphere of caution and conservatism permeates the organization.

A frequent complication is the gradual gathering at an intermediate level of individuals with strongly narcissistic features, who are able to adjust to excessive control on the top while maintaining an internal distance that protects them from the organization's paranoid regression; they are "narcissistically floating," one might say, in an organizational structure to which they adjust without a deep commitment. Such developments may lead to an association between the paranoid narcissistic leader and a lieutenant with antisocial features as his instrument for institutional control (the relationship between Stalin and Beria is a typical example).

THE ABSENTEE LEADER

The paranoiagenic effects of absentee leadership derive from the lack of availability, whenever group regressions occur, of task-oriented maintenance or reorganization of task systems and task boundaries, of corrective feedback, and of the quelling of rumors by authoritative information and directives from the top. Because absentee leadership weakens administrative structures and can result in chaos, group regression and authoritarianism tend to coexist. If the organization is relatively stable, if its products have an assured market, and if the external environment is stable, the underlying problems may last for many years. But absentee leadership may be the prelude to organizational breakdown in times of acute environmental change or crisis.

Various types of personality difficulties may be responsible for absentee leadership: a leader with a schizoid personality can exert leadership through written directives to a select group, but she is extremely reluctant to interact directly with her entire staff. Or the leader has been promoted beyond her technical expertise or interest and is occupying the position for other reasons—financial support, for example, or political influence. Or a highly narcissistic individual is more interested in the prestige provided by the position than in any investment in the organization's goals and tasks. Sometimes an individual may inherit leadership in a family business without having any personal interest in it.

Some absentee leaderships are undertaken deliberately for protective reasons, and provisions are made to avoid disrupting the organization. For example, a leading scientist in a highly specialized field may agree to head her professional institution to protect her particular field and then delegate actual leadership roles to a second-in-command.

With the provisions that the leader is conscious of her reasons for absentee leadership, that those reasons are public knowledge and her actions have public consent, and that a compensating leader is in place, the institution can function remarkably well. If a discrepancy exists between the formal organizational structure and the actual workings of the institution, there is risk of functional failure. Typical examples of such failure include a substitute leader who is overwhelmed by the organizational tasks, delegates them excessively to subordinates without clearly differentiating between strategic and tactical issues, overloads subordinates with problems that they cannot solve, and spends her own time with trivia rather than dealing with the central tasks of organizational leadership.

In the case of a narcissistic leader who simply goes through the motions, a ritualized fulfillment of organizational tasks may be expressed in chronic failure to fulfill commitments, evasive avoidance of decision making, and the growing isolation of component task systems within the organization. As a consequence, the overall integration of institutional components gradually fails, resources are allocated irrationally, political struggle across task-system boundaries erupts, and different departments and units become embroiled in chronic and often unnecessary contentiousness.

LEADERS WITH AFFECTIVE UNAVAILABILITY OR INSTABILITY

So far, in describing leaders and the paranoiagenic effects of their failure, I have described people who present a relatively stable or normal capability of affective deployments. Sometimes leaders whose intelligence, moral integrity, conceptual clarity, and technical expertise are exceptional may nonetheless suffer from personality problems that are expressed in the instability or unavailability of their ordinary affective responses. These are usually—but not always—leaders who have significant pathology of internalized object relations.

Perhaps the most distinct type here is the robot leader, an individual who has enormous difficulty in expressing his own emotions and in accepting emotional expression in those who work with him. People with strongly obsessive tendencies or schizoid tendencies, as well as some narcissistic individuals may present these characteristics. Highly efficient in their communication concerning technical issues, they lack a human quality and therefore frustrate the emotional needs, particularly the dependency needs, of those with whom they work, as well as exacerbate, by the absence of their emotional response, the paranoid tendencies among their subordinates. An organization's task systems may function effectively, but the individuals may feel isolated, vaguely insecure, and paranoid about their inscrutable leader.

The leader who is insecure in the realm of emotional expression may have the same effect as the absentee leader. If he is strong in exercising decision making and leadership functions in general, however, he may function well enough despite his robot characteristics. Leaders with these characteristics unconsciously attempt to avoid intense emotional conflicts because of the threat that significant aggression will evolve in these conflicts, and that fear communicates itself throughout the organization. This style of leadership discourages group processes within the organization, or, rather, it nurtures what might be called an amorphous crowd of equally self-controlled singletons, each having a sense of isolation and impotence, of not being able to influence the operations in the institution. Work may proceed satisfactorily but is typically experienced as exhausting because the dependent needs of the staff are being frustrated.

In contrast to this absence of affective deployment, leaders with other significant personality disorders, particularly dependent, infantile or histrionic, and borderline personalities tend to present intense emotional crises or temper tantrums as part of a leadership style that has disorganizing effects on their followers. Narcissistic, infantile, and dependent leaders may present themselves as overworked and exhausted and in dire need of soothing and support, which distracts their staff's attention from actual tasks and transmits a general sense of burnout throughout the institution.

Burnout symptoms—a general and persistent sense of exhaustion and of being overwhelmed—may also result from other leadership styles, particularly that of the narcissistic-charismatic leader who implicitly promises the staff complete gratification of all their needs, raises the level of expectation in unrealistic ways, and fails to set realistic limits to task performance. If the entire emotional life of the staff is to be gratified, in fantasy, at the workplace, burnout is a natural consequence. The emotional needs of the leader and the staff's attention to the leader's needs take precedence.

The temper tantrums of leaders with infantile or histrionic personality may, by direct expression of aggression in the context of organizational group processes, appear as a violent attack, an acute invasion of staff privacy—what amounts to a traumatic group experience that may repeat itself, frequently without the leader even being aware of having caused it. A dramatic decay of staff morale, high staff turnover, a chronic sense of frustration, failure, chaos, and fear may pervade the organization. The combination of such affective excesses with a paranoid leadership style may lead to a true gaslight atmosphere resulting in disastrous organizational dysfunctioning.

It is rare for people with such immature affective behavior to be promoted to head institutions, and even though they possess unusual capacities in other areas, they tend to remain at an intermediate level of leadership. Yet because their emotional outbursts are directed largely against subordinates, it may take time before senior leadership becomes aware of them. An individual with strong narcissistic, paranoid, sadistic, and antisocial features (such as Hitler) may ascend to a position of leadership as part of a fight-flight subgroup and then stabilize such emotionally violent behavior in the context of a controlled, totalitarian bureaucracy, with maximal paranoiagenic effects.

Yet another affective style that can be detrimental to organizational functioning is a certain superficial joviality that masks a deep emotional unavailability. Some narcissistic individuals adjust themselves only too well to the organizational hierarchical structure, ascend the hierarchical ladder by their remarkable flexibility, and end up in positions of authority where they apparently facilitate smooth functioning. But gradually a sense of unreality and emotional unavailability permeates the institution, needs for dependency are frustrated, and the staff's sense of trust is undermined. Often such apparent friendliness and flexibility go hand in hand with a passive and conventional style of task performance. Sudden crises in their administrative realm may be the first indicator that something has been simmering under the surface for a long time.

THE CORRUPT LEADER

I am referring here to the leader who consciously and blatantly exploits the organizational resources under his control for his own benefit, disregarding his responsibilities to the organization and to the task, and, in the process, damages the organizational resources and task performance. The simple wish to stay in power may be the dominant motivation for the leader's corrupt behavior, and this type of corruption is often to be found in a leader with a strong paranoid orientation and antisocial features, who visualizes the world as divided between friends and enemies and for whom all measures at the service of survival are justified. Here is an example of the "paranoid urge to betray" described by Jacobson (1971a); the paranoiagenic effects of this style of leadership stem more from the leader's paranoid behavior than from the corruption derived from it.

In contrast, corrupt behavior reflecting the leader's personal greed and rapaciousness may present in individuals whose behavior is predominantly antisocial, and where paranoid tendencies emerge only when their exploitativeness and greed is threatened. Often narcissistic personalities with infantile tendencies and immature superego development perceive their leadership role as an entitlement as well as an opportunity for gratifying personal aspirations, accumulating wealth, gratifying particular sexual or dependent needs, and rewarding those who collude with them. The complementary persecution and punishment of those who stand in the way of such exploitativeness or threaten the leader with public exposure create this style's paranoiagenic features.

A cadre of corrupt followers may create an entire layer of corrupt leadership. The group adopts the ideology that they constitute a leading class—for example, based on what they see as their historical rights, on their merits in ascending to leadership, or on the their entitlement to compensation for their unusual, heavy responsibilities. The scandals about corrupt leadership in organizations whose goals are philanthropic or that are nonprofit and in political elites of long-standing social or, in particular, totalitarian regimes are examples.

It is usually a hierarchically rigid organization (such as a large bureaucracy) with enormous power invested at the top that permits the corrupt leader to develop a corrupt circle of influence around him, and the paranoiagenic effects may take time to develop throughout the rest of the organization. Usually, however, particularly in large organizations with many hierarchical levels, implicit boundaries between the corrupt inner circle and the excluded outer circle tend to evolve, and, in the process, a sharp dividing line is drawn between the relaxed friendships on the top and the resentment, suspicion, and paranoid fears of the excluded. One might consider this the model of how psychopathic regression at one level generates a powerful paranoid regression at the next level. The relationship between the politburo, on the one hand, and the lower levels of hierarchy of the communist party, on the other, within the administrative structure of the German Democratic Republic is an illustration (Schabowski, 1991). In small organizations, corrupt leaders may be replaced without major organizational turmoil; in large organizations, the widespread nature of institutional corruption means that a corrective organizational change will trigger intense paranoid regression throughout; the threat to organizational survival under such circumstances is maximal.

Narcissistic individuals with infantile and antisocial tendencies are the personalities who typically develop corrupt leadership. The temptations I have referred to in earlier work (Kernberg, 1991) explain why many corrupt leaders may have a history devoid of antisocial behavior before their rise to power and can return to relatively normal social functioning after their deposition as leader.

DIAGNOSIS AND MANAGEMENT

The correction of malfunctioning leadership requires two things: a diagnosis of the leader's functioning and the organizational dynamics and structure within which it is taking place and management of the leader's malfunctioning so as to restore organizational health. The psychoanalytically oriented consultant has to be prepared to carry out this double function. Fortunately, for practical purposes, it is usually possible to harmoniously integrate organizational requirements with individual needs. A malfunctioning leader whose personality limitations are such that they do not permit him to carry out the corresponding organizational tasks needs to be helped to change his role. At the same time, this will facilitate the reorganization of the organizational structure. Reorganization of institutional structures or tasks results in breaking the cycle of individual and group regression that causes the leader to function at his worst.

It should be kept in mind that the leader's personality problems are frequently the first symptom of organizational malfunctioning, and that it is quite possible that they are really no more than a symptom; that the cause of the organizational malfunctioning lies elsewhere. But when the leader's malfunctioning is indeed a significant factor in organizational malfunctioning, as represented by the symptom of excessive paranoiagenesis, organizational and individual counseling can reinforce each other.

It is important to separate organizational requirements from the leader's psychotherapeutic needs. The consultant diagnoses the institutional tasks that are not being accomplished; she explores whether the leader understands which tasks he did not accomplish but could, or whether testing is necessary to determine that he has the capacity to do so. Whether, in order to carry out these tasks, the leader will need personal treatment in addition to the consultative-educational process provided by the consultant may have to be decided by the leader in the context of discussing the psychological issues involved in institutional management.

Organizational consultation from a psychoanalytic viewpoint has to start at the top, with full authorization by the leadership of the organization, and then proceed through the exploration of tasks, structures, and success and failures in those tasks under the condition of present or newly developing constraints. The study of group processes (by means of open-group meetings in which work experiences are shared with the consultant within each level of hierarchical and task-system structure), jointly with interviews of key leaders in managerial positions, should enable the consultant to make an institutional diagnosis and, as part of it, a diagnosis of personality styles of leadership.

Organizational counseling constitutes a second stage of the diagnostic enterprise. The institutional diagnosis must come first for it allows the consultant to differentiate leaders' capacities to change their functioning once the nature of the difficulties is clarified, and to diagnose the leader's ability to change. The organization should eventually be able to install and preserve a functional leadership and to carry out such changes as may be necessary to guarantee it.

An organizational consultation may itself temporarily increase paranoiagenesis; but fortunately, the liberating effect of an open ventilation of conflicts that previously went underground or were expressed only through the rumor mill tends to reduce paranoid developments. Much tension can be relieved by the consultative process, but there is also the risk of raising expectations of immediate improvement when changes may take time and be difficult to achieve. It is important, as part of organizational consultation, to discourage excessive idealization and messianic hopes, simultaneously with a focus on and resolution of the temporary accentuation of paranoiagenic regression.

If fundamental organizational changes are required that will affect the lives of many individuals in the organization, the exploration of these changes may first require a confidential consultation with top leadership, which may also temporarily increase paranoiagenesis. As soon as a point of closure has been achieved, however, there is an advantage in taking whatever corrective measures are available as quickly as possible and in making those measures public as quickly as possible. When the staff is fully informed of the facts, the reasons for change, and the nature of the change, paranoiagenesis tends to decrease even when the organization is in crisis.

I have been involved in two organizations that had to lay off a large number of staff in a short period, and, painful though the process was, it was achieved without further organizational regression because once the impending changes were announced, the need for the layoffs was universally recognized. The capacity of individuals and groups to trust their leaders when they are open and responsible is as great as their capacity for severe paranoid regression when organizational uncertainty prevails and there is no open communication about unresolved problems.

Part Three Therapeutic Applications

Chapter 10 A Systems Approach to the Priority Setting of Interventions in Groups

THE "NONCONCENTRIC" NATURE OF SYSTEMS IMPINGING ON GROUP LEADERSHIP

This chapter is a continuation of previous efforts to apply an open-systems-theory approach to the integration of various psychotherapeutic modalities, particularly group methods, within a psychoanalytic frame of reference (Kernberg 1973). It focuses on the boundary functions of the group leader, whether a consultant to a small study group exploring group dynamics for learning purposes, a group psychotherapist attempting to help patients with psychological illness, a leader of a task group, or a leader of an administrative group structure working within the hospital as an organization. My dominant focus, however, is on the task of the group psychotherapist.

Clinical analysis of the concrete boundary functions of group leadership reveals that instead of involving one universe containing a hierarchy of systems (each higher-level system being constituted by units representing systems of a lower level—as outlined by Miller and Rice [1967] in referring to living systems), a puzzling change occurs in the order of system levels from moment to moment, and "nonconcentric," overlapping hierarchies of system levels can be found. All these impinge on the group leader and demand an ever-shifting determination of which boundary functions are predominant at a given moment and what are thus the priorities for his interventions. One consequence of this is the temptation for the group leader to arbitrarily limit his focus of awareness to a certain fixed hierarchical sequence of systems as a more or less exclusive frame of reference, thus neglecting both the creative potential and the destructive threats implied in a broader awareness of the total hierarchy of systems impinging upon his decision making.

The most generally accepted hierarchy of systems involved in group processes is probably that which puts the individual—or her personality—as the subsystem, the group as the main system or "target system" (pers. comm., Durkin, 1972) under examination, and the social organization within which the group functions as the suprasystem of the series. Within psychoanalytic object-relations theory, internalized object relations constitute the subsystem of the target system, which is represented by the overall psychic structures (superego, ego, and id), and the complete personality is the suprasystem of the series. All these systems, from internalized object relations to social organization, can be placed within a single hierarchical continuum. If we wished to represent this continuum graphically, we could place concentric circles representing, from the center to the periphery, internalized object relations; overall psychic structures; and personality, group, and social organization. This is a typically unified concentric hierarchy. In groups, however, the situation is more complex.

From one viewpoint, the activation of basic assumptions in the group, fostered by lack of structuralization (lack of clearly defined roles and functions) and by the absence of an objective task relating to the external environment, promotes regression into personal psychopathology and threatens to absorb the group into intrapsychic and interpersonal conflicts of the members; personal psychopathology thus appears as a subsystem of the dynamics of the entire group. At the suprasystem level, the shared cognitive observations within the group of what is happening represents a conceptual system integrating this group's functioning with a general theoretical system; a purely intellectual analysis of group processes fostered by the group leader may obscure the emotional reality of what is being observed. This hierarchy of systems extends from a theoretical suprasystem describing group functioning (the "obsessive" pole of the continuum); through a middle zone of group dynamics—the "target system"; to individual or group psychopathology—the subsystem (individual or group acting out, representing the "hysterical" pole of the continuum).

From a different viewpoint, the examination of group themes and basic group assumptions activates powerful group processes, group cohesiveness, and magical hopes of gratifying basic emotional needs that are frustrated in ordinary reality. Insofar as expression of these needs also reflects a value system that affirms human openness, love, and sharing, it represents a polarity opposite to that of the realistic awareness of the transitory nature of the relationships of group members and of social and cultural constraints concerning discretion, privacy, autonomy, and individual responsibility. In other words, this type of group task—exploration of group dynamics—functions on the boundary of a subsystem that might be called psychotherapeutic culture and a suprasystem of ordinary social conventions. In addition, insofar as economic, political, racial, and other ideological conflicts of external reality are activated as part of the group processes being examined, the conflicts between ideal value systems expressed in the psychotherapeutic culture and the constraints given by social reality reinforce the opposition between the complex system of universal values shared in emotional communication on the one hand and rational adaptation to the "real world" on the other.

At this point, it becomes apparent that what is suprasystem and what is subsystem are no longer clear. Emotional regression to basic group assumptions appears to be close to the personality subsystems, while rational, adaptive considerations of social and cultural constraints seem close to the social environment as suprasystem. However, efforts to escape from the task of examining group dynamics by means of intellectual analysis of what constitutes the "real world" fosters individuation within the group, reaffirmation of individual differences and separateness in contrast to the shared group culture, and activation of characteristic individualized personality defenses of the group members. In contrast, the emotional climate of shared basic-group assumptions may link the group powerfully with the emotional realities of social conflicts of the "real world," for example, the experience of religious prejudice, that of the irrational subjugation of one social group to another, and the struggle against authoritarian systems.

The situation is more complex in the case of group psychotherapy than in group-dynamics groups, because the very fact that a group leader accepts the task of helping patients to improve from psychological illness adds new hierarchies of systems in terms of professional responsibilities to individual patients and to the group at large, in terms of time dimensions (the relation between change aspired to and time available), and in terms of the impact of the therapist's personal values on group functioning. Regarding the therapist's values, his commitment to help each patient as an individual may, at times, conflict with the technical requirement of focusing on the predominant group processes. A patient who may be helpful in expressing certain emotional conflicts of the group at large will not necessarily benefit from doing so. It is interesting that "failures" of group psychotherapy are often explored purely as "drop outs" (Yalom, 1970); the possibility that patients might not improve in spite of persistent attendance in the group is rarely explored. The issue of time as a constraint, particularly the question, "How much can this patient realistically be helped within the time limits of this particular psychotherapy group?" may be more difficult to evaluate than in cases of individual psychotherapy, because the extent to which focus upon individual patients occurs depends on overall group developments. Granting that working through group conflicts includes and facilitates working through individual conflicts, the uncertainty nonetheless is greater in groups than in well-designed individual treatment.

In systems terms, working through group resistances appears at the boundary between the activation of primitive group phenomena related to primitive levels of internalized object relations of the patients, on the one hand, and the focus upon individual transference reactions and their working through in the group, on the other (Astrachan, 1970; Durkin and Glatzer, 1972; Glatzer, 1969). In this continuum, it is again difficult to define suprasystem and subsystem in respect to common group themes. Insofar as basic group assumptions activate primitive object relationships in individual patients, pregenital conflicts and defenses may be activated and worked through in the process, and thus primitive individual psychopathology (especially borderline conditions) may be considered the subsystem of group basic assumptions. Insofar as the therapist's focus is upon the development of individual transferences within the group network of transferences, other aspects of individual psychopathology, particularly "higher level" pathological character constellations (Kernberg, 1973) may be explored and worked through in the group. In short, the target system of group processes appears on the boundary between higher levels of individual psychopathology on one level and lower or more primitive levels of individual psychopathology on the other.

To this point, I have tried to illustrate the proposal that the task of the group leader involves boundary functions among various systems that are related to one another in a shifting order of levels of hierarchy. These hierarchies include a hierarchy of value systems, a hierarchy of professional and technical requirements across the dimension of time, and the complex system relations between personality structure, group structure, and social structure. I propose that these cannot all be reduced to a unified hierarchy of levels of systems. In more general terms, all the levels of systems along the various hierarchies of systems mentioned cannot be represented graphically in concentric circles; they represent a "nonconcentric" overlap of hierarchies. In short, the nature of the systems among which the group leader carries out boundary functions is nonconcentric. The nature of these systems varies according to the main task determining the functions of the leader. The respective levels of subsystems, systems, and supraordinate systems may be activated so that a simple, graphic model that describes systems as evolving along one continuous dimension no longer applies.

This viewpoint is in contrast to approaches such as Miller's (1976). Miller, in attempting to integrate all living systems into a unified, general hierarchy, suggests that language and music are examples of "artifacts," that is, inclusions in some systems—inventions that carry out some critical process essential to a living system but that are not living systems as such. Unfortunately, he does not mention value systems in this connection. In any case, it is questionable whether cultural value systems can really be considered simply artifacts. There is an internal dynamic of change to cultural systems, and particularly to value systems across historical and social boundaries; in general, multiple boundary functions can be observed among cultural, social, and personality systems. Parsons (1964a, 1964b) has convincingly stressed the irreducibility of these systems into one continuum of hierarchical levels. However, his description of the dyadic interactions as a common subsystem of the cultural, social, and personality systems is closely related to my stress here on the group leader's observing ego as a subsystem common to all the hierarchies of systems impinging upon the group.

These considerations may be illustrated with the irreducible nonconcentricity of systems that impinge on the decision-making process of the leader of a psychiatric organization, such as a hospital or a department of psychiatry. The decision-making process of the leader involves boundary functions among the following systems: (1) value systems regarding the human and technical qualities required for treating patients with psychological illness (which corresponds to the amalgamation of highly technical, professional, and personal value systems); (2) administrative considerations regarding the optimal use of available staff resources; (3) political pressures reflecting the organizational environment within which the institution functions and which force the administrative leader into a search for managerial support and loyalty; and

(4) crucially at this time, financial pressures—such as managed care requirements—that shape the nature of the delivery of services. For example, the search for people with convictions in depth, both professional and personal, can (and usually does) clash with demands stemming from the scarcity of financial resources, political pressures, and such human factors as the uncanny administrative effectiveness of those whose only real convictions relate to the importance of keeping themselves employed or in positions of importance.

At the same time, functional leadership of a psychiatric institution, within which the exploration of the whole social process becomes a therapeutic technique, requires a level of open examination of leadership functions, an exploration that over a period of time relentlessly exposes the various conflicts between systems that overlap in the boundaries of administrative leadership. Efforts to reduce these conflicts in simpler terms, for example, along a unified hierarchy of moral and other value judgments or along a hierarchy of status-role concepts or along a "business-management" hierarchy of rational-technical considerations of social efficiency or in terms of a hierarchy of personality structures are all insufficient by themselves; administrative leadership usually pays a high price for seriously neglecting any one of these dimensions.

UNCERTAINTIES OF FEEDBACK
FROM THE PSYCHOTHERAPY GROUP
TO THE LEADER'S INTERVENTION

The interventions of the group leader are a powerful influence upon the development of the group culture, with its norms for "appropriate" or "inappropriate" ways for individual group members to participate, which shall be the main subjects explored here. Yalom (1970) summarized the abundant evidence indicating the model-setting functions of the group psychotherapist, and Astrachan (1970) showed how the therapist, acting as central regulatory agent, determines by his interventions whether the group will be focusing mostly upon individual psychopathology (what might be called sophisticated levels of transference developments related to relatively high-level character constellations) or to group processes (what might be called primitive transference dispositions related to primitive object relationships activated in the basic assumptions of the group). I stress here that because of the central regulatory function of the group therapist, the feedback he receives will largely depend upon his interventions, and thus by itself has limited value in either confirming or disconfirming the priorities for intervention that the therapist has set for himself. If the group therapist were simply involved in a boundary function among two or three hierarchically linked systems that constitute an ordered series of levels from subsystems to suprasystems, the decision-making process would be easier.

For example, if it were simply a matter of deciding whether to intervene regarding basic group assumptions that become major group resistances against group work or to intervene regarding particular interpersonal interactions that reflect major individual psychopathology (which had brought the group members to treatment in the first place), the therapist might decide which of these alternative steps to take in terms of relatively simple technical psychotherapeutic considerations. If it is true, however, that the group therapist (and the group leader in general) operates on a common boundary between multiple hierarchies of systems, the task becomes more complicated, and the limited informational value of the feedback to his past interventions for present priority setting means that he cannot rely upon it alone in deciding when to say what.

The same difficulty about checking on the accuracy of interventions obtains in individual psychotherapy or psychoanalysis; however, the development of a social system within the group and its dynamic interactions with larger social systems of which the group forms a part, and the development of a group culture that interacts with value systems of individual members, of the therapist, and of the institution or society at large, all increase enormously the complexity of the therapist's boundary functions and the level of uncertainty of what his major task is at any particular moment. In psychoanalytic treatment, the accuracy of interpretation of defenses can be evaluated by the amount of previously defended against unconscious material that now emerges; the danger of artificially forcing certain contents, of "brainwashing" the patient along the analyst's theoretical hypotheses or preconceptions, can be controlled by evaluation of the extent to which the patient's elaboration of new material remains intellectual, dissociated from other areas of conflicts, or leads to new, unexpected intrapsychic changes. The general psychoanalytic rule of thumb— to evaluate free association from the viewpoint of whether it focuses too much on either present or past material, on affective or intellectual expression, on the relationship with the analyst or matters external to the sessions—constitutes a built-in control of the risk that the feedback from the patient may simply be slanted to confirm the analyst's theories.

Within a group setting, as Astrachan (1970) states: "The therapist's understanding of the multiple ways in which he may act as a regulator of the group may even allow the therapist to listen more to the group, be less constrained by his own theory of therapy (for example, individual and group psychoanalytic, and social-psychologic) and at times shift his regulatory behavior (with awareness of what the consequences of such a shift will be) in response to a re-evaluation with the group of its needs and aims" (p. 116). This approach demands a clear understanding of the boundaries of the various nonconcentric systems that impinge simultaneously upon the group leader and a clear understanding of the particular "target system" (Durkin, 1964) of each of these hierarchies that relates to the group leader's function in the group. In other words, the group leader needs to be aware of most if not all the systems operating in his immediate boundary zone.

Thus, one obvious task of the group leader is to become aware of and define the hierarchies of systems operating upon the group he is leading; for example, a therapeutic group conducted within a psychiatric institution is involved in a particular social system, in addition to the larger social system that would affect psychotherapy groups both in private practice and institutions. A therapeutic-community setting contains subsystems relating to the staff, to the institution, and to the hierarchy of value systems of that particular treatment setting regarding overall treatment objectives. The simple awareness of the need to define as many boundary functions as possible increases the scope of the observational field of the group leader.

THE GROUP LEADER'S PERSONALITY
AS THE CRUCIAL COMMON
ORGANIZING SYSTEM

The crucial role of the group leader as a central regulator of all the forces operating within and upon the group corresponds, in terms of open-systems theory (Miller and Rice, 1967; Rice, 1963, 1965, 1969), to her boundary functions for the group. By the same token, the group leader occupies the intersection of all the hierarchies of systems involved. However, which aspect of the group leader occupies this boundary needs to be explored further. It is not her behavior but her personality that is involved in this boundary function.

More specifically, this boundary function of the group leader is represented by her self-exploratory function, the "observing part of the ego"—that aspect of her personality that centers upon her self-concept and the related internalized conceptions of significant others, including (but not on an exclusive basis) the group members. Insofar as the group leader's self-concept includes consciously held value systems (general ethical values as well as particular professional values) and her personal integration of the various roles she carries out (or expects herself to carry out or thinks she is expected to carry out) in the context of the group, the "observing ego" includes personality factors, cultural factors, and social factors (status-role "bundles"). In other words, the activation within the group leader of particular, differentiated internalized object relations, combined with the predominant aspect of her self-concept and with the predominant representations of external objects involved, reflect the activation of her ego identity. One might also say that it is the subsystem of individualized, integrated aspects of internalized object relations that is the predominant personality subsystem occupying the boundary zone between the various hierarchies of systems which cross at this nodal point. To put it more briefly, the group leader's ego identity and its most differentiated components constitute the nodal point at which all the other hierarchies of systems influencing task performance in the group meet. What follows are examples of the boundary functions of the personality of the group leader among nonconcentric hierarchies that ordinarily influence group processes.

The group therapist is frequently accused by the members of his group of "projecting" onto them his own internal conflicts. For example, when interpreting group transferences involving defenses against aggression, the group may unite in pointing out that the therapist seems to see only aggression against himself in the group and has disregarded the reality of all other matters. At that point, the group therapist must, indeed, explore to what extent his deeper personality factors, particularly the more primitive levels of internalized object relations or activation of pathological character patterns, are distorting his perceptions, or to what extent it is the pressure of basic assumptions that is bringing about the activation of internal dispositions in himself and heightening his awareness of what is going on in the group. At times, a masochistic therapist may artificially foster the increase of hostility toward himself; or a paranoid therapist may project his own aggression onto the group. In short, the therapist's observing ego carries out a boundary function between his own psychopathology and group processes.

Problems involving the development of a group culture with shared values that are in sharp contrast to those of the surrounding social system may serve as a second example. In the earlier example, the shared group disposition constituted the suprasystem; here, group values constitute the subsystem, while social values at large constitute the suprasystem. The group therapist's observing ego is again at the boundary between these two levels (group and society) along the hierarchy of value systems. This is an important issue, particularly when a generally humanistic group philosophy of openness, mutual respect, and expectation of personal growth and satisfaction linked to individual autonomy develops within the cohesive group; while the reality of interpersonal and social violence; the participation of the individual in economic, political, and social conflicts; and the individual's impotence in the face of these conflicts are all projected outside the group and (with a good basis in reality) attributed to the values of the "external" world. In broader terms, the danger exists of an idealistic, utopian value system developing in the group that will be thought to be the kind of ideal social reality toward which the individuals should adapt themselves, thus neglecting aggression, ambivalence, and unavoidable intrapsychic, interpersonal, and social conflicts. There also exists an opposite danger of "the group becoming a technocratic tool to adapt people to a social system without questioning the values of that social system" (pers. comm., A. Brocher, 1972). What, for example, is the meaning of "well-adjusted people" in totalitarian regimes?

This situation becomes particularly acute in group-dynamics groups, short-term training groups, or intensive but short group-therapy experiences (encounter groups, marathon groups, and so on), where rapid development of group cohesiveness and of a sense of emotional freedom and openness facilitates the development of a messianic group culture, a splitting off of aggression and projection of it onto the "external" society, and therefore a loss of the capacity for in-depth exploration of basic human conflicts. The group leader is placed right in the middle of the clash of opposing ideologies. To tolerate the contradictions between the values of the group and of society in terms of the primary task set for the particular group is no easy job, particularly when the therapist's own ideological convictions and conflicts regarding social values are involved. There are group therapists who, for reasons of their own psychological needs, exploit group processes to express their own dissatisfaction with society; others are afraid of the philosophical implications for themselves of what develops in the group. In any case, personality functions of the group leader are prominent in fostering or in preventing the carrying out of the boundary functions among conflictual value systems.

A third example is the clash between the group leader's value systems and the reality of the social organization within which she carries out group leadership functions. A typical example is the use of training groups for medical students or psychiatric residents by group leaders who have been influenced by a democratically inspired, functional-administrative theory of group and organizational processes, which is in contrast to the reality of the rigidly hierarchical and possibly authoritarian organization that is characteristic of some departments of psychiatry or medical schools. Again, the observing ego of the group leader carries out the boundary function between the social realities of the institution mirrored within the group culture and the conflicts in the group, on one side, and her own value system in clash with that social system on the other. The leader's temptation to act out her own rebellious reaction against the institution within which the group is training is intense under these circumstances, and such a pressure for acting out may bring about an unconscious or conscious stimulation of rebelliousness in the students toward the institution, a defiance that expresses the group leader's own needs. This rebelliousness has to be differentiated from other sources of activation of basic assumptions of flight-fight within the group. At other times, the activation of rebelliousness within such a group may be erroneously interpreted by the leader exclusively in intragroup or intrapsychic terms, thus neglecting the reality of the impact of the social system—the psychiatric institution—on the group processes. At times, when it is dangerous to speak out within a certain organization, to be encouraged to speak openly within a small group may be cruel.

A final example is that of the technical skills involved in the group therapist's decision making as to when experience should be encouraged, and when thinking. Again, the observing ego of the group therapist stands at the boundary between cognitive analysis of the meaning of what is going on and experiential unfolding of the emotional realities of individuals within the group and of the group at large. This last example mirrors the technical considerations in psychoanalytic treatment that determine the analyst's shift from focus on defenses to content, and his shift from emotional experience to intellectual understanding.

In all these examples, the observing part of the group leader's ego (the more conscious aspects of his self-system), or his higher-level internalized object relations (Kernberg, 1973), constitute a common sector of the various hierarchies of systems. In more general terms, aspects of the group leader's personality system constitute a common system of various hierarchies, and a central or target system for subsystems and suprasystems along nonconcentric systems impinging on the group processes. In other words, the personality of the group leader, in particular his self-observing function, occupies a crucial position in the decision-making process regarding which boundary function of the many involved has highest priority at any particular point, or, in simple terms, what are the type and order of interventions indicated at any point in time.

In individual psychotherapy, the more regressed the patient, the more the total behavior of the patient constitutes the major subject matter of the therapist-patient interaction. The patient's verbal and nonverbal behavior are explored by the therapist, whose free-floating attention permits him, under optimal circumstances, to set priorities for interpretation on the basis of all the verbal and nonverbal material available. In the case of the psychotic patient, where remnants of ordinary verbal and nonverbal communication are mixed with bizarre fragments of statements, attitudes, behaviors, and emotional expression, the therapist becomes a "container" (Bion, 1967), and the therapist's emotional reactions in trying to integrate within himself the perceptions of the fragmented communications of the patient constitute major source material on the basis of which the priorities for intervention and the type of intervention are selected and designed. It was the application of this method (of diagnostic integration of fragmented perceptions within the therapist) to the developments within small, closed, unstructured groups that permitted Bion to formulate his theory of basic assumptions characteristic of such groups (Bion, 1961; Rioch, 1970a). The steps of this diagnostic process include not only an effort of the group therapist to experience as fully as possible the total group situation in which he is immersed, and his internal clarification of the major "organizers" within all this informational input, but also the question of how his understanding can be formulated. The group therapist also has to ask himself whether such a formulation will foster understanding by the group, what criteria could assure him (by means of the study of feedback to his verbal interventions) that his hypothesis was basically correct, and what effects it had (regardless of its correctness).

DIAGNOSTIC USE OF THE GROUP LEADER'S PERSONALITY IN TERMS OF PRIMARY TASKS AND THEIR CONSTRAINTS

To act as a container, the group therapist needs an optimal awareness of the origin of the stimuli which impinge upon her self-exploratory awareness. If it is true that her self-awareness reflects the activation of various levels of nonconcentric hierarchies of systems, then the task of sorting out which stems from where, and which is more important may at first appear overwhelming. The less defined the task of the group leader, the more the danger exists that she will be unable to set rational priorities for her interventions. In an extreme case, the person who is put into a leadership position for a group but given no "instructions" other than to keep herself in "power" (whether this is her own choice or she is put into this position), will probably destroy the understanding and the work in the group she is supposed to lead. The more restricted and precise the definition of the task, the easier it will be for the leader to explore information impinging from many systems in terms of this task and its constraints. Bion, when defining his task as observing the processes going on in groups conducted by him and organized for the purpose of learning about such group processes, effectively restricted the range of his primary observations and interventions to what are now known as the work group and the basic-assumptions group (Bion, 1961).

A group leader who sees as his main task the facilitation of the freest possible emotional expression and interaction among members of the group (for example, in following a naive personality theory according to which the fullest expression of emotions in groups or elsewhere reflects a universal ideal of health for all individuals) has a relatively simplified set of priorities for his interventions. The situation becomes much more complex for group leaders operating within various systems and performing various tasks simultaneously. For example, an administrative leader of professional groups working in psychiatric institutions may have to combine tasks along administrative, group-dynamic, technical-professional, and interpersonal-intergroup dimensions. The group psychotherapist working over a long period with the objective of helping individual patients is concerned with systems of individual psychopathology; with group processes facilitating or inhibiting the full expression, examination, and resolution of individual psychopathology activated within the group; and with professional responsibility and accountability for patients' functioning outside the group situation. His considerations along time dimensions become complex in that he has to evaluate immediate feedback from the group in terms of its long-term effect, the selective capacity of various individuals to learn from the group experience, and the realistic time limitations for treating unresponsive patients (who might respond to other modalities of treatment) as measured against such negative effects as changes in group composition.

Perhaps the most dramatic example of multiple hierarchies of systems impinging on the decision-making process of group leadership in psychiatric practice is given by the leaders of therapeutic community settings. If the main purpose of the therapeutic community is open, therapeutic exploration of the social processes affecting the patient-staff system within an institution, the primary focus of community meetings should be the exploration of commonly shared, emotionally significant perceptions and reactions within the community's social system. If, however, the primary task of the therapeutic community is to maximally activate the patients' capacity for helping one another by sharing mutual observations and understandings and by participating responsibly in decision-making processes, then the primary focus would be on the individual patient's complete interaction with other patients and staff members, on shared decision making regarding significant problems affecting individual patients, and on generally open expression of mutual feelings and reactions among patients and, within certain limits, among staff and patients. If, finally, the primary task of the therapeutic community is expressed as the wish for a more democratic, egalitarian social system that would permit patients to increase their self-esteem, autonomy, and effectiveness, the primary focus of the therapeutic community would be on democratizing the decision-making process and trying to decrease the distance between staff and patients and between various disciplines with traditionally hierarchical relationships.

It is, of course, easy to resolve the potential contradictions of the major focuses of these varying approaches by assuming that they are all primary tasks that complement one another, and that the overall objective of the therapeutic community is to do justice to them all. In practice, however, these various primary tasks constrain one another, and thus conflicts between actions derived from them need to be explored; choices must be made; and priorities have to be set.

Unfortunately, priorities of intervention in therapeutic community settings are often set in terms of a simplistic crisis orientation, so that whatever seems to be in danger of getting out of hand first is explored first. The usual effect of such control by crisis intervention is the neglect of the treatment needs of individual patients—that is, of the primary reason patients entered the therapeutic institution in the first place. This is not due to willful or unintentional patient neglect but to the uncontrolled absorption of staff resources, time, and communication channels when group leaders have abandoned effective priority setting on the basis of clear delimitations of primary tasks and constraints.

The following are typical examples of multiple systems from various hierarchies that impinge on the therapeutic community and of symptoms that illustrate the neglect by the community leadership of diagnosis and management of critical boundary functions among those systems. This neglect usually derives from the faulty setting of primary tasks and definitions of constraints (constraints to the primary and secondary tasks, constraints among these tasks, priority setting among tasks in terms of constraints).

The leader of the therapeutic community may see her task as that of "consultant," aimed to clarify the social system, particularly the social constraints operating on the therapeutic community itself. For example, she may help the group become aware of contradictions in hospital policy regarding patient privileges or dealing with "forbidden" behaviors without taking responsibility for acting as the liaison with the hospital administration or helping the therapeutic community clarify its task by establishing or developing such liaisons to seek an appropriate solution to the problem. In effect, what this leader is doing is creating awareness of problems without helping the group find functional channels for their resolution. Thus, she helps split the group from the broader social system of the hospital. This is an example of "teasing" by means of incomplete "knowledge." Such teasing creates or aggravates pathological reactions. A more general implication is that no one can make an effective examination of the realities of the social system that impinge upon a subunit of the institution if the basic structure and functions (and dysfunctions) of the administrative system are neglected.

Another example of neglect of primary task and boundary functions is the development of a therapeutic community model that emphasizes joint staff and patient meetings so much that special needs of individual patients "slip through" the net of the community organization. Thus, the therapeutic community becomes unsuited for the treatment of such patients. What started out as a method to help treatment may end up as an end in itself that acts counter to treatment needs. In addition, shifting from group processes to individual cases, even when individual cases are selected in terms of overall group themes, may consume so much time and energy that major decisions involving individual patients have to be made hurriedly in informal meetings; as a result, the patients' tendency to split staff can be expressed for a long time before it is fully diagnosed and discussed at the group meetings. Also, the effort to explore in the here and now the major interpersonal issues affecting decision making may be so influenced by the patients' behavior in the group that contrary evidence (even glaring contradictions in the patient's behavior in the group as compared to that outside the group) is missed. For example, a severely regressed patient starts improving, adjusts to the requirements of the therapeutic community, becomes a model patient; this behavior is rewarded and reinforced without anyone examining what brought about the change and to what extent the patient has avoided facing contradictions in himself by adjusting to the group pressures in the community.

SOME FREQUENT ILLUSIONS AND THEIR IMPLICATIONS FOR GROUP LEADERSHIP

The Exclusiveness of the Here and Now

To analyze conflicts, behaviors, and general issues within groups in the here and now only may represent a dangerous, though tempting, method of simplifying by ignoring the number of systems and hierarchies of systems impinging upon the group. Also, it may create the illusion that there are a smaller number of constraints on primary task performance. In practice, focusing on the here and now may mean focusing only on basic-group assumptions—on the group's and individual members' behaviors—or on manifest (in contrast to covert or unconscious) behavior. This approach may be justified under particular experimental conditions; for example, the study of group phenomena in nonstructured, nonpatient groups that do not function within an organized institution and do not extend over a long period. (The various "non's" indicate various systems that may rightly be disregarded because of the particular experimental conditions.) Unfortunately, one often finds the exclusive focus on the here and now in various groups that are linked through intragroup and intergroup processes to institutional conflicts at large or in psychotherapy groups extending over a long period and including patients with varying types of psychopathology and varying levels of ability to benefit from the group process.

The Unitary Nature of Breakdown

The illusion of the unitary nature of breakdown throughout hierarchies of systems may almost be considered a travesty of systems theory itself. In practice, the characteristics of dysfunction and structural alteration within a system are considered appropriate and sufficient to characterize dysfunction and structural breakdown at other levels of the same hierarchy or even within other, more distantly related hierarchies. The most frequent example of this occurrence is when psychopathology is attributed exclusively to conflicts within group processes. Thus, psychosis would be caused exclusively by distortions in the family, by social group pressures, or by the group pressures surrounding the individual in the hospital. The implication is that an exclusive focus on group conflicts, particularly on basic-assumption processes, will resolve psychosis. Psychopharmacological approaches would therefore seem unnecessary or even contraindicated; an analysis of psychopathology in terms of individual personality structure would be unwarranted; and appropriate change in our culture or the social system will do away with psychosis.

The painful nature of learning, including the awareness of limits of knowledge (as the student or observer or group leader moves from her respective target system to levels of systems which are progressively more distant from her original base and therefore add enormously to the number of tasks and constraints in simply clarifying boundary functions), gives rise to the temptation to find a single clarifying theory or unique instrument that will resolve all paradoxes and contradictions within a supposedly unitary system. The primitive emotional experience of total bliss related to the activation of an "all-good," fused self-object image constitutes one potential answer to all questions in groups. The search for an ecstatic group experience that can clarify with one stroke all the contradictions of society is illustrated by the various group movements that have sprung up throughout history; and, closer to home, in the cults in this country in recent years. Instant intimacy as the great releaser and cure of all social, cultural, and individual ailments, or "body harmony" or universal love demonstrate the inappropriate export of one subsystem of human experience and psychological structure to various social and cultural systems.

The Possibility of Resolving Contradictory Demands Through One Stable, Hierarchical Set of Priorities

The psychoanalytic community of a Latin American country was split on the question of whether disregard of social conflicts by analysands needed to be interpreted as an important sector of psychological denial. One group of analysts felt that an analysand's lack of involvement in social struggles was an expression of his psychopathology, fostered by a sick society that was opposed to necessary change. Another group felt that this focus represented the artificial introduction of social issues into the psychoanalytic situation, the impingement of the analyst's political convictions on his technique, and a loss of the technical position of neutrality; it was contradictory to basic psychoanalytic principles. Let us call the first group of analysts *political activists,* and the second group *technicians.* In terms of the actual political spectrum involved, the activists were on the Left, the technicians on the Right.

In another Latin American country, the government developed radical new social policies; these policies, in the opinion of one group of psychoanalysts, constituted a threat to individual rights and to the freedom that is indispensable to psychoanalytic treatment. The political activists in this case planned to suspend their patients' sessions in order to participate in a national strike against the government. The technicians criticized what they saw as a loss of technical neutrality by the political activists and criticized them for attempting to influence their patients in terms of a political ideology. Here the political activists were to the Right, the technicians to the Left. In both countries, social change was taking place; in my opinion, each example brings home the limitations of technical answers ("neutrality") found under conditions of rapidly shifting value systems in the society. Neutrality is protected by social stability and is less clear in its definition than appears to be the case under ordinary circumstances. It cannot be placed within an exclusively technical system and depends also upon a "nonconcentric" hierarchy of cultural values. At the same time, to abandon the technical concept of neutrality in terms of social or political ideology may be an easy way to avoid painful and irresoluble conflict—but only at the cost of uncontrolled and uncontrollable influences of the psychoanalyst's personality and value systems on the patient.

The implication is that there are multiple, irreducible systems that impinge on the perceptive functions of the group leader, on his observing ego; irresoluble conflicts exist that can be dealt with only at a particular time and in terms of the broadest possible awareness of the various systems, subsystems, and suprasystems involved. Thus, training in depth is essential for group leaders, at least in the areas of those levels of hierarchies of systems which are closest to their main task. A group psychotherapist should have knowledge of individual psychopathology, individual psychotherapy, group processes, and, if he performs group psychotherapy in the context of an institution, intergroup phenomena and administrative theory. A leader of sensitivity groups should have acquired, in addition to a solid knowledge of group dynamics and administrative theory, a sufficient knowledge about his own psychological functioning and psychopathology to enable him to determine the origin of his perceptions of group processes. The psychiatrist in charge of therapeutic community methods needs to combine solid clinical knowledge in the area of psychopathology, diagnosis, and treatment with sufficient knowledge of the professional expertise of other professionals with whom she works, as well as of group dynamics, her own psychological makeup, and administrative theory.

There are many excellent psychotherapists who are poor group leaders, regardless of whether they function in administrative roles or as group psychotherapists; there are group psychotherapists whose understanding of administrative theory, intergroup processes, and characteristics of functional leadership of task groups is so minimal that they can do little as consultants in these latter areas. There are good leaders of sensitivity groups who are poor psychotherapists and administrators. Group leaders will vary in their technical and personal skills and in their level of knowledge regarding the target system they work in, the boundary systems related to it, and their awareness of their own limitations. However, an optimal training situation for group leadership would offer sufficient experience in the boundary areas of their specialty for them to learn more about their capabilities and limitations.

Only a broad and deep level of potential knowledge that can be "switched on" at a particular moment along various dimensions can offer a meaningful answer to the questions a group leader must constantly ask himself: What is going on? What is the reason for my confusion in diagnosing what is going on? How do I formulate what is going on in terms of what I am here for? What, in my understanding at this moment, matters to the group and needs to be communicated to it, again in terms of my main function? What stands in the way of my achieving the understanding or ability to do my job at this point? In other words, a rapid and ongoing diagnosis of what the group leader's primary task is, what his secondary tasks are at every point, and what the major constraint is for the primary task are essential. Also, the nature of group resistances, of countertransference in the leader, and the built-in constraints from various sources (time, social situations, lack of authority of the leader, lack of knowledge, hidden agendas) need to be assessed.

It is easy to dismiss my plea for knowledge in depth along the dimensions mentioned if one considers the enormity of practical demands for group leadership, the limited nature of time for the training of psychotherapists, and the social demands on the mental health profession. However, if poor leadership interferes with the work of individuals, groups, and institutions, and if we are as yet at the beginning of the technical as well as the conceptual exploration of boundary areas within social systems, lack of training in multiple disciplines and areas for group leaders is, from a social viewpoint, highly damaging and self-defeating.

THE DANGERS OF AND PRECONDITIONS
FOR USING "ONE'S OWN SELF"

The crucial function of the group leader's self-exploration in determining which hierarchies of systems predominate in the perceptions impinging upon him, and what the conflicts between various levels of these hierarchies are, points to the need for maximum self-awareness by the group leader. Because of the increase of stress on the group leader at the time of decision making, specific personality defenses against stress may become activated and influence his decision-making process excessively, thus reducing his capabilities. What follows are some typical examples of this development.

Group leaders with strong narcissistic personality features (Kernberg, 1970) may obtain particular narcissistic gratifications from being the center of group processes, in which they nurse unconscious (or conscious) fantasies of having the godlike capacity to influence the lives of the group members. Narcissistic personalities are drawn to positions of group leadership and, for brief periods, may do well in such functions. Yet their lack of ability to discriminate in depth between various personality aspects and their lack of commitment in depth to value systems (which is characteristic of narcissistic personalities) combine to decrease their awareness of the impact of clashes of value systems and of the personality systems of group members and themselves. At the same time, leaders with narcissistic personalities may be strongly aware of primitive processes in themselves, and of the activation of these processes by group pressures, so that they may be sensitive to the development of basic-group assumptions, particularly as these assumptions determine the group's emotional attitude toward the group leader. Thus, narcissistic personalities may be quite effective in diagnosing basic-group assumptions, and, by enacting the unconscious expectations of the group, particularly regarding grandiosity and power, they may gratify the assumptions of dependency and messianic hope of the group, to the detriment of the group members' cognitive learning (including learning on the basis of endurance of uncertainty and conflicts). It may be that good leaders of short-term sensitivity groups or encounter groups who are poor psychotherapists or poor administrators generally have narcissistic personality structures.

A group leader with a strong predominance of obsessive traits may be poorly equipped for broad, flexible, rapid decision making because he is unable to "contain" the total emotional situation that impinges upon his observing ego. This may be the reason some excellent administrators or individual psychotherapists make poor group psychotherapists or group-dynamics leaders.

Some psychotherapists with severe character pathology who function on a borderline level may do well with certain severely regressed patients and also with handling complex group situations under particular structured conditions. They may be able to do so in spite of their obvious interpersonal difficulties under ordinary social circumstances, in executive leadership functions, and in psychotherapeutic treatment of relatively nonregressed patients. These group leaders draw on their awareness of primitive object relationships within themselves; they are attuned to primitive processes within the group; and if the total group structure provides control and containment (for example, within a limited group-dynamics situation or a well-structured therapeutic community setting), their ability to function may be greater than one might expect given their serious ego distortions.

Perhaps the worst types of group leaders are those who combine severe narcissistic features with an ego-syntonic depreciation of learning, emotional depth, and moral convictions; the combination of ignorance, superficiality, and opportunism derived from these disorders is a typical basis for the exploitation of the messianic hopes of others, the indulgence in personal grandiosity, and the endless search for instant intimacy in group experiences.

For a group leader to set his intervention priorities accurately and effectively he needs: (1) a clear understanding of the primary task and task constraints operating upon the group; (2) knowledge in depth of the various subsystems and suprasystems impinging on the target system of his "observing ego" (the higher level, internalized object relations actualized in his ego identity); and (3) tolerance of the nonconcentric (or irreducible) nature of the conflicts between the various social, technical, cultural, and value systems involved in his boundary functions.

The search for knowledge, for emotional depth, and for moral commitment does not make the task of the group leader easy; however, these are indispensable personality preconditions for an optimal priority setting of interventions in complex group situations. One final precondition is that the group leader be able to tolerate uncertainty and to be aware of contradictions for which there might be immediate action in terms of present priorities but no definite solution. To tolerate uncertainty, however, does not mean to justify a defensive ambiguity. Leadership roles must be defined clearly, and ambiguity has nothing to do with a technical, neutral position of the psychotherapist. Modern theory of leadership has questioned the traditional assumption that leaders are born, but while leadership can be learned, not every person has the capacity for this learning, nor does breakdown in leadership always reflect unresolvable conflicts on the boundary among systems impinging on the leader. Sometimes failure in leadership is simply personal failure, and acceptance of personal failure in leadership functions is one more constraint that the group leader, like all leaders, must accept.

Chapter 11 The Therapeutic Community: A Reevaluation

In my more than two decades of experience with therapeutic communities in hospital settings, I have been in a position to observe the therapeutic effectiveness and potentially damaging effects of various treatment methods. The therapeutic community has transformed the more traditional methods of hospital treatment, opened new roads to the inpatient and day-hospital treatment of severe character pathology, and shed new light on the optimal administrative requirements for psychiatric hospitals. Some of these insights were not only unforeseen, however, but unintended.

Whiteley and Gordon (1979), after pointing out that *therapeutic communities* is one of the most misused and misunderstood terms in modern psychiatry, offer their own definition. The therapeutic community, they say, "is a specific, specialized treatment process utilizing the psychological and sociological phenomena inherent in the large, circumscribed and residential group" (p. 105). In this respect, it is an intensified extension of milieu therapy (which was described by these authors in an earlier chapter), "which has more general implications and applications for patients of all categories in the mental hospital community" (p. 105). In the course of their excellent chapter reviewing the history and developments of therapeutic-community models, Whiteley and Gordon introduce an additional aspect to their concept of the therapeutic community, namely, that the community have an ideology. Both Main and Jones—key originators of therapeutic-community models—stressed their belief in the value of democratizing treatment processes, in aiming for a "therapeutic setting with a spontaneous and emotionally structured (rather than medically dictated) organization in which all staff and patients engage" (Main, 1946), or in flattening the hierarchical pyramid, blurring roles, and opening communication as expressions of a democratic therapeutic environment (Jones, 1953).

It is from this combined technical and ideological conception of the therapeutic community—as a treatment modality and as a democratization of the treatment process (versus a hierarchical and authoritarian social organization of the hospital)—that the therapeutic advantages, shortcomings, and problems of this approach emerge.

Therapeutic-community concepts may also be defined by contrasting them with the team approach to diagnosis and treatment that is prevalent in contemporary psychiatry. Whereas both rely on the participation and collaboration of various types of mental health professionals, the team approach distributes decision-making authority functionally among various disciplines according to the task. In the therapeutic community, in contrast, the opposition to hierarchical distribution of authority is an end in itself. In the therapeutic community the aim is to minimize the hierarchical levels that typically stem from professional expertise, academic degrees, and job titles and to maximize the democratic decision-making process. In addition, the psychotherapeutic advantage to the patient of being treated by and within the therapeutic community is felt to supersede that of the ordinary team approach.

Stanton and Schwartz (1954), in their classic study of the effects of breakdown in staff morale and of covert disagreements among staff on the pathological excitement of patients, particularly the activation of the "special case" syndrome, highlighted the impact of the hospital's social and administrative structure on the functioning of individual patients: social pathology reinforces individual psychopathology. Caudill (1958) illustrated how the isolation of patients from staff that is encouraged by the hierarchical hospital structure contributes to the crystallization of a culture of the patient group, a culture that has powerful effects on the treatment of individual patients as well as on the functioning of patients as a group. He describes how the induction of the patient role, the peer pressure among patients to socialize and to accept the doctors' value system—together with the patients' general opposition to authority (particularly that of nursing staff)—fosters a mutual ignorance between patients and staff, stereotyping, and alternations between permissiveness and restriction in the form of cultural ground swells, which strongly influence all the treatment carried out in the hospital. Belknap (1956) and Goffman (1968) stressed even more sharply the regressive and degrading effects of the traditional hierarchical system in large hospitals, where the deterioration of patients' self-respect and a general prison atmosphere were the result of arbitrary and authoritarian control exerted by the lowest echelons of the hierarchically organized staff.

Main (1957) provided a crucial counterpart to all these findings; his article was in particular a theoretical and clinical complement to Stanton and Schwartz's work. Main concluded that the "special case" may induce a pathological activation of conflicts among staff that reflect, in the interpersonal field, the activation and projection of the unconscious conflicts of the patient's internal world. This finding represents the single most important bridge between the understanding of the hospital as a social system and the understanding of the activation of pathology of internalized object relations of patients in that social system.

The concept of therapeutic-community treatment emerged as a direct challenge to the regressive and antitherapeutic effects of the traditional, hierarchical psychiatric hospital organized on a medical model. Although various authors described the essential aspects of the approach differently, the basic idea, as derived from Jones (1953) and Main (1946), emphasized the following features: (1) community treatment, in which staff and patients function jointly as an organized community to carry out patient treatment. Patients actively participate in and are co-responsible for their own treatment; (2) therapeutic culture, in which all activities and interactions relate to the goal of reeducating and socially rehabilitating patients. The optimal functioning of patients in the therapeutic community would be the first phase in promoting their optimal functioning in the external community; and (3) living-learning confrontation, in which an open flow of communication between patients and staff provides immediate feedback regarding observed behaviors and reactions to them. An exploration of the functions of these behaviors in the here and now, and of alternative, experimental behaviors would help the patients to cope in the therapeutic community and in the external community.

Therapeutic-community treatment depends on group meetings—of small groups, large groups, and task groups—to facilitate open communication, to generate pressure in the direction of socialization and rehabilitation, and to foster a democratic process of decision making.

In addition to small-, large-, and task-group meetings, three particular types of meetings are common to therapeutic-community models. First is the community meeting, which includes all patients and staff. Its aim is to examine the complete social environment in which staff and patients participate—the distortions of and interferences with the community's social life—with a free flow of communication in this meeting. The group also considers whether antidemocratic or authoritarian processes are developing and if so, how to change them. Second is patient government. Regardless of the specific form such government takes, therapeutic-community models tend to encourage patients to organize and to participate in the social and decision-making processes. Third is the staff meeting, which complements patient government. Here, democratic decision making among staff allows staff to study how they are influenced by administrative and other pressures, as well as by their interaction with patients. The staff meeting permits the democratic distribution of authority for tasks to be done, in contrast to hierarchical decisions from above.

PRECONDITIONS FOR THERAPEUTIC CHANGE

A number of assumptions regarding therapeutic change are included in therapeutic-community concepts. First, it is assumed that patients as individuals and as a group are able to help one another. Second, that patients functioning in a group setting may react in "normal," appropriate, and responsible ways; group reactions will contrast with those caused by individual patients' psychopathology in interactions outside the group setting. Third, by the same token, that staff as a group may function pathologically and antitherapeutically, despite the maturity and skills of individual staff members displayed in private encounters. In fact, in agreement with these assumptions, I think that the pathology and social effectiveness of groups does not coincide with the pathology and social effectiveness of their individual members; and clinical experience has confirmed these assumptions.

Fourth, it is assumed that authoritarianism is antitherapeutic and that decisions made on the basis of power rather than reason work against the best interests of the patients. This assumption is correct if one defines authoritarianism as taking responsibility for making decisions beyond what is functionally warranted. But I suggest that there exists a functional, in contrast to an excessive or inappropriate or nonfunctional, authority; the true opposition, therefore, should not be between authoritarian and democratic decision making but between authoritarian and functional decision making. With this qualification, I agree with the general assumption, abundantly documented in the literature, that authoritarian treatment systems can have a negative, sometimes devastating effect on the patients' welfare. An authoritarian hospital administration may transform treatment arrangements, distorting them so that they will confound the therapeutic team trying to apply them. Such distortions in treatment arrangements can promote a pseudoadaptation of the patient to the hospital system and militate against the development of his autonomy and growth. An authoritarian hospital structure, almost by definition, interferes with an open, ongoing evaluation of the hospital as a social system and practically eliminates the possibility of expanding hospital-milieu treatment by the therapeutic use of the hospital as a social system.

Fifth, in contrast to authoritarian treatment systems, therapeutic-community concepts imply that democratization of the treatment process is therapeutic per se. Democratization increases the patient's self-esteem, the effectiveness of his functioning, and the honesty of his communications; it is directly growth promoting. In light of my experience, I believe that this assumption can be challenged. Democratization of the decision-making processes in hospitals has often had complex and unforeseen results, both therapeutic and antitherapeutic.

Sixth, public, collective decision making is assumed to be therapeutic because it fosters democratic processes. Later, I shall examine the illusions implied in this assumption.

Seventh, it is assumed that patients can help one another as individuals and, in the process, develop interpersonal skills, creativity, and ego strength. On the basis of my experience, this is usually true; by the same token, however, patients can also have destructive effects upon one another. For every "David and Lisa" who help each other, we can find a psychopath who may potentially drive another patient to suicide.

The most important precondition for a therapeutic community is that it be functionally integrated with the administrative structure of the psychiatric or general hospital in which it operates. This might seem trivial were it not that, in practice, leaders of therapeutic communities are often naive about the implications of the administrative structures, boundaries, and constraints of their institution. Even the literature on the therapeutic community does not sufficiently consider the relation between the therapeutic community and the overall institutional organization.

Thus, for example, Edelson (1970) in *Sociotherapy and Psychotherapy*, although explicitly describing the administrative and professional implications of the relation between hospital administration and the director of sociotherapy, in fact presents models of organizational functioning in which no clear administrative structure links, say, the authority vested in the therapeutic community with that of the overall hospital administration. Although he acknowledges the potential for stress and conflicts in his model, his proposed solution is a consultative one, not organizational or administrative. I mention Edelson because he is one of the most sophisticated theoreticians in this field, a man who is not prone to replace a study of administrative constraints with a declaration of ideological convictions. If the therapeutic community is to openly explore the social system actualized by the patient-staff community, it must activate as well all stress and latent conflicts in the system, with consequent influences on the political dimension of the decision-making process in the institution. A purely observational, clarifying, and informative approach to conflicts in the social system, couched in technical and neutral interpretive terms, cannot be carried out without its in turn implying an active participation in the conflicts of hospital administration. The proof is the frequency with which one encounters the following scenario: An enthusiastic group develops a therapeutic-community model in a sector of the hospital; an "ideal society" is formed that generates gratification, excitement, hope, and perhaps a messianic spirit that infects both staff and patients. This is followed by bitter disappointment because of the lack of understanding and apparent rejection of this ideal society by the institution as a whole. A final stage of disappointment follows, in which the task is abandoned, the therapeutic community collapses, and the leaders either transfer into a different system to start the cycle all over again or into private practice.

In practice, a therapeutic community has a necessary size limitation: the combined patient-staff community should number somewhere between sixty and eighty participants at most. This means that therapeutic communities can be established only in small psychiatric hospitals or in relation to relatively small inpatient or, particularly, day-hospital services within a larger hospital. It is no coincidence that some of the more successful models have operated within small psychiatric hospitals, where the complexities of relating to larger administrative structures are less evident.

When the leader of the therapeutic community fully understands the organizational structure of the institution and the level and stability of the authority delegated to her—and, therefore, to the therapeutic system she is in charge of—the limits of the authority vested in the entire community as well as in its individual members can be considered when conflicts within the therapeutic system and across the boundaries of the therapeutic community are studied. An authentic boundary function of the leader of the therapeutic community requires clear administrative arrangements linking the community to its environment, and the community leader should be able to define them. In the last resort, ideological—in contrast to technical—convictions about democratic political organization often influence leaders of therapeutic communities and the staff members who share their convictions to operate as though they constituted a minority party in an authoritarian state. Unconsciously, they confuse exploration of the social system with the political means to change it. The therapeutic aim of the therapeutic community becomes conflated with the political aim of democratization of a health-care institution. Eventually, both staff and patients pay the price for this confusion between a technical-therapeutic setting and a political system that has no clearly defined tasks or differentiated boundaries.

The support of the administration for the therapeutic community needs to be worked out by the leaders of the therapeutic community with the hospital administration and constantly redefined and renegotiated. This implies an additional precondition for establishing a therapeutic community, namely, that the leader be able to carry out a political function in terms of boundary negotiations—that is, not in terms of democratic concepts but in terms of effective ways of influencing individuals and groups across task-determined boundaries in the institution. This precondition can be broadened into a definition of the basic skills required for leadership of the therapeutic community, such as a solid knowledge of small-group, large-group, and task-group functioning and management; of individual psychopathology and of the influence of individual psychopathology in distorting small-group processes in the environment; and of psychotherapeutic principles. These requirements hint at the problems inherent in training good leaders.

Still another precondition for the development of a therapeutic community is the clear definition of authority, of the roles and functions of each individual staff member as well as of formally organized, interlocking groups. The authority delegated to the therapeutic community must in turn be distributed within it in functional ways. The danger is that although group processes facilitate shared decision making, they may also blur the assignment of responsibility for carrying out decisions made in group settings, as well as obscure the nature of the system of inspection, control, and monitoring of community functions.

Another danger is that traditional roles and expertise that have been "imported" into the therapeutic community will be underutilized or that authority will be delegated to people without appropriate technical skills.

An egalitarian approach that neglects the differences in capacity, skills, and training of individuals may prevail, but it leads to inefficiency and waste of available human resources. The deskilling that occurs in small and large groups under the effect of regression into basic-assumptions–group functioning is made worse by the failure to use available skills that is caused by lack of administrative clarity within the therapeutic community. In this connection, as Rice (1969) pointed out, there is an advantage in maintaining a tension between task groups and task sentience, on the one hand, and professional sentience groups (represented by the loyalties within each particular group of mental health professionals that have consolidated into a team), on the other, as a protection against the regressive features that develop when task and sentience systems coincide.

THREATS, CHALLENGES, AND FAILURE

Therapeutic communities have often been perceived as a threat by the traditional administrative and professional leadership of psychiatric hospitals. Insofar as the authority vested in the medical profession is being challenged in the name of a doctrine of egalitarianism, the threat is real. In addition, a functional analysis of the relation between the expertise and skills required by various professions and the amount of authority distributed to medical and nonmedical personnel highlighted authoritarian distortions and, by implication, threatened traditional power structures. As well, the open examination of the functioning of the hospital as a social system could not but spotlight ever-present problems in the hospital's administrative structure and functioning. Such an examination perforce becomes a monitoring of the administrative process, with all the political implications and challenges therein. It may be argued, of course, that this is a healthy development for some petrified hospital systems, but the proponents of therapeutic communities should not be surprised by the active or subtle opposition they provoke.

The therapeutic community is also a threat to the traditional patient-doctor relationship and to the traditional relationships between interdisciplinary staff members. In terms of democratizing life in a psychiatric hospital, this is an advantage; but in terms of using therapeutic resources to their best advantage, it can have unforeseen, sometimes negative consequences. Relatively uneducated staff in the lower echelons of the hospital hierarchy may find themselves given more authority but at the same time receiving more direct scrutiny. Consequently, their relationships with their administrative and professional supervisors will become ambiguous. The contradictions between social inequality, inequality in salaries, and differences in work expectations dictated by the environment in which the hospital functions and the development of an egalitarian atmosphere in the therapeutic community sharpen the awareness of real social conflicts and contradictions that are beyond the therapeutic community's ability to resolve. Simmering resentment and unresolved guilt at various hierarchical levels may increase tensions among staff members and further complicate the analysis, let alone resolution, of tensions in the social system of the therapeutic community. All this increases the danger that professional efficiency will diminish in all areas.

Therapeutic communities can also become a real or perceived threat to the patients' treatment. Because of the number of individuals involved and the effort to maintain a relatively open flow of communication, patient meetings, staff meetings, and, particularly, the community meeting itself can easily acquire characteristics of large-group processes; the regressive effects of large-group processes can affect individual patients' development in antitherapeutic ways. Elsewhere (Kernberg, 1976, chap. 9; 1980, chap. 11) I pointed to the danger of regression of patients as a group to basic-assumptions–group functioning when functional, task-centered leadership is not available, when the tasks carried out by patients are not meaningful, when the delegation of authority from staff to patient is ambiguous, and when the patient group's own leadership is ineffective. Under these circumstances, patient groups may become intolerant of individuals, establishing a dictatorship of the group that acquires characteristics of a primitive morality, and allow personalities with narcissistic and antisocial features to assume leadership positions. Staff may contribute to this regression by an ideologically determined denial of differences among individual patients, an implicit expectation that all patients have the same needs and should be expected to react or participate in similar ways. Patient and staff groups may enter into an unconscious collusion that interferes with the autonomous development of individual patients and fosters an uncontrolled invasion of privacy that corresponds to the total group's acting out of aggression against individual members.

In addition, groups may develop an exaggerated need for formality and ritual as a defense against violence (which large groups, in particular, tend to generate), a defense that may be functional for the group but restrictive with regard to individual patient needs. The control of unstructured group processes by the most regressed patients—the chronic monopolizers, the manipulators, or the most violent—may significantly distort first the content of meetings and later, the allocation of resources, thus reducing many patients' treatment time.

Unacknowledged and dissociated sadistic tendencies in individuals may infiltrate the group process in the form of accentuation of bureaucratic rigidity, which serves to control violence while expressing it in subtle ways; this excessive formalization of group processes, combined with rigid conventionality (particularly regarding sexual issues), may throw the therapeutic community back to restrictive group processes of latency and early adolescence. Under the conditions of Bion's (1961) basic-assumptions–group developments, all the negative effects of group processes increase. The very concepts of egalitarianism, democracy, and trust in the beneficial effects of open communication may feed into the messianic expectations inherent in the dependent or pairing basic-assumptions group's development, thus creating an unrealistic hospital environment that hampers the functional reentry of patients into the external world. Under regression into fight-flight conditions, the exacerbation of social struggles that derive from intrastaff tensions may naturally blend with patients' search for ad hoc "parties" and militant ideologies that rationalize violence.

As mentioned before, some of the literature and clinical approaches to the therapeutic community clearly favor democratic decision making. The assumption seems to be that the ultimate authority for decision making should reside within the temporary community constituted by patients and staff. This assumption fails to consider the difference between political processes and administrative structures. It confuses decision making in an open community without fixed institutional boundaries by political elections and negotiations among political parties with the functional requirements of therapeutic institutions with a limited number of boundaries, tasks, and constraints that determine their survival. To put it simply, what is needed for optimal functioning of a psychiatric institution is a functional administration, not a democratic one. In fact, the replacement of a functional by a democratic organization may lead to distortions of the relation between authority, responsibility, and accountability, thus to the re-creation of an authoritarian structure as opposed to a functional one.

Another theoretical problem with therapeutic-community concepts is their implication that society at large contains no intrinsic contradictions. Proponents of therapeutic communities are often unaware that building up an "ideal society" within a hospital can easily merge with patients' needs to deny their own conflicts—both intrapsychic and interpersonal—as well as the real contradictions in the external world. Hence the patients adapt to hospital life but fail to prepare for reentry into the external environment. At a different level, there may be a subtle assumption that everyone is essentially good, and that open communication permits the elimination of those distortions in perceptions of self and others that are the ultimate cause of pathological conflict and pathological psychic structure. This philosophical concept denies the existence of unconscious intrapsychic sources of aggression, a striking contradiction of what staff and even patients themselves can observe in patients in a psychiatric hospital.

To assume that patients are victims of irrational social forces and are, in fact, expressing these forces and that a rational society (one without intrinsic contradictions) will permit a full restoration to health is appealing but naive. It is probably not a coincidence that the idea of the therapeutic community had particular appeal for the counterculture of the 1960s and 1970s. In the late 1990s the utopian quality of the ideas and assumptions of many of the models is more transparent.

Failure to differentiate social from intrapsychic factors influencing psychopathology may lead to a faulty application of systems theory to the psychotherapeutic situation. The assumption that patients' psychopathology directly reflects contradictions in the environment can result in the therapist's locating the etiology exclusively in the social system. Here Main's approach and Bion's description of group processes diverge sharply from Jones and his focus on social psychopathology in community psychiatry applications of the therapeutic community that were fashionable in the United States in the 1970s.

Because it is easy for group methods to proliferate in a psychotherapeutic community, eventually the same issues and problems can be discussed from different perspectives at different places without regard to the economy of human resources involved. There is, further, the ubiquitous possibility that splitting mechanisms will be activated by the simultaneous discussion of the same issues in different settings. In theory, all information flows together in the community, staff, and patient meetings; in practice, however, crowded agendas and increasing diffusion of information militate against integration of information. In the long run, the loss of privacy may be a lesser evil than the waste of time and human resources that occurs when treatment modalities and techniques are not differentiated from one another.

Edelson (1970) attempted to solve the problem of the relation between sociotherapy and psychotherapy by keeping them completely separate. That solution artificially isolates the patient's dynamics as manifested in his psychotherapy from observations of those dynamics in the therapeutic community; it impoverishes both psychotherapy and social modalities of treatment.

To neglect the relation between therapeutic-community concepts and the theory of administration has important clinical consequences for the functioning of the therapeutic community. If the leader of the therapeutic community lacks administrative skills, the system might break down. In practice, the leader's lack of administrative skill can be seen in his failure to monitor therapeutic functions, to distribute resources adequately, and particularly to establish priorities at various meetings. The consequences of the leader's administrative inadequacies will be reflected in a lowering of staff morale. The staff will feel overworked, overwhelmed with responsibility, drowning in a flood of information. The gatekeeping function of group leaders deteriorates when no clear set of priorities has been established for the administrative aspects of the therapeutic community. This internal chaos may be the counterpart of the breakdown of communication between the therapeutic community and hospital administration at large that is a consequence of the neglect of the administration's knowledge of the therapeutic community in the negotiation of the community's external boundaries.

The time element is of crucial importance in determining the success or failure of the therapeutic community. In units for acutely regressed patients, with rapid turnover owing to general shortness of stay, and acute medical problems requiring urgent attention, therapeutic-community approaches seem to work least well. In contrast, for patients with chronic characterological difficulties who are in inpatient units that have slow turnover or in day hospitals that offer extended lengths of stay, therapeutic communities are at their most useful. In this, I agree with Jones, who originally stressed that therapeutic-community approaches were indicated for patients in these circumstances.

In addition, again related to the dimension of time, the short-term (one to six months) effects of therapeutic communities may be strikingly different from the long-term effects; the advantages of therapeutic communities appear strongest over a shorter period, and the problems manifest themselves only in the long run. In the short term, the activation of patients' potential for helping one another, the highlighting of internal contradictions of the social-treatment system that often can be resolved as part of this diagnosis, and the exciting and exhilarating effects of group processes strengthen the bonds between patients, among staff, and between patients and staff, and increase the potentially therapeutic knowledge that can be gained quickly about patients. In the long-term (six months to one or two years), however, the following phenomena make their appearance.

The agendas of community meetings and all decision-making groups tend to become overloaded. Efforts to stimulate patients and staff to participate freely typically result in group resistance and the emergence of basic-assumptions groups, in the development of passivity among patients and staff alike, in long silences and wasted time, or in the eruption of such an abundance of primitive material that determining community priorities takes up inordinate time. Efforts to solve these problems by making the meetings more formal can lead to bureaucratization, which slows down the decision-making process—and once more the agenda becomes overloaded. Gradually, the need for administrative decision making, and the negotiations between the therapeutic community and the external environment that give rise to reality pressures, foster a new, informal network of decision making. Paradoxically, this ad hoc administrative structure may work very well, but it may also be perceived as running counter to the idea of shared decision making; it will thus require further analysis and lengthy negotiations of otherwise obvious community needs.

Patients with strong manipulative and violent potential, who are impelled to test the limits of their power and control, present another problem. What are the responsibilities of staff to protect these patients as well as the rest of the community from violence? For example, the power struggles that usually evolve around patients with anorexia nervosa or patients who use suicide attempts to control their environment create agonizing conflicts for the nursing staff and sharpen the contradictions between efforts to protect the idea of permissiveness and the need to control life-threatening acting out. What for individual cases may seem to be functional decision making—in the sense of a gradual, painful process of rational analysis, explanation, outlining, and implementation of a treatment plan—may combine with similar processes involving other patients to create impossible time constraints.

All these features can wear out the staff; because the exhaustion is at first masked by the messianic spirit, excitement, and high morale that therapeutic communities engender in the short run, the dangerous overstretching of staff can be obscured for some time. Eventually, however, staff exhaustion, particularly that of the nursing staff, can lead to requests for increased staffing, a need for the senior medical staff to spend more time with nursing staff, the development of passivity among staff—who continue to attend meetings but with increasing passivity—and the ascendance to leading positions in the therapeutic community of both staff and patients with narcissistic personality features.

The lack of commitment to any strong conviction that charcterizes narcissistic personalities, their lack, therefore, of perception of intrapsychic stress and the conflicts it causes, and the ease with which they superficially adapt to group processes—particularly when they are the center of attention—gears them to a leadership style that promotes pseudointimacy and tends to erode deep feelings, as well as undermining quality control on the service (Kernberg, 1980b, chap. 11).

One other manifestation of staff exhaustion and regression is an increase in staff members' self-absorption. Over a period of time, the proportion of time directly spent with patients gradually decreases, while the number of group meetings involving staff increases. At the same time, the leaders frequently "burn out": after three to five years, service chiefs who are interested in and committed to therapeutic communities tend to abandon their positions out of exhaustion.

A question that usually tends to be avoided is the cost-benefit ratio of the therapeutic community in comparison with that of traditional psychiatric hospital treatment. The simultaneous development of alternative models in autonomous services permits some typical findings. Earlier findings indicated that when insufficient staff is available to treat patients—such as in severely neglected large state institutions—group methods can lead to an increase in patient-staff contacts and the humanization of hierarchically rigidified channels of communication between patients and staff. But the need for individualized patient treatment is not met by such an organizational shift, and a process of "natural selection" takes place whereby some patients with severe character pathology can be helped while others withdraw even farther from therapeutic involvement.

By contrast, in a modern psychiatric hospital with adequate patient-staff ratios, multidisciplinary approaches, and ample senior psychiatric staff, therapeutic communities can lead to more intense, individual patient treatments and can enrich the unit's understanding of the patients and thus their treatments and the techniques geared toward helping them. This positive effect, however, tends to be neutralized in the long run, as group meetings occupy the time of the most experienced members of the staff, reducing their availability for individual patient contact; in addition, the least skilled staff members are rather passive in group meetings; they neither participate nor—necessarily— learn much, while their skills in relating to individual patients are underutilized. In short, human resources are being distributed irrationally and uneconomically.

This phenomenon is made worse by the therapeutic community's neglect of and withdrawal from the external institutional environment of the hospital unit, a development that is commonly encountered. Work in the therapeutic community generates an emotionally intense yet protected atmosphere, so that the staff wishes to remain with its patients, rather than encourage an open flow of other staff and trainees through the unit for short periods to learn about and eventually export knowledge of the new treatment modality. Therapeutic communities are sometimes the least tolerant of short-term students and trainees.

Another factor in the unequal distribution of resources is the fact that some of the most violent and manipulative patients manage to consistently draw attention to themselves in dramatic ways and receive more than their share of treatment resources. Indeed, this is one of the most persistent features of therapeutic community functioning. In theory, all patients are presented with the same model of social treatment; in practice, inappropriate behavior may be rewarded by increased attention, while other patients fade into the background. And, because of the chronic overloading of agendas, no compensating mechanisms are available to benefit the neglected patients.

Individual staff members may not take responsibility for what happens to patients between group meetings, a danger that is maximized when so many decisions regarding individual patients are arrived at in such meetings. Neglect of individual patients also stems from a neglect of the analysis of the external circumstances surrounding a patient's treatment. The patient's family is often perceived as an intrusive outside force, and communications with family members may decrease as the staff becomes totally engaged in the internal world of the therapeutic community. Thus, the patient's reentry into society may be more difficult.

Quality control tends to suffer when staff members are so intimately involved with one another that the senior staff finds it awkward to make decisions about promotions, firings, and the like. By the same token, it becomes difficult to judge whether sufficient learning is occurring. One would expect relatively junior or inexperienced staff members to eventually be able to take over the therapeutic community functions, thus permitting senior staff members to dedicate their time to individual work with patients or to research and educational activities. But this rarely happens.

In the initial enthusiasm and excitement caused by staff and patients working together, personality conflicts among staff members tend to be submerged in their striving for common goals. In the long run, however, such issues reassert themselves. Often, however, they cannot be included in the analysis of staff conflicts because the theory behind the therapeutic community and its democratic decision making has no room for unsolvable personality clashes; for the sake of peace, distortions in the administrative process may evolve. Paradoxically, personality issues now may become more important than they would be in the hierarchical style of hospital administration, where strict rules, regulations, and bureaucratic expectations tend to decrease the direct impact of individual personalities.

I earlier mentioned the stress between the leadership of the therapeutic community and the hospital administration that derives from the failure to integrate therapeutic-community and administrative theories. In practice, the therapeutic-community staff uses these conflicts to create a fantasy structure, in which the community is a protected, ideal island within the institution, an island where staff and patients help one another, where staff members protect one another from acknowledgement of shortcomings, mistakes, and outside criticism. This idealization leads to the transformation of community boundaries into barriers (pers. comm., Robert Michels, 1980). By projection, the institution's critical concern for the effectiveness of the functioning of the therapeutic community reemerges as a sense of attack from outside forces—enemies who, in reality, have to carry out analyses of cost-effectiveness, staff performance, and staff morale. In terms of the social resources provided for treatment purposes, the therapeutic community may now appear to be geared more toward fulfilling the needs of the staff than those of the patients. If the shortcomings of the therapeutic community are first diagnosed from the outside rather than from within, the criticism will perpetuate the community's myth of being an ideal world crushed by an envious, materialistic, and autocratic organizational environment.

BLUEPRINT FOR THE FUTURE

How can we preserve the eminent advantages of the therapeutic community—its therapeutic use of the hospital or day hospital as a social system; the activation of patients' potential for contributing to their own treatment; the development of skills and responsibilities of staff at lower echelons; the increasing knowledge about the interaction between the internal world of patients and the structured conflicts in the environment; the corrective emotional experiences provided by the therapeutic community; and the increase in staff morale—without falling prey to the serious, sometimes devastating, disadvantages of this powerful therapeutic tool?

Above all, the indications for the therapeutic community settings need to be sharpened. Severe character pathologies, borderline personality organization, patients with severe, chronic regressive features who, while not psychotic, would not be able to sustain a psychotherapeutic process on an outpatient basis are all ideal subjects for therapeutic-community treatment. There is an enormous advantage in having specialized services that are treating such patients adopt therapeutic-community models. The usefulness of such models for chronically regressed schizophrenic patients is more questionable; they would certainly require careful experimental comparison with more standard combinations of psycho-phenomenological, rehabilitative, and psychotherapeutic-management treatment of schizophrenia. But the therapeutic community is not currently well suited for acute psychotic illness requiring hospitalization.

The organization and implementation of a therapeutic community must include a clear administrative structure, a clear link to the administrative structure of the psychiatric institution in which it functions, and a clear definition of tasks, authority, responsibility, and accountability of all involved. Staff members should be chosen for their specific expertise and professional background, periodically evaluated regarding their performance and learning, and restricted to their appropriate roles.

All staff members have a common, nonspecific human function in interacting with patients, namely, that of using their personalities to resonate with patients' personalities, of understanding their own emotional reactions to patients, and of using that understanding to diagnose both the total pattern of the patients' internal world and the activation of their intrapsychic conflicts in the interpersonal field. This nonspecific function, however, must be complemented by a differentiated, specific function that varies from discipline to discipline and corresponds to the professional skills required for the total treatment of the patients. At a different level, the team spirit (task sentience) should never completely override the loyalty within the various professions: it is important to protect the separateness and interaction of task sentience and professional sentience.

One implication of the proposals I have offered is that the hierarchical structure of lines of authority must be preserved for the sake of functional decision making, allocation of responsibilities, accountability, and the evaluation of staff performance, program effectiveness, and alternative treatment modalities and administrative arrangements. Staff members should be expected either to learn and become more independent in their functioning or else to accept demotion to relatively nonskilled functions that leave them less involved in complex discussions about patients and the community's dynamics.

Working relations between staff members should show a respect for boundaries of privacy, in contrast to the exciting, erotized, and exhausting stripping that may become part of the intimacy and staff self-evaluation in the therapeutic community. By the same token, hierarchical leaders must encourage internal critical staff evaluation instead of automatically defending "inside" staff against "outside" criticism. The contradiction between shared decision making, on the one hand, and the preservation of hierarchical lines of authority, on the other, reflects the healthy preservation of a real dynamic tension in the world at large, in addition to a concern for essential administrative requirements.

For practical purposes, it is extremely helpful to differentiate what Rice (1963) described as executive conferences from executive meetings. Executive conferences include anyone who is providing information that is fundamental to decision making in addition to the decision makers themselves; executive meetings are composed only of the decision makers. This clarification can be crucial in preventing regressive processes, particularly in community meetings and in other large-group meetings. If everyone knows whether the final decision will be taken at that meeting or whether it will be deferred, unnecessary expectations and disappointments can be prevented, and rational choices concerning the appropriate authority to make a particular decision can be assured. This eliminates embarrassing deterioration of therapeutic-community settings, such as when a group of patients participates in a "vote" on whether a potentially suicidal patient should be given a weekend pass.

By implication, democratic—in contrast to functional—decision making has a very small place within optimal therapeutic communities.

Regarding the actual functioning of group processes, it is imperative that clear priorities are set for the subjects to be discussed and that the lowest priority issues are dropped once allocated time limits have been reached. One reason for delegating certain decision-making authority to individual staff members— rather than subjecting the issue to a broader discussion—is the low priority of the issues involved. By the same token, strict limits should be set to time allocated for all activities, and this means mercilessly reducing the number of all group meetings, including community meetings, to the minimum necessary to carry out high-priority functions. Charting all the meetings in which patients spend their time may spotlight unnecessary overlap of treatment methods.

Speaking more generally, I would like to see a systematic review of the individual developments of all patients and an evaluation of the extent to which patients are obtaining a fair share of total treatment time. One reason for restricting patients is to free staff time for other activities that are essential for patients in general; there must be a clear consciousness throughout the therapeutic community that staff time is its most valuable commodity and needs to be carefully rationed. To illustrate the opposite trend: staff members are often only too happy to talk individually with patients who feel an urgent need to communicate to a particular staff member. Such intense individual contacts lend themselves to splitting processes and to a distortion of use of staff time. They should be included in the overall evaluation of time dedicated to individual patients.

Each patient requires, at all times, one staff member with final authority, responsibility, and accountability for his or her treatment development. The authority and responsibility may be flexibly delegated to other individuals and even to groups, but the accountability cannot be delegated. This necessarily restricts the scope of community decision making regarding each individual patient. In general, decisions arrived at by staff and patients in group meetings regarding individual patients should be an exception to the usual practice.

One of the greatest potential strengths of the therapeutic community is that it allows the analysis of functional task requirements for the best patient treatment, so that tasks can be redistributed functionally. This functional decision making should and can be carried out within the context of an administrative analysis of what patients' total needs are, what the total available resources are, and how to use them optimally. For example, an activity therapist may be more interested in doing group therapy (under the heading of resocialization or living-learning experiences) than in teaching specific skills to patients; or a psychiatric social worker may be more interested in intensive family therapy than in participation in the patient's rehabilitative efforts with various community support systems. All staff members should be encouraged to shift to functions needed by patients rather than functions reflecting their own preferences.

Finally, there is a great advantage in having alternative, competing therapeutic systems sponsored by the same institution. In contrast to a monolithic doctrine that promotes a basically similar treatment model throughout a hospital, there should be highly specialized, relatively autonomous units that can experiment with different treatment philosophies and arrangements, thus facilitating the study of therapeutic and cost effectiveness, and the creative development of new treatment models. This implies building a research function into therapeutic-community models. It should include both consideration of therapeutic-effectiveness and cost-effectiveness studies. A study of pure cost effectiveness often neglects optimal treatment methods that require time and extreme specialization of care; a neglect of the financial and administrative constraints of treatment methods often leads to a concept of treatment that loses its relation to social reality.

Part Four **Applications to Psychoanalytic Education**

Chapter 12 Institutional Problems of Psychoanalytic Education

Psychoanalytic education is suffering from serious disturbances, which, by analogy, can be examined as an illness affecting the educational structures of psychoanalytic institutes and societies. After describing the symptoms of this illness, I shall explore its causes and suggest a possible course of treatment. My objective is not to present ideal solutions but to provide a theoretical frame that might facilitate such solutions.

THE SYMPTOMS

Psychoanalytic education today is all too often conducted in an atmosphere of indoctrination rather than open scientific exploration. Candidates, graduates, and even faculty tend to study and quote only their teachers, often ignoring alternative psychoanalytic approaches. The amount of time and energy given to Freud, in contrast to the brief and superficial review accorded other theorists—including contemporary psychoanalytic contributions (other than those of dominant local authorities)—and the rigid presentation and uncritical discussion of

Freud's work and theories in the light of contemporary knowledge give the educational process a sense of flatness.

Candidates are systematically prevented from learning the details of their faculty's analytic work. They are usually even sheltered from sharp disagreements within their own institute, so that, at best, they may learn about these at society meetings rather than as part of their formal educational program. In case seminars and personal supervision, candidates learn only about cases treated by themselves and other candidates; the psychoanalytic techniques used in these cases will likely reflect the inexperience of the person providing the treatment. The more senior the analyst, the less he shares his analytic experience with students. Illustrating the teaching of technique with selected vignettes is not the same as fully presenting ongoing clinical material to students. The only experience candidates get in the best way to perform psychoanalysis comes from their own personal psychoanalysis and from their reading. If it is true that candidates' own analysis is highly contaminated by their transference and that the literature case material is highly distorted by a variety of factors and thus of questionable value as a model of psychoanalytic technique, the failure to offer experience in optimal techniques is the most astonishing and rarely discussed aspect of psychoanalytic education.

A candidate who is authentically dependent on his training analyst may identify with his analyst's analyzing attitude. But even under optimal conditions, the candidate will not learn general technique. That the candidate may learn and identify himself with his analyst's style is a far cry from his learning about his analyst's theory of technique. And unless this method of learning is enriched by exposure to optimal psychoanalytic technique, it may end up as a ritualized and cliché-ridden mode of approaching patients. Candidates with narcissistic pathology, who are attuned to all their training analyst's interventions and thought processes as these reveal themselves in his eventually predictable behavior, miss the opportunity to learn about psychoanalysis from their own unconscious.

It hardly needs to be stressed that all published clinical data reflect a carefully selected segment of any psychoanalysis, typically of those aspects in which the psychoanalyst was either successful or, if unsuccessful, managed to learn from and overcome that momentary failure. This selectiveness conveys an idealized and unrealistic conception of the true nature of psychoanalytic work.

The reluctance of senior analysts to share their clinical experience and technique (as reflected in extended, detailed case presentations) with their junior colleagues is carried to extremes with candidates. There may be good reasons why a candidate's own training analyst should not share other clinical experiences with her, but I can see no good educational reason for the general practice of training analysts not sharing their ongoing clinical experience with candidates as a group or with individual candidates in the supervisory relationship.

Preventing candidates from learning about the difficulties and uncertainties of psychoanalytic practice and technique leads, under the best of circumstances, to a subsidiary symptom: the candidate's unrealistic idealization of psychoanalytic technique and of the senior members of the faculty. It can happen that senior members of the faculty who never discuss a case, present a paper, or publicly share their work are even more highly idealized.

The ultimate authority of most institutes is vested in the training analyst; the authority of the faculty suffers by comparison. This apportioning of authority results in a fragmentation of the supervisory and monitoring process throughout a candidate's training. Particularly in large institutes, it is as though each seminar leader and each supervisor were operating in a vacuum. Opportunities for communication among faculty members regarding the candidate's functioning are minimal. Individual faculty members feel that they have little influence on the overall evaluation and progress of the candidate. Although such fragmentation of the faculty may protect some candidates against arbitrary persecution from a single senior faculty member with inordinate influence, a public faculty discussion of discrepant views about a particular candidate offers greater protection against arbitrary evaluations. In large institutes, the information from seminar leaders and supervisors tends to be transmitted to a committee rather than to the entire faculty, further fragmenting and depersonalizing the supervisory monitoring functions of the candidate's educational progress. In small institutes, where the people who train also teach and supervise, a cautious attitude tends to prevail, focusing on the training analyst of a particular candidate, as though any criticism of the candidate might reflect on the training analyst, or any negative evaluation of the candidate might be considered an attack on her training analyst.

In fact, the assumption that the candidate reflects the power or influence of her training analyst is so pervasive that Greenacre (1959) describes it as having created a convoy system, in which training analysts safely monitor the voyage of their analysands through the perilous seas of the training years. These training analysts reflect the loss of the analytic attitude and the institutional corruption of the analytic process.

Linked with this phenomenon is the implicit assumption that the "real" psychoanalytic education is the training analysis, that supervision is secondary and courses only tertiary aspects of training. The often implicit additional assumption, that monitoring a candidate's learning and capability in the light of anything but his own training analysis is of doubtful value, contributes to the self-demeaning consequences of the supervisory and instructional faculty's lack of sufficiently shared knowledge and authority. Insofar as seminar leaders who are not training analysts also contribute to the underestimation of their own didactic functions, the junior faculty implicitly contributes to this self-devaluation.

The traditional assumption that training analysts should report on the candidate's progress, a highly questionable, longstanding custom, has now been recognized as a major cause of distortion of the psychoanalytic process in the training analysis itself, and as the origin of the still-existing practice of the candidate's having a "first analysis" for the institute, and a "second analysis," after graduation, for themselves. In a review of the literature, Lifschutz (1976) convincingly argued for the nonreporting training-analyst position. The general shift in the policies of psychoanalytic institutes toward restricting or eliminating reporting by training analysts is an encouraging development.

Behind the tradition of reporting training analysts is the assumption that supervision, seminars, group discussion, and faculty evaluation are less important than the training analyst's presumed knowledge about the value and capacities of her analysands. The faculty's self-protective withdrawal from candidates who are perceived as particularly privileged or untouchable and "compassionate graduation" of inadequately performing candidates who have remained in training for many years are other typical symptoms of the failure to invest adequate authority in the faculty.

A lack of accountability of the faculty for candidate evaluations is the counterpart of its lack of sufficient functional authority. Under the influence of changes in the educational systems in universities and medical schools, candidates as a group now tend to have more authority and specific channels for redress of grievances, but psychoanalytic institutes—as reported by the national organization of candidates (Franzen, 1982)—are characteristically vague and imprecise in describing the requirements for candidate acceptance, progression, graduation, and channels of communication and grievance redress.

This situation is complicated by a specific characteristic of psychoanalytic education that is usually ignored. I am referring to the paranoid atmosphere that often pervades psychoanalytic institutes and its devastating effect on the quality of life in psychoanalytic education. Members of some South American psychoanalytic institutes speak of the phenomenon of the "unhooked telephone": the fact that candidates' criticism of faculty, which largely consists of training analysts, is inhibited because the candidates are in personal analysis with those same training analysts. Thus candidates as well as graduates and faculty have to be extremely careful about what they say about training analysts in the presence of students and colleagues who may still (or again) be in analysis with these analysts. Training analysts, of course, are in the unhappy position of having to hear through their candidates (particularly at times of strongly negative or split-off negative transference) what their colleagues and students are saying about them. The assumption that the training analyst's narcissism is healthy enough to keep him or her from taking offense is, as we well know, an illusion.

Several phenomena play off one against the other and strengthen the paranoid atmosphere that pervades many psychoanalytic institutes. Candidates' displacement, splitting, and acting out of the negative transference may be expressed in underground criticism of the senior faculty, particularly when the institute does not provide ordinary channels for students and faculty jointly to evaluate the educational process. The narcissistic lesions absorbed by senior training analysts through the phenomenon of "unhooked telephones" may increase their countertransference reactions to their own candidates and the displacement of these reactions onto other training analysts and candidates, thereby increasing their paranoid reactions toward the institution.

The training analysts' acting out of countertransference reactions frequently takes the form of confidential communications about candidates to other training analysts, often expressed in subtle gestures or pregnant silences. Dulchin and Segal (1982a, 1982b) have pointed to the breakdown of confidentiality about candidates' analyses in one psychoanalytic institute, and it is reasonable to assume that this is a widespread phenomenon, particularly in institutes that still have reporting policies. Although reporting is officially disappearing from psychoanalytic institutes, it tends to linger in this informal way.

A consequence of these developments is that senior faculty members develop the attitude of being an in-group, sharers of secrets, in contrast to the out-group of junior faculty, who are not training analysts, and to the candidates. As Roger Dorey (pers. comm., 1983) has pointed out, this actualizes the fantasy of the secretive oedipal couple and the excluded children that is prevalent in psychoanalytic institutes. The paranoiagenic (Jaques, 1976) atmosphere of psychoanalytic institutes, the threat of persecution that permeates them, is the counterpart of the institutionally sanctioned and fostered idealization (particularly of senior training analysts) that also pervades them.

The apparent or real arbitrariness in junior faculty and training analyst appointments is another easily recognized problem in psychoanalytic education. It is an open secret that appointments of training analysts often are politically motivated, that the qualifications of the analyst may be less important than his or her reliability in matters of local politics. This corrupting aspect of psychoanalytic education is often apologetically rationalized as the unavoidable repetition of "family life" (with, for example, intergenerational conflicts, sibling rivalry, and primal scene material) in psychoanalytic institutes. But the failure to make a distinction between an educational institution and a family reflects a failure to develop and preserve an organizational structure that is oriented to the tasks to be performed. Such a failure directly causes paranoiagenic deterioration of the institution's social life and functions.

My point—arbitrariness in the appointment of faculty—could be misunderstood as a rejection of the necessarily subjective criteria, the personal judgments that must enter the decision of whom to appoint as a training analyst. That is not what I mean.

What I question is the lack of explicit, public policies and criteria for the selection of training analysts and the lack of explicit, public information regarding the locus of and the accountability for the decision making. The formal locus and the real locus of decision making are often very different. The policy of "gently tapping" selected graduates, rather than explicitly encouraging candidates for training analyst appointments to demonstrate their interest in the job, illustrates the social hypocrisy surrounding such appointments, a hypocrisy that poisons the atmosphere of psychoanalytic institutes.

The lack of explicit criteria for appointments of faculty in general, and the lack of explicit policies and criteria to control the quality of faculty functioning and particularly of training analysts' functioning, reflects the political nature of these appointments. In addition, avoiding giving explicit criteria for when faculty, particularly training analysts, should retire, and the proverbial conspiracy in institutes to protect incompetent training analysts are equally well-known problems. Here the lack of discussion of the actual clinical work of senior training analysts has one more negative consequence.

A final symptom of the illness of psychoanalytic institutes is the diminished creative thinking and scientific productivity of their faculty, students, and graduates. A narrow intellectual frame, determined by the locally prevalent views within the broad theoretical spectrum of psychoanalysis, intellectual toadyism or kowtowing to venerable fathers of the local group, petty "cross sterilization," and discouragement of original thinking are painful indicators that all is not well with psychoanalytic education.

Cross-sterilization is manifest in the suspicious and envious way new ideas are received, in the faculty's fearfulness in expressing new ideas that might challenge local dogma, and in the general collusion in publicly applauding rehashed formulations while privately deprecating the monotonous repetition of concepts that, by the same token, also reassure the faculty that nothing new threatens its present convictions. The net effect is that scientific work and original thinking decline. One could ask whether the general scientific domain of psychoanalysis actually has anything new to say. But the exciting developments at the boundaries of psychoanalytic theories and technique belie such a narrow and pessimistic view.

IMMEDIATE CAUSES: PRIMARY-TASK AND ORGANIZATIONAL STRUCTURE

So much for the symptoms. Now to determine their causes. I have chosen to approach the problem by first examining the organizational structure of psychoanalytic institutes and then examining their primary tasks (or aims); for if there is a discrepancy between the primary tasks of an organization and its structure, problems must follow. In what follows, I explore the relation between primary tasks and the administrative structure of psychoanalytic institutes.

What are the primary tasks of a psychoanalytic institute? And how would different concepts of such tasks relate to a corresponding, functional administrative structure? I propose four models of education, each of which corresponds to explicit aims that have been formulated as desirable primary tasks for psychoanalytic institutes. Each of these models demands a specific organizational structure that corresponds to its specific aims. The models are an art academy, a technical trade school, a theological seminary or religious retreat, and a college at a university. I shall examine the theoretical implications of these models, the corresponding organizational structures that are functionally linked to them, and the actual structure of psychoanalytic education in light of these models.

In the first model, the art academy, the primary task of psychoanalytic education is to train expert craftsmen and artists. This model assumes that psychoanalysis is more than a technique, it is an art; and specialized training in craftsmanship will enable the apprentices to express their creativity. This model fits with the highly individualized nature of psychoanalytic training, with the tutorship and mentorship aspects of psychoanalytic education and criteria for progression, and with the assumption (characteristic of many institutes) that one ideal technique exists that needs to be mastered as a basis for subsequent creativity within that art. Discussion of various theories would be circumscribed by the need to establish their relation to the ideal technique. Some psychoanalytic institutes, in fact, operate as though such an ideal technique,elevated to perfection by the local masters, existed and that learning this technique from their masters is the optimal way for candidates to absorb and master it.

There is, however, a striking contradiction between the art academy model and the way institutes actually function. Unlike the art teacher in the art academy, the senior training analyst works in privacy, and his techniques remain shrouded in secrecy. To conform to the aim of the art academy, psychoanalytic training would have to allow candidates to observe and judge the process of a psychoanalytic treatment carried out by their local masters. In addition, the focus would have to be on the nature of the product or outcome of the actual psychoanalytic work rather than on the nature of the personality structure facilitating this work. The supervisory and seminar structures would become much more important for the evaluation of the candidate's work.

The second model, that of a technical or trade school, takes the primary task of psychoanalytic education to be the learning of a clearly defined skill or trade, with no emphasis on artistic creativity. Teachers would be able to document their mastery of psychoanalytic skills without assuming or pretending that personal inspiration or creativity is required. Psychoanalytic institutes, according to this model, would be highly specialized trade schools with a program of efficient training and monitoring of the student's progress until the optimal level of skill has been reached. An essentially bureaucratic structure of institutional organization might be similar to that of other specialized technical schools, such as those that focus on industrial and technical skills in applied arts.

Most psychoanalysts would probably reject this model and consider it a degradation of the analyst's personality attributes and personal creativity and the artistic aspects of psychoanalytic work. It needs to be pointed out, however, that, insofar as emphasis is currently being put on the careful monitoring of the progress of the candidate's skills, without any emphasis on the public display of corresponding skills by the faculty, the institute does resemble a trade school, where a student can learn accounting techniques, budgeting, and financial analysis without observing his teachers performing such tasks in their personal work.

Less obvious, but more important, the trade-school model highlights the advantages of a bureaucratic organization that has explicit criteria and professional standards for both teachers and students. Such a model provides a system for objective monitoring and qualifications, which reduces arbitrary, subjective judgments made privately; it provides for an easy system of checks and balances between students and faculty and for redress of grievances of both students and faculty. The responsibility of the trade-school administration to give diplomas only to students with socially acknowledged and sanctioned technical expertise also provides a clear accountability of the institution. This protects its members from arbitrary redefinitions of the nature of the work or the qualifications for admission, progression, and graduation.

This model illustrates Jaques's (1976) thesis that bureaucratic systems of organizations, at their best, reduce paranoiagenic features in the organization. Such a reduction may have salutary effects upon psychoanalytic institutes, which, as mentioned earlier, are particularly paranoiagenic. However, because psychoanalysts tend to conceptualize psychoanalysis as an art and a science, they would probably reject this model.

A third model considers psychoanalytic institutes as theological seminaries or religious retreats and psychoanalysis as a system of religious beliefs. Although psychoanalysts would probably vehemently reject such a model, insisting on the scientific, in contrast to the religious and ethical nature of psychoanalytic theory, there are important features of psychoanalytic education as it is actually carried out that would justify such a designation.

First, the religious assertion of faith in the existence of a deity and the essentially irrational nature of such a faith are not unlike the psychoanalytic conviction about the truth of psychoanalytic theory, particularly about the unconscious. This sense of conviction is usually traced to an emotional experience connected with the discovery of the unconscious in oneself and the experience of psychological change following upon this discovery. In both the religious and pschoanalytic instances, a highly subjective personal experience—an emotional encounter with the unknown—rather than rational analysis constitutes the basis of the educational program.

In addition, this deeply transforming emotional experience is carried out in the context of an intense relation to another person, idealized and experienced as a spiritual guide. That spiritual mentor is complemented by other mentors, who focus on the limitations, shortcomings, mistakes, and inadequacies of the student's performance, while sustaining the assumption that they speak from a higher level, which the student must reach through ongoing self-exploration as well as through absorbing the teachings of the masters, in particular, the original master, Freud.

The idealization of Freud in psychoanalytic education is illustrated by the detailed, frequently obsessive and relatively noncritical study of his work, the invocation of his ideas whenever new developments in the field appear to threaten them, and the genealogical retracing of psychoanalytic training from a candidate's own training analyst to his training analyst to one of the original disciples and finally to Freud. All these features reflect an extraordinarily emotional investment in the original founder and his beliefs, quite similar to religious practice.

Above all, the quality of faith required to undergo a process that is explicitly designed to face an individual with the unknown, and the shrouding in secrecy of the work and the personality of those who help the student, reproduce the emotional atmosphere of monasteries and religious retreats. The exposure of the personality of the trainees to minute scrutiny, while the personalities of the teachers are kept as secret as possible, is also characteristic of religious education.

But although the organizational structure of psychoanalytic institutes may be similar to that used for theological training, psychoanalysis should stand or fall as a science and not as a system of emotional belief.

This leads us to my fourth model, that of the psychoanalytic institute as a university college, as an institution for the transmission, exploration, and generation of knowledge, including the transmission of methodological tools for the generation of new knowledge. That this knowledge should have a practical application, namely, helping human beings in distress, in particular, giving psychologically ill people psychological treatment, places psychoanalytic education close to the model of medical schools and other helping professions and fits with a definition that Freud (1922) gave of psychoanalysis as a theory of the mind, a method of investigation of unconscious processes, and a method of treatment. Such a model would include the following as major organizational requirements.

First, the candidate must have personality characteristics that allow her to explore her own unconscious and learn how to explore the unconscious of patients without undue risks to herself or to others. In addition, she would have to be exposed to and educated with a critical sense regarding all theories and techniques; she should be expected to learn the latest developments in the theory of technique, rather than a closed system of beliefs, and to accept the uncertainty resulting from a critical examination of all knowledge, theories, and procedures in the light of all available evidence. She would have to absorb not only Freud's writings but also those of psychoanalysts who had reached theoretical or technical conclusions that differed from Freud's.

The faculty would have to tolerate scientific debate, to expose their theories and actual clinical work to the critical analysis of the students. Faculty selection, while necessarily containing a subjective, personal element, would depend on publicly known criteria and sanctioned procedures that were open to review by a legally designated authority; the institute would be accountable for the selection, monitoring, and ongoing reconfirmation of faculty.

Both faculty and student bodies would have independent organizations that could challenge the actual carrying out of policies by the administration in the light of such publicly sanctioned policies; and the hierarchical relation between the director and her administrative subordinates in the institute would be balanced by the sanctioned authority of the faculty. This model may be the most congenial to the aspirations of most psychoanalysts, but it fits poorly with the actual structure of psychoanalytic institutes.

My conclusion is that a serious discrepancy exists between the prevalent, explicitly formulated or implicitly acknowledged aims of psychoanalytic education and the dominant organizational structures that characterize psychoanalytic institutes. Although psychoanalytic educators believe that they are teaching both an art and a science, they have structured their institutes to correspond most closely to a combination of the technical school and the theological seminary. If instead, psychoanalytic educators adopted a model that combined the features of the art school and the university college, they would be closer to achieving their aims and would eliminate the problems I listed earlier.

UNDERLYING CAUSES: PSYCHOANALYTIC
TREATMENT IN AN INSTITUTIONAL SETTING

Having examined the relation between the primary tasks and the organizational structure of psychoanalytic education, let me now turn to a motivational analysis of the distortions in these relations. By analogy, one could call this the unconscious motivations determining the psychopathology of psychoanalytic institutes. The simplest explanation one might be tempted to propose in analyzing the discrepancy between primary task and organizational structure in psychoanalytic institutes is that a self-perpetuating power elite of training analysts exploits the exacerbation of idealization processes that is inherent in psychoanalytic training to consolidate its power and achieve the related narcissistic gratification by exercising control over a small social organization.

Inasmuch as a desire for power is a universal human quality, the power exerted by education committees, particularly when they also function as executive committees of psychoanalytic institutes, may gratify an important human motivation. One might speculate that because senior faculty tend to be older (late middle age and old age), the correspondingly waning gratification in creativity, productivity, and sexuality may also reinforce the power motive. The financial security of older training analysts and their distraction from the ordinary uncertainties of aging may play an important role here.

These are universal conflicts and motivations, however, and they cannot be attributed exclusively to psychoanalysts; the functionally excessive or authoritarian power that a senior group of training analysts obtains from their institution must reflect further issues. Frequently, when senior analysts step down from positions of power and authority, they are immediately able to point to the distorting nature of their former positions (see, for example, Keiser's 1969 and Arlow's 1972 analyses of problems in psychoanalytic education, which point in many ways to the symptoms I mentioned earlier).

In addition, political minorities within an institute may begin by protesting against the institute's authoritarian structure; should they themselves reach positions of power, however, they might easily become as authoritarian as those whom they have replaced.

In addition to the problems associated with the individual desire for power, the widespread ignorance of the importance of organizational structure, and the regressive consequences of group processes activated under conditions of nonfunctional administrative structures, there are other, underlying sources of insecurity pervading psychoanalytic institutes and psychoanalysis as a profession. These insecurities derive from the nature of the work of psychoanalytic institutes, namely, the uncovering of the unconscious in the context of institutional boundaries, and the particular effects of this operation upon candidates and training analysts alike. Using a fashionable contemporary analogy, one might say that the therapeutic process of psychoanalysis liberates radioactive products; the dispersal of this radioactive fallout, which ordinarily occurs in psychoanalytic treatment performed in an open social setting, is impeded by the constraining and amplifying effects of the closed environment of the psychoanalytic institution.

In ordinary psychoanalytic treatment, much of the transference and countertransference is dispersed in the form of displacement, working through, and via the ordinary dilution of the emotional impact of the psychoanalytic session as patient and analyst move in completely separate social environments between the sessions. The advantages of this arrangement in protecting the technical neutrality of the treatment situation and in reducing the potential for transference and countertransference acting out are evident. In contrast, the training analysts' treatment of candidates occurs within the confines of a shared social setting and organizational structure; this creates opportunities and temptations for transference and countertransference acting out and for amplification of these powerful emotional forces within the institution.

Both the training analyst and the candidate-analysand are more exposed to each other than is the case in ordinary psychoanalytic treatment; they are more vulnerable to their directly exerted and indirectly expressed mutual influence, and yet each is perceived as inordinately powerful by the other. The training analyst is exposed in terms of her accessibility to direct observation and information by the analysand, and the analysand is more directly exposed in terms of his accessibility to direct observation and indirect information by the training analyst.

Displacements of the transference, splitting the transference onto other members of the faculty, and acting out the negative and positive transference at seminars and in supervision all contribute to making the training analyst more vulnerable to her candidates' acting out. The training analyst actually exerts power in the reporting institutes, but the experience of her as extremely powerful is present in nonreporting institutes as well, for she is part of the administrative structure of the institute, a senior and influential member of the faculty.

This radioactive fallout is a basic cause of disturbances in the psychoanalytic institute and of the activation of primitive defensive operations in the institution to deal with them. Why primitive defensive operations? Because as we have seen, when people function in groups, and especially when these groups exist in an organization that is structurally out of tune with its primary tasks, regressive group processes tend to become operative (see chapters 1, 4, and 8). The exploration of the dynamic unconscious carried out in multiple therapeutic psychoanalyses within a social organization increases the regressive potential of group processes to an intensity that is probably matched only by institutions that are tightly controlled by authoritarian leadership.

Idealization processes and an atmosphere of persecution are practically universal in psychoanalytic institutes. Jointly, these mechanisms also point to the prevalence of splitting operations: the division of the institutional world into idealized and persecutory objects. Although these regressive features could be reduced, if not eliminated, by an organizational structure that was optimally adapted to the organizational tasks, the opposite usually takes place. Because psychoanalytic institutes have not attempted to develop functional administrative structures, the prevalent defenses of idealization and feelings of persecution have contributed to pushing the organizational structure into further reinforcing these defensive operations.

At the center of the activation of these prevalent defensive operations is the idealization of the training analysis and the training analyst. In a somewhat oversimplified generalization, one might say that the technical-school model in combination with the theological seminary or religious-retreat model is unconsciously geared to prevent the open examination of the training analysts' work or the open exploration of their theoretical systems and techniques. The idealization of the training analysis reflects the unconscious need for personal and institutional security, control, and certainty, which would shield all concerned from the radioactive fallout of the psychoanalytic process.

I recognize that there are also external sources of insecurity that have an important impact on psychoanalytic education. But I am focusing here on the internal sources. These derive in large part from the mutual effects of the psychoanalytic institution and the training analysis.

To begin with, the need for the training analyst to maintain a position of technical neutrality in regard to his candidate-analysand has powerful and unforeseen consequences on the nature of psychoanalytic education. Some of what follows has already been referred to in the psychoanalytic literature on the problems of the dual nature, the combined therapeutic and educational objectives of the training analysis. What I wish to stress, in particular, are the consequences of this dual nature of the training analysis for psychoanalytic institutes and psychoanalytic education.

The training analyst's efforts to shield his personality characteristics, viewpoints, idiosyncrasies, and institutional conflicts from his candidate-analysand induce him to be more secretive in his institutional functioning. There is an ongoing confusion between, on the one hand, the training analyst's need to maintain privacy in connection with his personal life, his emotional reactions, and his countertransference and, on the other, the appropriateness of his taking a public stance on organizational, educational, clinical, and professional issues. This confusion tends to foster the ideal of the "anonymous" analyst, a person who is assumed to have perfect moral standards, a completely neutral personality, vast human understanding, comprehensive psychoanalytic knowledge, and no convictions or opinions on non-psychoanalytic topics.

In the case of the reporting training analyst, that secrecy leads to hypocrisy and dishonest manipulation, even if the training analyst is otherwise essentially honest: the contradiction inherent in hiding one's personality in order *not* to influence the candidate's analysis while actually influencing the candidate's academic progression behind his back has been one of the most problematic aspects of psychoanalytic training. Fortunately, the practice is gradually disappearing from even the most traditional institutes. But the training analyst still tries to conceal his professional functions from the analysand-candidate. This unrealistic attempt to be a nonperson is unwarranted.

The training analyst's going underground on the professional level is a well-rationalized manifestation of insecurity regarding his method and operates in unconscious collusion with the candidate's assumption that it is the training analyst who "knows" about the candidate's unconscious, rather than the candidate being himself the one who is finding out about his unconscious with the help of the training analyst. Roustang (1982) rightly points out that the analysand's fantasy that his own analyst "is the one who knows" should be analyzed until the analysand realizes that all interpretations are only hypotheses. The analysand has to learn that new knowledge will emerge in unexpected ways from his own unconscious by means of free association and the exploration of the transference; this process may have been facilitated by his analyst's interpretations, but it is essentially a surprising—and often moving and startling—discovery of the unknown in oneself.

In addition, the idealization of the training analyst as the one who knows is realistically reinforced by the fact that the training analyst is also an essential part of the educational institution. Unanalyzed idealizations of the training analyst, reflected in the analysand's identification with him and in her related wish to become an analyst and a training analyst as well, are never resolved. Arlow's (1970) discussion of this problem in psychoanalytic training is relevant here, as is his comment (1972) that in the British Psychoanalytic Institute, where candidates have the opportunity of entering either Kleinian or Anna Freudian seminars, the seminars they select are almost invariably determined by the orientation of their training analysts.

As both Arlow and Roustang point out, the candidate's unanalyzed ambivalence against which the idealization is a defense is expressed in splitting off the negative transference onto other training analysts and, eventually, onto other psychoanalytic schools and orientations, with the consequent maintenance of the idealization of one's own training analyst and institute and, ultimately, of Freud, all of which then perpetuate blind spots regarding such idealizations— perpetuate, too, the "family romance" of generations of candidates. My main point here is that the training analyst may unconsciously use "technical neutrality" as a disguise, a rationalization for his unconscious wish to maintain the candidate's idealization of him.

It used to be thought that the analyst's office should contain nothing that might reveal something personal about him, that it should look rather like a monk's cell, so as to reinforce the idea of technical neutrality. These excesses are now a thing of the past. Yet the behavior of many training psychoanalysts still seems to reflect the fantasy that technical neutrality is equivalent to having no personality. Behind the training analyst as a person without qualities is there the fantasy of the training analyst as the person who pretends not to be God?

This issue is related to the current controversy over the extent to which the transference is based both in the patient's past and in the reality of what the patient observes in the analyst or is based exclusively in the patient's past, a controversy that neglects the fact that the transference usually crystallizes around real aspects of the analyst's personality, exaggerated and distorted as a consequence of the patient's unconscious transfer from experiences in the past. To differentiate the reality of the stimulus for the transference from the transference per se as a distortion or an exaggeration of that stimulus has always been a primary technical task.

That an analyst may defensively deny the reality of the stimulus he provides for the patient's transference is a product of countertransference. To describe a proneness to countertransference reactions as complementary to the development of the transference is very different from calling the transference itself a compromise formation between contributions of patient and analyst. The training analyst's wish to eliminate himself as a faculty member in the psychoanalytic institute only serves to perpetuate the analysand's unresolved idealization of him, the institute, and of the psychoanalysis itself.

Another major issue derived from the candidate-analysand's relationship with his training analyst is the assignment of roles automatically carried out during psychoanalytic exploration. To the extent that the candidate is exploring his unconscious motivations—his repressed or dissociated libidinal and aggressive impulses—the training analyst carries out the dominant function of a reasonable and mature ego, while the id or the unconscious aspects of the superego are activated in the candidate.

This development, true for all psychoanalytic treatments, becomes a danger for the candidate-analysand because it again fosters his idealization of his analyst-teacher as unusually mature, and a danger for the training analyst because it fosters in her an internal sense of pressure to live up to such expectations in her other educational functions as well. Idealization corrupts its object. Collectively, the faculty is under pressure to reinforce the image of the rational and reasonable superbeings the candidates' collective fantasies expect them— and unconsciously induce them—to be.

In addition, the training analyst's control over the candidate's treatment gradually tempts her to extend that control to the educational process. We tend to underestimate the training analyst's temptation to extend the control over her candidates because the two are submerged in the same social institution. The early history of psychoanalysis is the product of more than the paternalistic tendencies of the forefathers.

Conflicts that arise in connection with the classroom are frequently interpreted as acting out of transferences, and the first solution to be heard is, "Back to the couch!" This attitude reinforces the idealization of the training analysis; it also obscures possible shortcomings in the institute's educational program. Faculty and students come to share an unconscious image of the institute as a huge couch behind which sits the collective body of training analysts and on which lies the collective body of students.

The training analysts' fantasy of omnipotence expressed in the order "Back to the couch" can also be perceived in the faculty's tendency to blame the training analyst for her candidate's shortcomings. Education committees, admission committees, and progression committees have a habit of throwing questioning glances at the training analyst whose candidate is misbehaving; the training analyst maintains the obligatory silence and struggles with the resulting guilt feelings. Rarely, a highly narcissistic training analyst may be tempted to terminate prematurely the analysis of a particularly notorious candidate. Other narcissistic training analysts may never let go of their candidate-analysand to avoid launching a less-than-perfect product of their work on the institute. Many institutes now try to avoid discussing the candidate's progression in the training analyst's presence. The information nonetheless usually reaches the training analyst, particularly if resentment against the candidate exists elsewhere or if the institute is small.

As a member of an educational institution, the training analyst carries out implicit and explicit administrative functions. When he supervises or conducts a seminar or participates in committee work or represents the institute at the local society or at the national level, he carries out a boundary function, that is, a function of communication between two connecting systems at whose boundary he stands. For example, as a teacher, the training analyst is at the boundary between the group of students he is teaching and the institute; he should, therefore, clarify the needs, expectations, and distortions each has about the other. This managerial or leadership function is essential to all social organizations; it would not be worth mentioning, were it not that it happens to be in precise conflict with the requirements of training analysis.

The training analyst must maintain strict silence about what he learns from his patient-candidate about what goes on in the institute in order to minimize the danger of the "unhooked telephone" syndrome mentioned earlier. At the same time, the training analyst is in a position to hear about his candidate-analysand from many sources, particularly if the candidate's behavior is unconsciously provocative. The training analyst now also has to be able to absorb, contain, and tolerate such information about his candidate without acting on it. He must keep himself open to exploring his internal reactions to such information in the light of his candidate-patient's material and transference developments. In other words, the training analyst must maintain a *barrier* between his candidate-patient and the institute in connection with these double vectors of acting out, even as he must act as *liaison* between other students and the institute.

It is not surprising but it is unfortunate that the training analyst tends to extend this barrier function to his other educational activities in the institute, thus causing a breakdown of boundaries between groups, task systems, and faculty and students, even as he lets his functions as a member of the faculty contaminate the boundaries between himself and the candidate. The result is that the training analyst may commit indiscretions in regard to his candidate or have emotional reactions to third parties about whom his candidate has spoken.

The analyst in private practice does not have to experience the normal limitations of personal authority regarding other people, required in ordinary social organizations. Furthermore, she is protected from the regressive pull that even reasonably well-functioning organizations exert from time to time over their members. These circumstances may foster a false sense of personal maturity and autonomy in the analyst. An ivory-tower attitude characterizes the training analyst in full-time private practice, especially those whose patients are not generally severely pathological and include a number of "normal" candidates. The reanalysis of colleagues, often rightly considered difficult, is nonetheless very different from the ordinary spectrum of patients of nontraining analysts. In fact, the temptation for prestigious psychoanalysts to gradually select an ever-healthier spectrum of patients may increase this exclusive attitude, which enters into a sharp and even violent contrast to what is required of her in a psychoanalytic institute.

The sense of power and security the analyst enjoys in her office is legitimate in that her technically appropriate control of the psychoanalytic situation is also socially sanctioned. It is only natural that the analyst seek the same gratifications of power and security from her institute. But when the wish or need to control is transplanted to a psychoanalytic institute, it immediately fosters a hierarchical system of social control and authoritarian management, which is rationalized by the training analysts as a group on the basis of the need to preserve their anonymity.

Another and related issue is the temptation for the training analyst to displace repressed or dissociated sadistic and narcissistic needs onto the psychoanalytic institute. To represent reason and rationality behind the couch is one thing; to avoid the expression of frustrated, dissociated, repressed, or projected narcissistic and aggressive impulses in the course of organizational interactions is another. We assume that psychoanalysts' sexual needs are sufficiently fulfilled outside their professional situation that, under ordinary circumstances, they will not create problems within the institute. The sexual barrier between analysts and patients naturally extends to that of training analysts and candidates in psychoanalytic institutes. The same is not true, however, for the expression of narcissistic needs, of the frustrated exhibitionism of the "silent" analyst behind the couch, and of sadistic needs stemming from many sources. Dissociated sadistic needs, usually well controlled in dyadic and triadic relationships, are often acted out in social organizations. Psychoanalytic institutes provide special channels for narcissistic gratification and injury.

The uncertainties attending the selection of candidates, their progression and graduation, and the selection of training analysts are real. They are compounded, however, by vague and diffuse institutionalized ideals of perfection and by those ideals' counterpart, suspiciousness and rigidity at all points of transition. Arlow (1972) called attention to the oedipal roots of the initiation rites in psychoanalytic institutes. I expand on his formulation by including the collective institutional temptation to project dissociated sadism onto the guardians of the gate—those who are delegated to carry out selection procedures and supervise other initiation rites. A former chair of a committee that qualified candidates for membership in the American Psychoanalytic Association told me how, in contrast to his usual behavior, his role as chair had made him rigid and suspicious, and how, retrospectively, he perceived himself as the policeman of the organization, although he had never been given any explicit "orders" to behave in this way.

Arlow suggested that the counterpart of the unresolved idealization of the training analyst is the unconscious fantasy produced by the status of the newly appointed training analyst: he has successfully rebelled against the father, which leads to a guilt-determined identification with the father as the aggressor and the consequent temptation to dominate and suppress the next generation of candidates, graduates, and nontraining analysts alike as potentially dangerous usurpers.

This unconscious identification with an aggressor may be reinforced by unconscious envy of the candidate as the immature, regressed, and therefore guilt-free representative of gratification of instinctual needs that are forbidden to the supposedly mature and rational training analyst. The exaggerated conventionality and even puritanism that sometimes permeate older and larger institutes and the inordinate outrage (and implicit sexual excitement) that follows any breach of sexual boundaries within the psychoanalytic organization illustrate this development.

The conscious fear and presumably largely unconscious enjoyment of crisis and chaos at times of organizational conflicts in institutes may also be related to the projection onto the institute of intolerable instinctual impulses. The suspicion aroused by "dissenters," the relief when a split in the institute finally creates "external" enemies, and the transformation of psychoanalytic theory into a self-sustaining belief system that becomes the ideology of an in-group (the guilt-determined alliance of the brothers) contain both oedipal elements and the preoedipal defenses and group valences characteristic of regression in the basic-assumptions groups described by Bion (1961).

Thus, as a consequence of the problems derived from the nature of the work done in psychoanalytic institutes—namely, the activation of the dynamic unconscious in training analysis—additional complications develop. These include unconscious fears that the institution will be invaded by uncontrollable instinctual forces, fears that strengthen the senior faculty's experienced need for an authoritarian, hierarchical organization as a security system. We can see the temptations for establishing a theological seminary or religious-retreat model of organization. The hierarchical organization and religious ideology also protect the senior group of training analysts' institutionalized fantasy of omniscience.

In spite of the explicit and genuine conception of psychoanalysis as a science and an art that predominates among psychoanalysts and that would optimally be expressed in corresponding institutional models of organization, powerful forces tend to transform the ideology of psychoanalytic institutes into that of a religious organization or, rather, transform its structure into an organizational structure that would be most commensurate with a theological seminary.

Psychoanalysis, in this transformation, is no longer a scientific theory to be continually reexamined but a doctrine that also has an implied value as a Weltanschauung, a view of the world that readily explains the unconscious motives and resistances of those who do not agree with it. Psychoanalysis thus becomes a powerful ideological instrument in combating the unfaithful, in using unconscious motivation of others as a social weapon. Personal imperfections in the behavior of individuals in the psychoanalytic institution are understood as signs of regression to be cured by a return to the couch. The institutionally activated aggression of the members of this psychoanalytic community is gratified by the attack on out-groups; their dependency needs are gratified by the unremitting idealization of their training analysts—teachers of past generations, down to Freud; and their sexual, particularly oedipal needs are symbolically gratified in the family-romance fantasies described by Arlow (1972).

It could be argued that all these characteristics of psychoanalytic institutions are an extension of the historical circumstances of the origins of the "psychoanalytic movement," of Freud's struggle to protect his revolutionary discoveries against the hostility of the organized academic "science" of his time. Roustang (1982) mentions Freud's paternalistic personality, the cult of that personality engaged in by his immediate followers and reflected in the efforts to maintain an unnecessary secrecy about his personal life, and the historical enactment of a sequence of oedipal dramas involving Freud's disciples and relatives. Roustang points to the intimate connection between these historical aspects of psychoanalytic institutes and the current pathology of their unresolved idealizations in the transference. Mahony (1979) called attention to the intimate connection between these same historical circumstances and aspects of Freud's writings. I find these historical analyses interesting but propose that the organizational distortions in psychoanalytic institutes are self-perpetuating, that they are due to active institutional processes that go beyond a purely historical explanation. I have attempted to specify some of these processes here.

We can assume that if the organizational distortions of psychoanalytic education were resolved—if the administrative structure of psychoanalytic institutes were altered to correspond to an explicit concept of the aims of psychoanalytic education—new challenges and difficulties would emerge in response to new developments at the boundaries of psychoanalysis as a science and a profession. The revolutionary developments in, for example, neurochemistry, infant development, small-group psychology, and philosophical inquiries pose potential challenges to psychoanalytic theory that may facilitate new research and discoveries within psychoanalysis itself. When psychoanalytic education remains excessively concerned with protecting idealization processes within the institution, however, persecutory fears may easily be projected onto the external environment, and new scientific developments in other fields may be perceived as threats to psychoanalysis.

The predominant educational culture—for example, the different educational systems in other countries—may stimulate corresponding educational structures in the world's psychoanalytic institutes as well, often without a conscious effort or even awareness of this connection (Edward Joseph, pers. comm.). It is striking that in spite of these potential environmental influences, psychoanalytic institutes in many countries and in very different social, cultural, and educational environments suffer from very similar problems related to the internal structural and conflictual issues I have been exploring. The resolution of these internal constraints may also contribute to a more creative interchange of educational philosophy across the institutional boundaries of psychoanalytic institutes.

SOME GENERAL PRINCIPLES OF TREATMENT

In what follows, I suggest strategies for institutional reorganization that deal with the immediate and underlying causes of the stagnation of psychoanalytic education. By these guidelines I do not imply that there is a single solution for all institutes; I offer rather a theoretical frame from which to explore alternative solutions and their respective advantages and disadvantages. If it is true that the underlying causes of the problems in psychoanalytic education have to do with intrinsic qualities of the psychoanalytic situation, we must be prepared to live with conflict and the limited effectiveness of all corrective measures. It seems reasonable, however, that significant improvement of the educational functions of psychoanalytic institutes is possible.

First, it is essential that the administrative model or models correspond to explicit goals of psychoanalytic education. The combined model of a college and an art academy is the most promising for psychoanalytic education. There are undoubtedly technical aspects of the training that would respond well to the integration of aspects of a technical-school model. If psychoanalysis is, among other things, a helping profession, standards of technical sophistication for the profession are an important aspect of psychoanalytic education.

By the same token, aspects of the theological seminary or religious-retreat model, with its central focus upon faith, are probably unavoidable because particularly in the early stages of learning about psychoanalysis, much work on oneself and with patients has to be carried out without any immediate evidence of the specific effectiveness of that work. To open oneself to exploring one's unconscious requires an act of trust that has a religious aspect to it (or a religious attitude is one expression of basic trust).

With these reservations, however, a model based predominantly on the college and art school seems to me optimal. It should be kept in mind that I am referring to *models* and not to how universities or art schools actually function. Conflicts will always be found in all human institutions, and this holds true for universities and art schools as well. If the primary task and the organizational structure are in harmony, the self-regulatory functions of colleges and art schools can *limit* the disturbances derived from unavoidable human factors. A university college model of organizational structure would imply full academic freedom for the faculty and rewards for scientific productivity (as opposed to rewarding submission and subservience to local ideologists and kowtowing to the masters); it would generate both the faculty's and the students' interest in scholarly and scientific work. This could electrify psychoanalytic seminars and transform them into focal points for the generation of new knowledge in psychoanalysis.

To place functional authority in the hands of the faculty—supervisors, seminar leaders, and lecturers—would go a long way toward reducing the pathological idealization of the training analysts. The students would know that their progress depended on performance in the classroom, and under the supervision of and in open interchanges with their teachers.

This model would offer clear, precise criteria for admission, progression, and graduation. It would mean that decisions made about students by committees were publicly known and that there were public channels of redress of griev- ances. The faculty would have the obligation to share its evaluations with the students; and a clear system of evaluation would go far in diminishing the paranoid atmosphere within institutes.

The selection of faculty would also have to correspond to clear, publicly expressed criteria and would be carried out by committees that were account- able for their decisions. The selection of training analysts, particularly, would have to be based on explicit criteria and on a selection process that permitted all eligible psychoanalysts to apply for faculty positions and be ensured a fair chance. That subjective judgments operate in the selection of faculty, particularly training analysts, does not mean that the criteria according to which these judgments are made should not be public, nor that those who make such judgments should not be held accountable for them. Within a university model, it should not be difficult to devise systems that guarantee a fair selection and monitoring of faculty. This alone would help reduce the paranoiagenic atmosphere of psychoanalytic societies and institutes. I am not proposing to make public the reason a particular analyst was not appointed; rather, the method, the procedure, and the locus of the discussion and decision must be public, so that the person affected by the decision knows who made it and why. The committee's discussion would not be public, but its chair or a representative should be authorized to discuss the issue with the applicant if he or she wished.

The task is to destroy the perception—and the reality—that a privileged group of training analysts exists whose selection depends as much on personal and political factors as on their professional capacities. One problem connected with this is the number of training analysts appointed by a given institute. Institutes in various countries have experimented with selecting training analysts on the basis of explicit standards and requirements, complementing the appointment of a large number of training analysts by allowing the candidates to freely select their training analyst from a list provided by the institute.

In other countries some institutes have opted for "democratic" methods of selecting training analysts. Training analysts are all "full members" of the society, who were elected by a members' vote; thus, strictly academic criteria are replaced by a purely political mechanism. The trouble with this method is that it is based on a fallacy. The expectation that democratic solutions will solve the problems of arbitrariness reflects a confusion between organizational requirements of an educational system and the political governance of a community.

Democratic decision making may protect individuals in institutions from arbitrariness, but it does not ensure that the aims, or primary tasks, correspond with the organization's structure. The quality of the product—in this instance, the competence of the training analyst—may suffer equally whether the institution is authoritarian or democratic. The appointment of a large number of training analysts who are required to meet set standards is probably the best way to demystify the function of training analysts and to produce a healthy competition for academic excellence among them.

By the same token, limiting the number of candidates that any one training analyst may treat analytically at a time should help to eliminate the "convoy" phenomenon in which a training analyst has a large cohort of candidate-analysands. Training analysts would thus treat a broader spectrum of patients. Generally speaking, if a large number of faculty members offer seminars and supervision, it may also diminish the control over certain key courses held by a small, self-perpetuating group. Again, the selection of seminars and seminar leaders should be based on educational criteria, not political, democratic ones.

Clear lines of organizational structure are the essence of the university model: there are clear administrative boundaries but no boundaries or restrictions on the transmission, exploration, and generation of new ideas.

I do not favor having analysts report about their analysand-candidates. At most, the training analysts might report what day the training analysis started, the number of sessions held each month or year, and the date the analysis was either interrupted by one or both participants or was completed. This arrangement would offer a reasonable compromise between the need to know whether a candidate has been or is in analysis as part of his training requirements and an otherwise complete separation of the training analysis from all other educational functions of the institute.

"How to Catch a Psychopath" could be the heading beneath which lie all the reasons given in support of the reporting training analyst. But a true psychopath may conceal psychopathic behavior from his own training analyst. Against the argument that only the training analyst will be aware of a candidate's serious psychopathology is the fact that much concealment goes on in reporting institutes, typically expressed in the practice of a candidate's undergoing a second analysis "for himself." Those in favor of the reporting system justify it on the grounds that it can uncover unsuitable candidates. But I see no reason why a training analyst cannot interrupt an analysis with a candidate she thinks is unsuitable without prejudice to the candidate's request for another training analyst. I believe that the damage done by the reporting system is ten times worse than any safeguards it provides, and I strongly endorse Lifschutz's (1976) analysis of this issue.

Keeping training analysts truly separate from the educational and supervisory system of their own candidates puts greater pressure on supervisors and seminar leaders to evaluate the candidate's progress, and this is a salutary pressure. Supervisors and seminar leaders thus have an increased sense of authority and responsibility, and this in itself can positively influence the educational atmosphere. And once training analysts are reassured that their responsibility is exclusively to their candidate-analysands, they in turn may experience a greater level of freedom in their handling of transference and countertransference.

A university model implies open scientific discussion and the sharing by training analysts of their own cases in scientific meetings, which include both graduates and candidates. It seems reasonable that training analysts should not present their own cases to a seminar involving their own candidates, but this should not be a problem in any but very small psychoanalytic institutes. Training analysts should not, however, have to refrain from teaching seminars in which their own candidates participate. The supervisory situation may be a particularly favorable opportunity for senior analysts to share their experiences with their supervisees. At the same time, the supervisors would have the responsibility for communicating honestly their evaluation to their candidates-supervisees, an essential aspect of a functional educational system.

The model of an art academy for psychoanalysis would be expressed in the opportunities for candidates to learn from the analytic work of faculty and training analysts, in addition to learning psychoanalytic technique through their own cases and those of other candidates presented in supervision and in seminars. The tendency for only junior faculty to present case material in junior-senior faculty gatherings would gradually disappear. The subservience of junior faculty toward senior faculty would also lessen, both because the appointments of training analysts would be institutionalized, formalized, and subjected to the checks and balances of an academic institution and because sharing the universal difficulties in analytic work would help reduce the irrational idealization of senior colleagues.

The introduction of some bureaucratic organization with formal policies and procedures, publicly known mechanisms of redress of grievances, and socially sanctioned authority and accountability at all levels is a challenging but not impossible task. These policies and procedures might combine the best aspects of a university model with that of a technical school.

The proposed changes in the structure of psychoanalytic education, which tend to strengthen the university college and art academy models at the expense of the technical school and, particularly, the theological seminary or religious-retreat models, should go a long way toward reducing the pervasive idealization and persecution processes that plague psychoanalytic institutes. The firm protection of the boundaries of the personal analysis of candidates, matched by the open participation of training analysts in all other aspects of the educational process, and a fair, rational, and open system of selection, monitoring, and progression of both candidates and faculty may not eliminate the conflicts created by institutional psychoanalysis, but they would facilitate the creative use of the awareness of these conflicts for deepening psychoanalytic understanding and knowledge and developing psychoanalytic technique. Adopting these measures would significantly contribute to reactivating the excitement of psychoanalytic education and help generate new knowledge in the field.

Chapter 13 Authoritarianism, Culture, and Personality in Psychoanalytic Education

A senior candidate at a psychoanalytic institute was assigned a patient who had murdered her infant son. The candidate considered the case unanalyzable, while his supervisor, the leader of the institute and a very powerful personality, insisted that it was an acceptable analytic case. The other senior psychoanalytic consultants had agreed with the candidate that psychoanalysis was contraindicated, and the candidate therefore refused to continue the analysis, referring the patient instead for psychotherapeutic treatment. Afterward, his supervisor voiced continued objections to the candidate's graduation, although in the opinion of the rest of the senior faculty, the candidate had fulfilled all the requirements for graduation. Many extra-official meetings took place among the senior members of the faculty to explore whether it would be possible to help the candidate graduate by circumventing the leader's veto. The lengthy postponement of the candidate's graduation eventually became an open secret throughout the institute, increasing the already existing atmosphere of fearfulness and cynicism about psychoanalytic training.

When individuals function in groups, and especially when these groups exist in an organization that is structurally out of tune with its mandate, regressive group processes tend to be activated. In the relationship between training analysts as a group and candidate-analysands as a group, the effect of multiple transferences and countertransferences operating simultaneously upon all participants is to increase the need for protective, defensive operations by both groups, actions that transform these groups into nontask-related sentience groups (Miller and Rice, 1967). (*Sentience* here refers to the emotional bonds that influence group formation and cohesiveness.) To the extent that this group cohesiveness is not directly related to the task—in this case, psychoanalytic education—the nontask groups develop defensive processes that are in conflict with the educational functions of the organization.

Idealization processes and an atmosphere of persecution—reflecting the projective management of aggression—are the most immediate, practically universal consequences of group regression in psychoanalytic institutes. Jointly, these mechanisms also point to the prevalence of splitting operations, or the division of the institutional world into idealized and persecutory objects. These regressive features might be reduced, if not eliminated, by an organizational structure that was optimally adapted to the organizational tasks, but because of the administrative distortions I outlined in chapter 12, the opposite happens.

At the center of the activation of these prevalent defensive operations is the idealization of the training analysis and the training analyst. This idealization is fostered by the training analyst's insecurity, which derives from many sources: the confusion of the technically neutral analyst with the "anonymous" analyst, the effects of the training analyst's going underground professionally, and the limitations to the analysis of the idealization of the training analyst by the candidate-analysands that stems from the candidates' nonanalyzed identification with their training analysts as professional models, a problem that Arlow (1972) and Roustang (1982) explored in great detail.

In chapter 12, I recommended that strategies be developed for institutional reorganization to reduce these symptoms. My recommendations depend on a model that combines aspects of the art academy and the university college and that has a corresponding administrative structure.

I have been able to observe as a participant the functioning of at least three psychoanalytic institutes: the Chilean Psychoanalytic Institute in Santiago, the Topeka (Kansas) Institute of Psychoanalysis, and the Columbia University Center for Psychoanalytic Training and Research. In addition, I have been a guest student and faculty member at other institutes, and I have been a consultant on institutional problems to psychoanalytic institutes in

Europe, Latin America, and North America. My observations derive from these experiences.

I believe that the principal cause of authoritarianism in psychoanalytic institutes is the *motivated* discrepancy between explicit educational goals and the administrative structure. The unacknowledged influence of the surrounding culture—from prevalent political crosscurrents (particularly those of totalitarian ideologies) and from the educational system generally—and the personalities of the psychoanalytic leaders have the potential to contribute to authoritarianism in subtle and not-so-subtle ways. Sometimes even ordinary social conventionality may be transformed into a focused oppression.

The most immediate effect of a nonfunctional administrative structure is the development of authoritarian tendencies among the staff. Chaos also follows, but because organizations continue to operate, this chaos is usually complemented or followed by authoritarianism. The immediate symptoms of authoritarianism can include fearfulness, submissiveness, rebelliousness, and passivity. In psychoanalytic institutes, idealization and paranoiagenesis become dominant under such circumstances.

Authoritarianism depends on the extent to which the faculty's power and exercise of that power are appropriate to the faculty's functions. This is particularly true of training analysts as a group. That is, authoritarianism depends on how functional this power and authority are. Faculty may be "powerless," that is, may lack the power needed to carry out its tasks, or faculty power may be greater than necessary for the task. This is the definition of *authoritarianism.* Ideally, power must be adequate for legitimate authority, which is in turn defined by the level of power needed to carry out required tasks (Kernberg, 1979). We saw an example of authoritarianism at the beginning of this chapter.

THE SURROUNDING CULTURE AND
INSTITUTIONAL BLIND SPOTS

One can see how the concepts of technical neutrality and acting out differ in different cultures, and these differences influence the definition of acting-out behavior. In Santiago, Chile, in the 1950s and 1960s, I noted that it was culturally acceptable to avoid paying taxes. A rather liberal, European attitude toward sexual morality also existed; that is, there was a dual morality that combined the authority of a paternalistic culture with that of the Catholic church. Divorce was frowned upon, although extramarital affairs, particularly by men, were tolerated. These cultural mores were reflected in the institute's attitude toward the sexual behavior of patients and candidates.

Topeka, Kansas, on the other hand, which is in the heart of America's Bible Belt, had a completely different culture during those years. For example, citizens were expected to pay taxes. In fact, a strong moral attitude informed that social responsibility in Kansas, as it did in the United States generally. On issues of sexual morality, the Topeka institute also reflected strong views: divorce was not only accepted; it was often considered a reasonably mature solution to marital conflicts. Extramarital affairs, however, were frowned upon. This attitude corresponded to that in the prevailing local culture. These cultural differences lent a marked contrast to the attitudes of the analysts toward their patients' clinical material. In fact, a joke circulating among psychoanalytic candidates in Topeka who had immigrated from various Latin American countries had it that in the United States, a man would have all the women of his life in sequence, while, in Latin America, they were available simultaneously. And a training analyst in Topeka, wanting to be helpful, once warned me that she had observed me the day before kissing my wife in a movie theater. She was concerned that such a public display might endanger my future appointment as a training analyst!

POLITICAL IDEOLOGY

In Chile, during the presidency of Salvador Allende, a sharp split took place between the leftist supporters of the Allende government and the centrist and rightist opposition to it (including center-left Social Christians). This division extended to Marxist-oriented training analysts identified with the Allende regime and non-Marxist training analysts identified with the opposition. A Social Christian candidate happened to be in analysis with a Marxist training analyst. The training analyst interpreted the candidate's participation in a physicians' strike against the Allende government as a submission to the capitalist ideology that represented his oedipal father. The candidate protested, stating that he did not want to discuss politics with his training analyst. The training analyst then suggested that the candidate terminate the analysis and agreed to continue only after a lengthy and painful discussion with the institute's education committee. When he heard that he was still assigned to the same analyst, the candidate, panic-stricken, left the country to continue his psychoanalytic training elsewhere.

Technical neutrality is based upon the implicit assumption that the analyst and patient share a common cultural and ideological background. The repro-duction in the analytic situation of ideological conflicts in the political culture that destroy this underlying consensus may lead first to a breakdown of func-tional preconditions for analytic work and consequently to authoritarianism. Transforming psychoanalysis into a Weltanschauung may threaten the analyst's position of technical neutrality.

EDUCATIONAL SYSTEMS

In the United States, a few psychoanalytic institutes are associated with a university, particularly a department of psychiatry. This connection can signifi-cantly influence the educational procedures. In the university, knowledge from other scientific fields can "intrude" upon psychoanalytic seminars. When there is no university connection, however, and the faculty members have large private practices, isolation of the psychoanalytic institute can develop, which increases the risk that the educational program will be narrow and insulated. In some places, departments of psychiatry with a biological orientation might have almost no faculty with a psychoanalytic orientation, while an unaffiliated psychoanalytic institute might lack challenge from developments in biological sciences at the boundaries with psychoanalysis. This separation tends to restrict scientific inquiry and debate and to "flatten" psychoanalytic education.

In addition, psychoanalytic institutes in university departments of psychia-try can suffer from departmental chairs' changing attitudes toward psycho-analysis. Yet when a department chair of psychiatry appreciates the contribu-tions of psychoanalysis, the corresponding intradepartmental psychoanalytic institute exposed to the challenge and stimulation of an academic ambience may enrich its curriculum with exciting programs, stimulate a scholarly atmo-sphere, and make innovations in its educational programs. One of the reasons for the increasing attraction of Columbia's Center for Psychoanalytic Training and Research to candidates in recent years has been its encouragement of a scientific dialogue within its department of psychiatry and its development of interdisciplinary symposia and conferences with Columbia University.

THE PERSONALITY OF THE LEADER

Roustang (1982) points to the paradox that Freud, who critically described the irrational relationship between leaders and followers in organized institu-tions, should have been the author of "On the History of the Psychoanalytic

Movement" (1914). Freud's paper clearly indicates, says Roustang, his conviction that a scientific commitment to psychoanalysis coincided with loyalty to his (Freud's) ideas, whereas any questioning of key psychoanalytic concepts represented unconsciously determined resistances to truth. We might dismiss Freud's relationships with his immediate followers as an irrelevant historical curiosity if they were not intimately linked to subsequent psychoanalytic history. Roustang calls attention to a contradiction inherent in psychoanalytic movements: The goal of psychoanalysis is to resolve the transference. But psychoanalytic education attempts to maintain the transference that psychoanalysis tries to resolve. If fidelity to Freud, the charismatic founder of psychoanalysis, were a requirement for becoming a psychoanalyst, the members of psychoanalytic societies could not be scientifically independent. The contradictory tradition has persisted, as Roustang makes clear in his discussion of Lacan.

It could be argued that the tradition of the structural arrangements of the psychoanalytic movement initiated by Freud and consolidated in the prevalent characteristics of psychoanalytic institutes is primarily responsible for the authoritarian developments I summarized in chapter 12. Although I respect the historical origins of authoritarian features of psychoanalytic education, I maintain that it is the nature of the very task—psychoanalytic treatment in an institutional context—that, in activating organizational defenses, particularly along the lines of the group regression of training analysts and candidates, tends to perpetuate the distortion between task and structure. Yet the personality of the leaders in each psychoanalytic institution also has a significant influence on institutional functioning.

The chair of the department of psychiatry at a leading Latin American university from the late 1940s to the mid-1960s was also the founder of the local psychoanalytic association and its institute. A strong leader, he was concerned chiefly with the development of new ideas, and he was remarkably free of the need to impose these ideas (and his will) on those working with him. In fact, the dynamics of the institute centered around the faculty's effort to systematize and normalize psychoanalytic education, while the leader's emphasis was on the revolutionary content of psychoanalytic thinking and the need to continue to explore new territory. As a result, a strong personal leadership coincided with an informal structure of psychoanalytic education. Although it is true that the enthusiasm and commitment that accompanied this early generation of psychoanalysts contributed to the high morale of the institute, the informality of the leader's relation to both faculty and candidates balanced the natural division between training analysts and candidates. During his tenure, idealization and paranoiagenesis were remarkably low.

An institute of psychoanalysis within an important North American university in the 1950s and 1960s was headed by a senior training analyst who was simultaneously medical director of the corresponding department of psychiatry, of which the institute was a part. This leader was a powerful personality, both admired and feared, and his strong personal leadership of the psychoanalytic community included the institute. There, the atmosphere at seminars and in the supervision of candidates was remarkably tense. The cautious and at times fearful attitudes of candidates as individuals and in groups was striking. The leader was less concerned with the particular orientation of psychoanalytic education (the institute was firmly identified with American ego psychology) than with loyalty to himself and to the institution. The emphasis on the structure of the institute resulted in the usual hierarchical organization of teaching and the latent division between faculty and candidates and between training and nontraining analysts.

The founder and leader of another North American university-based psychoanalytic institution had left a very traditional, free-standing institute to set up a new psychoanalytic institute within a department of psychiatry at a prestigious medical school. He had expressed a strong commitment to psychoanalysis as a science and believed in a strong, centralized leadership. The level of authoritarian pressure he had generated was concretely revealed to me many years after his retirement. By then, a new generation of training analysts developed under his influence was dedicated to transforming an authoritarian administrative structure into a functional one.

Under the leadership of a young director, the institute developed an administrative structure that corresponded remarkably well to the requirements of the combined university college and art academy model I previously suggested as being ideal. This leader's commitment to psychoanalytic education that fostered a spirit of inquiry and an open discussion of the broadest range of psychoanalytic thinking, that encouraged research, and that, above all, carefully limited the authority vested in training analysts and faculty placed this institute in a central role in the intellectual life of the American psychoanalytic community. The level of idealization and paranoiagenesis at the institute was low, just as it had been in the Latin American institute mentioned, in contrast to the first North American institute discussed.

Similar variations in the level of idealization, paranoiagenesis, and authoritarian structure, however, may be observed in institutes where strong, personalized leadership is not present or is defended against by bureaucratic or political arrangements. In the 1960s and 1970s a struggle was in progress at still another North American psychoanalytic institute between a group of senior psychoanalysts who maintained a firm control of the institute and an out-group that included both a minority of training analysts and a large number of nontraining-analyst faculty who were challenging the rigid control of their institute, particularly in the appointment process for training analysts, a system that had become highly politicized. The level of idealization and paranoiagenesis at this institute was high, and the tension and anxiety of candidates as well as nontraining analyst faculty was strong. Here an authoritarian structure evolved without any strong personalized leadership.

An authoritarian structure can evolve in a system that is characterized by collective leadership, and a functional institution can evolve in a system with strongly individualized leadership. The effort to correct for authoritarian institutional structure by the development of democratic processes can backfire because, as I pointed out earlier, when political decision making replaces task-oriented decision making, functional authority can also suffer. For example, the appointment of members of the faculty by a secret vote of all members of a psychoanalytic society may be democratic, but it is not the best way to pick faculty. It can politicize the membership around an ideology that is tangential to the functional needs of psychoanalytic education. A few psychoanalytic institutes in Europe suffer from this problem.

In chapter 12, I focused on some major corrective measures that can reduce the negative effects of the development of paranoiagenesis and idealization. These include eliminating the reporting functions of the training analyst; developing a public, functional method to train, select, and monitor faculty; discussing training analysts' own clinical work; organizing faculty and candidate relationships to facilitate open communication, redress of grievances, and corrections of distortions in the educational process; demystifying all aspects of the selection, progression, and graduation of candidates; and encouraging candidates to participate individually and in groups in exploring and adding to psychoanalytic knowledge.

Perhaps the most pernicious effect of authoritarianism on psychoanalytic education and psychoanalysis generally is the restriction and "flatness" of the teaching and learning of psychoanalysis. A willingness to consider alternative theories and practice is essential for scientific development and education.

Chapter 14 Thirty Ways to Destroy the Creativity of Psychoanalytic Candidates

Some years ago, I was discussing with a colleague ways to increase the creativity of candidates in psychoanalytic training, when she told me with a smile: "Our problem is not so much to foster creativity as to try not to inhibit the creativity naturally stimulated by the nature of our work" (pers. comm., Lore Schacht, 1991). Her comment triggered memories and observations I have made in the course of studying, teaching, and participating in psychoanalytic education in various psychoanalytic societies and institutes. After gathering these observations and discussing them with colleagues, I have put together in a *negative* format the positively phrased plea for the nurturing of psychoanalytic creativity that I make elsewhere in this book (see particularly chapters 12 and 13). It is my hope that seeing the situation presented in a completely different light may stimulate some creative thinking—and, even more, action—among my colleagues in psychoanalytic education. As an excellent overview of present-day problems in psychoanalytic education, Wallerstein's (1993) summary of the fifth International Psychoanalytic Association conference of training analysts in Buenos Aires may serve as an important background.

The following list of ways to *inhibit* the creativity of psychoanalytic candidates is not exhaustive, although it does cover dominant reasons that creativity is being effectively inhibited at our institutes.

1. Slow down the processing of applications; delay accepting candidates; slow down the provision of information to candidates. This in turn will help to slow them down. If candidates' progress is systematically slow and cumbersome, if their written case material is subjected to numerous revisions, and, particularly, if long periods of waiting in uncertainty become a regular part of their educational experience, they will tend to become slow to respond and to take initiative. The slower the process of acceptance and progress, the more the candidates themselves will avoid the final steps to graduation, autonomy, and joining the membership of their psychoanalytic society. And they will take longer to produce scientific contributions, if indeed they ever do.

2. As instructors, insist that candidates read Freud's works carefully, completely, and exhaustively, in chronological order, making sure that they learn his precise theory at every given point. Freud's writings can be put to good use in damping candidates' interest in thinking for themselves. Teachers should convey the clear message that any critical analysis of Freud's conclusions has to be postponed until students have read everything (and until they have much more experience and knowledge in the psychoanalytic field). To begin with, students need to know what Freud thought: it is helpful, therefore, to disconnect the teaching of Freud's writings from all outside or contemporary critiques of his work, from contemporary controversial issues, and from real, important clinical problems. The protection of Freud's work from contamination by other theories or critiques will do wonders to decrease candidates' interest in further developments in psychoanalytic thinking.

The instructor should keep in mind that he needs to teach the *conclusions* Freud arrived at, not the *process of Freud's thinking*. In fact, if the students acquire a grasp of the methodology of Freud's thinking, which was unavoidably revolutionary, it might lead them to dangerous identification with his originality and thus defeat the purpose of the isolated and exhaustive focus on his conclusions (Green, 1991).

3. Assign some of Freud's most creative and important papers at the beginning of each new seminar. Go into great detail about everything Freud said in these familiar articles and stress his conclusions. This reassuring repetition of the permanent aspects of Freud's work, combined with the special emphasis given these works in the curriculum, will desensitize students to his contribution—a lulling process that can be much enhanced by asking students to write

extensive summaries of Freud's work or to orally summarize for the class what they have all just read. One may further the process by giving examinations on the content of Freud's entire work as a precondition for progressing to other seminars.

4. Be wary of candidates who tend to question the views of any major theoretician or contributor who is a favored author of your particular psychoanalytic institution. Convey clearly that critical thinking is welcome as long as it leads to a confirmation of your dominant leader's views. Make sure to reward those students who are excited and fully convinced by what you assign to them (except, of course, the contributions of "deviant schools": these should arouse appropriate incredulity and indignation among students). If you show your appreciation, tactfully but consistently, of those students who agree with the official view of your institution, the temptation to develop new, different, questioning, or divergent views should gradually disappear (Giovannetti, 1991; Infante, 1991; Lussier, 1991).

5. Try to protect candidates from participating too early in scientific meetings of your psychoanalytic society or from being invited to gatherings where respected colleagues may sharply disagree with one another. This can be justified by pointing out that the personal training analysis should be undisturbed by premature external influences, particularly those that might threaten the anonymity of the training analyst. Within a small psychoanalytic society, it is always possible to justify forbidding candidates to attend psychoanalytic society meetings because in such small groups one might not be able to avoid contacts among candidates and their analysts outside the sessions. This in turn justifies the isolation of the teaching institute from the active scientific world of psychoanalytic thinking.

6. Carefully control elective courses. These are often used by junior members of the faculty to present new and challenging ideas. Watch over elective seminars in general and remain alert to the possibility that they may disturb the harmonious, integrated approach to psychoanalysis that corresponds to your society's or institute's dominant views.

7. Maintain a strict separation between undergraduate and postgraduate seminars. Fortunately, most psychoanalytic institutes have an intuitive understanding of the importance of avoiding a premature mixing of candidates and graduate analysts in the same seminars: the candidates are too likely to discover uncertainty and questioning attitudes in the graduates that they themselves are learning to suppress. This may disturb a healthy idealization of the effectiveness

of psychoanalytic training and dispel the illusion that there are enormous differences between candidates and graduates.

8. The preservation in the students of a healthy respect for their elders may be achieved by assembling teams of senior training analysts and junior analysts interested in becoming training analysts to teach certain courses or seminars. Maintain a clear hierarchy of older and younger members of the faculty. If the junior analyst respectfully bows to the senior analyst's views, and conveys by her overall behavior her unquestioning acceptance of senior authority; if, in fact, she shows uncertainty as to the extent to which she may take initiatives in teaching a particular seminar, it will strengthen the message that one must not question established authority. You may support the hierarchy by simple means: for example, reserve the front seats of professional meetings for senior faculty.

9. Increase graduation rituals by whatever means you can find: this is a field with great potential. For example, you can ask the candidates to write up a case for graduation, and then subject their manuscripts to numerous revisions and corrections. Through this experience the candidates acquire a healthy respect for the enormous difficulties of writing an acceptable paper for publication.

You may require the candidate to present a paper before the psychoanalytic society. The discussants should be the most senior members of that society (who may not have written a paper themselves for a long time). Their demanding expectations of what a scientific paper should include may be communicated by their exhaustive criticism of the candidate's presentation.

Alternatively, a committee made up of senior psychoanalysts may convey the same message. In some countries, this effect has been obtained by a secret vote by all members of the society as to whether a candidate's paper fulfills the criteria for admission to the psychoanalytic society. When significant political divisions within the society make young graduates automatically drift to the power group of their own training analysts, the qualifying scientific paper can become an excellent source of anxiety about the dangers connected with scientific work (Bruzzone et al., 1985).

10. Stress that it takes many years of clinical experience before one's understanding of psychoanalytic theory and technique, not to speak of applications of psychoanalysis to other fields, are profound and solid enough to justify the attempt to contribute to the science of psychoanalysis. Raise delicately but early the question, To what extent do candidates' attempts not only to present papers but to have them published reflect unresolved oedipal competitiveness or

narcissistic conflicts? If junior psychoanalysts publish papers, make sure that senior members of their society approve their manuscripts before they are submitted for publication. This custom should be common knowledge among the candidates; it may help reinforce their fear of publishing. Naturally, avoid stimulating candidates to put new, original ideas into writing. Writing should be a chore, an obligation—never a pleasure or an early source of pride that one contributed to the science of psychoanalysis while still a student (Britton, 1994).

11. Point out that psychoanalysis is understood and carried out properly only in places far away from one's own institute and preferably in a country whose language is unknown to the student. If the demands of the training are such that the students cannot spend an extended period of time in that distant, ideal land, they may become convinced that it is useless to attempt to develop psychoanalytic science in a place so far from where the true and only theory and technique are taught. And that conviction will last.

12. Discourage candidates from premature visits to other societies or other institutes and from participating in congresses, meetings, and analytic work at other institutes. This holds true, particularly, for those gatherings in your own city, region, or country, and complements the idealization of far-away places or of languages that your candidates don't know. Fortunately, some psychoanalytic societies and institutes have erected powerful walls against intrusion by foreign visitors—except those very occasional invaders who will be shot down in a well-prepared meeting—and in many parts of the world it would be difficult for a candidate to transfer from one institute to another, from one country to another, and even from one city to another without having to overcome multiple obstacles. This helps avoid potentially damaging comparisons, the awareness of psychoanalytic institutes' and societies' experiments with new educational methodologies, and the contamination by a spirit of change and innovation.

13. Always assign double the number of publications that one could reasonably expect students to absorb from one seminar to the next. Ask students to present summaries to their colleagues, test the extent to which they have read these papers in detail, and, as I mentioned before, include those works of Freud's that they have already read. The message can be strengthened by not assigning any paper that was published fewer than twenty years ago: this makes it clear that the really important contributions have already been made and that little is to be expected from recent or new developments in theory or technique, including, of course, any ideas that might be germinating in the minds of the students.

14. Make it a strict principle that candidates should never participate in a seminar given by their own training analyst. This is in contrast to the practice at some institutes where the decision to attend those seminars is open to joint exploration by analyst and analysand. In fact, make sure that candidates do not show up at meetings, panels, or any professional gatherings where the transference might be disturbed by objective information about their analyst's professional work, lest the anonymity desirable for analytic training be disturbed. Anonymity fosters unanalyzable idealization and healthy insecurity (see chapter 12).

15. Give prominence in reading lists to the works of the leading members of your own institute, ideally to be taught not by their authors but by the authors' students, former or present. Assign concordant articles that reinforce the views of local leaders, and include one or two dissident views only to show these views' weaknesses. Complement a focus on reference lists by assigning a scientific paper or case study as part of the requirements for progress, with a careful emphasis on the need to quote the locally preferred theoreticians in support of the observations of the student's paper.

16. Avoid exposing students to alternative psychoanalytic schools for as long as possible. In seminars for advanced students, briefly review particular papers that represent dissident or deviant approaches in the context of offering balance, and criticize them appropriately. Invite leaders with different viewpoints to brief seminars that may only exceptionally include students, graduates, and course instructors. The latter may participate to ensure that students witness the dismantling of the representative of the alien view. One-day seminars in which the views of a leading dissident are attacked respectfully but firmly may contribute to the reassurance that the local school knows best, that the student's mind can rest at peace, and that new ideas, though dangerous, can be robbed of their subversive potential.

17. Always ask the least experienced candidates to present cases to the more experienced candidates and faculty. It should never be the most experienced analyst who presents a case to a candidate's group. The uncertainties of the work and the inevitable mistakes that even senior analysts make will erase a sense of self-criticism, fear of reprimands, and the natural modesty of candidates who are starting their professional work. The conviction that graduates do much better work than candidates, that training analysts do much better work than graduates, and that older training analysts do much better work than younger ones, will add to the self-doubts of the candidates.

18. Make sure that some unusually critical or rebellious candidates who

threaten the atmosphere of harmony at seminars, challenge their senior instructors, or dare to talk publicly against training analysts in the presence of their analysands (and who are likely, of course, to report such conversations in their sessions) are gently kept back or pressured to resign. It is not too difficult to do this, for example, by long delays in approving their supervised analytic cases. One may also arrange meetings of their seminar leaders in which the problematic candidates are critically discussed. The information about these discussions should get back to the candidates in question only indirectly, through personal advisers or ombudsmen, who, in friendly ways, should convey the negative attitude that exists in the institute toward them. If a candidate receives sufficient information through third and fourth parties of what is said about him, it will eventually either change his attitude about the institute in the desired direction or will lead him to resign. Once a candidate has resigned or been asked to resign, do not mention his name again, and maintain a discreet silence about the whole affair. The message that something frightening and dangerous has occurred about which nobody wants to speak will have a powerful impact on the student body.

19. Briefly summarize the entire psychoanalytic theory and technique, referring to the highlights of Freud's thinking and providing students with an introductory history of psychoanalysis, stressing that their knowledge of all these areas will be deepened later. This is a recent method for dampening students' excitement about psychoanalytic training in an informal, preparatory year of classes. As many candidates will already have studied psychoanalytic theory at various levels, the process of dulling by repetition should begin at this introductory level. The sense of not knowing fully what will be taught and the impatience to explore these issues more deeply can be created in this way. When joined with a routinized simplification of basic concepts, this uncertainty will rob students of their excitement when, much later, they finally do explore the issues in detail. And, naturally, you may use this method to induce a loss of interest in any course taught at an introductory level, insinuating that the "real stuff" will be presented later.

20. Do not teach an up-to-date course on psychoanalytic technique. Concentrate on Freud's introductory papers on the psychoanalytic method and on his case studies: the Ratman, the Wolfman, and Dora. Little Hans will, of course, have already been covered in the comprehensive study of Freud's work, but now these papers may be read again to teach the general principles of psychoanalytic technique. If candidates acquire knowledge elsewhere about new developments and alternative approaches to the psychoanalytic process

(as, unfortunately, is almost unavoidable), their anxiety over their own lack of familiarity with the different approaches of say, ego psychology, the French schools, and the British schools will make them increasingly insecure about their work. This will dampen their confidence in their ability to contribute to the challenges that our present-day patient population presents to us. If, at the same time, the subtle message is conveyed that psychoanalytic work is really an art that will be mastered intuitively, and that growth and intuition will depend on the candidates' progress in their personal analysis and in supervision, anxiety may help inhibit candidates for a long period (Arlow, 1991).

21. Talk to the candidates as little as possible. In fact, the candidate should experience a natural continuity between being a patient in analysis and the relationship with her supervisor. The supervisor should listen carefully and silently to the candidate's presentation of work with her patients, offering an occasional comment illustrating what the candidate has done wrong. This should keep the candidate uncertain and humble. Her effort to construct, for herself, the mental frame that determines her supervisor's views will occupy her mind to the extent of significantly influencing her work with her patient. The candidate should feel that following her supervisor's advice without question and demonstrating to the supervisor that she has made the kind of interpretation that she thinks the supervisor would have made will absolve her from responsibility for severe mistakes in her work.

This development will prevent the process by which the candidate might otherwise integrate for herself a theory and a personal frame of technique that evolves and changes creatively as she tests her views in the treatment situation while respecting the patient's autonomous development. If supervisors never come together to discuss their educational approaches to supervision, and if a complete split is maintained between the faculty who teach psychoanalytic technique and the supervisors of control cases, chaos and confusion may bring about the candidates' awareness that it will take many years before they will master analytic skills sufficiently to dare to contribute creatively to them.

22. Report on the development of the candidates in analysis with you in order to increase paranoid fears. A certain level of paranoid fear, the counterpart of the idealization processes fostered by the training analysis, permeates most psychoanalytic institutes as a matter of course. Yet all social organizations struggle with such developments. Paranoid fear may contribute to discouraging candidates from independent work, courageous initiatives, and challenging inquiries.

The tradition of reporting training analysts, that is, of training analysts' informing the education committee about the readiness of their analysands to start classes or to take a first control case, and so on, has been the most paranoiagenic instrument invented as part of psychoanalytic education. It is regrettable that this instrument has now been eliminated and even declared unethical by most psychoanalytic institutes. Fortunately, the irrepressible tendency of some training analysts to indicate silently, by small gestures, what their true feelings are about various candidates is still being kept alive. This attitude may be fostered by the use of the system of "unhooked telephones," that is, the use of what candidates tell their training analysts about what other candidates have been saying about them to inspire retaliatory moves by these training analysts. At the least, fear of the consequences of a careless comment is a healthy support for paranoid developments (Dulchin and Segal, 1982a, 1982b; Lifschutz, 1976).

23. Do not give candidates full or adequate information about requirements for graduation, expectations, rules, regulations, and channels for redress of grievances. Do not inform candidates regularly about how they are progressing, how they are viewed by teachers and faculty at large. Let them know about their shortcomings or failures only in the indirect ways I have already described. Supervisors should not be outspoken or explicit with their supervisees, who will learn only indirectly from their advisers, the director of the institute, or by rumors how they are being evaluated. This may contribute powerfully to reinforcing paranoid attitudes. It is perfectly legitimate to refer all candidates' questions to the official brochure and to avoid periodic information gathering and information sharing. In some institutes, the director meets with the entire candidates' body; this tends to create an atmosphere of relaxation, in which autonomy is fostered and challenges to authority may occur. This should be avoided.

24. As senior leaders of the local psychoanalytic community, carefully monitor the messages you convey; they are extremely important. Manifest, outspoken indications of insecurity and fearfulness over scientific writing by the most senior and powerful training analysts may foster the candidates' healthy identification with them. An even more effective example may be represented by the old-fashioned but still-existent "convoy" system. A small number of senior training analysts are the most desirable analysts in their local group and may have so many candidates in personal analysis that they have no energy left to go to scientific meetings, let alone participate actively in the scientific work of the society. To protect the purity of the transference, they may never open their mouths in public, and the mutual friendships, alliances, and rivalries between

those candidates in analysis with one of the great masters feed into a stabilizing idealization and passivity. This model is highly effective in inhibiting candidates' independent and critical thinking.

25. Seek to maintain a relatively uniform student body in terms of the professional aspirations of your students. The true analyst should wish only to do psychoanalysis, to experience the freedom of working in his office with analytic patients. He should be averse to diluting analytic work by applying it to other aspects of his professional background, such as carrying out psychotherapeutic work with severely regressed patients, children, or psychotics, participating in academic pursuits outside the psychoanalytic setting, performing research, or assuming institutional leadership.

Major challenges to psychoanalytic theory and technique occur at the boundary of the professional field. Avoiding an investment in such boundary pursuits protects the purity of psychoanalytic work. It also avoids challenging and potentially subversive questions being raised regarding the limits and applications of psychoanalysis. Do not accept or train the maverick who wishes to learn psychoanalysis to apply it to another realm of professional endeavor, the philosopher interested in the boundaries between philosophical and psychoanalytic understanding, or the empirical researcher seeking to complement her neuropsychological background.

If such a protective selection of candidates has been carried out effectively, then you may tolerate a few "special students" interested in the intellectual aspects of psychoanalysis. But you must clearly keep them separate from the student body, limit their attendance at clinical seminars, and, in short, imply that a gulf exists between true analytic training and secondary enterprises. Do not give partial clinical training to academicians from other disciplines. These outsiders should always know that you disapprove of unauthorized clinical work and that they can never understand psychoanalysis fully if they are not in a full-fledged clinical training program.

26. Relegate all interdisciplinary scientific inquiry to the advanced stages of training, tucked into elective seminars in the last year of courses, which are taken only after the basic identity of the candidate can withstand the diluting and potentially corroding effects of the psychoanalytic approach to art, societal problems, philosophy, and research in the neurosciences. Avoid particularly bringing in studies of peripheral sciences at a point when psychoanalytic theory is just beginning to be explored, as, for example, when psychoanalytic drive theory needs to be assimilated without contamination or questioning from alternative models or schools of human motivation; or when relating psycho-

analytic technique to alternative psychotherapeutic methods; or, for example, when teaching the psychoanalytic theory of depression, introducing prematurely the relation between psychodynamics and the biological determinants of depression that might threaten an authentic psychoanalytic conviction.

27. Refer all problems involving teachers and students, seminars and supervision, and all conflicts between candidates and the faculty "back to the couch." Keep in mind that transference acting out is a major complication of psychoanalytic training and that there are always transference elements in students' dissatisfactions. A candidate's inordinate leaning toward asking challenging questions, doing imaginative thinking, or developing alternative formulations usually has profound transference roots and should be resolved in the personal analytic situation. This means also that the faculty must remain united, that teachers faced with challenges from individual students or from the student body at large must stick together. A united faculty provides a firm and stable structure against which the transference regression of the student body can be diagnosed and referred back to their individual psychoanalytic experiences.

28. Seek to inhibit the creativity of the faculty. A faculty whose creativity is inhibited is most likely to unconsciously reproduce the process in its relationship with students. All my principles and recommendations will be inadequate if the teaching faculty is imbued with a spirit of creativity of its own.

This is the major challenge for the training analysts' group: What can you do in a psychoanalytic society to inhibit the creativity of its members? Long experience has taught us that the hierarchical extension of the educational process into the social structure of the psychoanalytic society is easily achieved and can be most effective. Here, what is particularly helpful is the development of powerful barriers at each step of the candidate's progress, from institute graduate to associate member of the society to full member to training analyst to education committee member or to person in charge of a major, ongoing seminar. Make sure it is clear that allegiance to powerful political groups is more important for advancement than professional or scientific achievements. Make sure that the ways to proceed from one step to the next are uncertain and indefinite enough to keep a constant air of insecurity and paranoia in the society. Have frequent secret votes to determine progress at all levels, making it clear that such votes are influenced by the political processes in your group.

29. Above all, maintain discretion, secrecy, and uncertainty about what is required to become a training analyst: how these decisions are made; where and by whom; and what kind of feedback or mechanism for the redress of griev-

ances exists for anyone who is fearful of the traumatic implications of being considered and rejected as a training analyst. The more the body of training analysts keeps itself separate from the rest, but united in being the center of authority and prestige, the more the inhibitory effects of the selection process will influence the entire educational enterprise. This is your most reliable and effective tool for keeping not only candidates but the entire faculty and the entire society in line.

30. Keep in mind, when uncertain about dangerous developments that may challenge proved methods of inhibiting the creativity of candidates, that the main objective of psychoanalytic education is not to help students to acquire knowledge in order to develop new knowledge but to acquire knowledge to save well-tried formulas from dilution, distortion, deterioration, and misuse.

Always remember: Where there is a spark there may develop a fire, particularly when that spark appears in the middle of deadwood. Extinguish it before it is too late.

Part Five **Ideology, Morality, and the Political Process**

Chapter 15 The Temptations of Conventionality

My objective in this chapter is to explore from a psychoanalytic viewpoint the nature of the appeal of mass culture, particularly as it is communicated by the mass media. I focus on the relation between the structural characteristics of mass culture and the latent expectations and dispositions of its consumers. I shall be examining the regressive effects of group processes on the consumers of mass culture, as well as the striking correspondence between the conventional aspects of mass culture and the psychological characteristics of the latency years.

SOME CHARACTERISTICS OF MASS CULTURE

I return to Freud's definition of mass psychology because it contains ideas that are relevant to my thesis. As I mentioned in chapter 3, Freud (1921), in defining mass psychology, proposed "to isolate as the subject of inquiry the influencing of an individual by a large number of people simultaneously, people with whom he is connected by something, though otherwise they may in many respects be strangers to him" (p. 70, translation mine).

I am defining *mass culture* as those forms of cultural expression that appeal to individuals under conditions in which they are influenced by real or fantasied masses, that is, under conditions where mass psychology operates upon them. I am concerned less with the question of the "operators"—who or what manipulates mass culture (a question explored in detail by Horkheimer and Adorno [1971], Bourdieu [1979], and Brantlinger [1983], among others)—than with exploring common characteristics of mass culture and the basis of its appeal.

My definition of mass culture dovetails with its traditional definition in the American and European sociological literature of the 1940s and 1950s (Rosenberg and White, 1957; Brantlinger, 1983), when *mass culture* referred to industrialized, mass-produced products intended for mass consumption (Howe, 1948; MacDonald, 1953; Rosenberg, 1957). Previous discussions of mass culture focused on such questions as whether it is a product of contemporary, industrialized society that "packages" pseudoculture to satisfy the economic needs of the producers, cheapening the consumer's taste in the process; whether it is an instrument for social control, packaging gratifying, nondisturbing entertainment in order to implant the dominant ideology of the society; whether it is the consequence of the ascendancy of the poorly educated and nondiscriminating masses, who by their sheer numbers and economic power dilute both high culture and traditional folk art; or whether it reflects the changing sociological characteristics of modern urban society, which fosters "other-directedness" rather than "inner-directedness" (Riesman, 1950), or, in a more recent version, the characteristics of a "culture of narcissism" (Lasch, 1978).

My focus is primarily on the entertainment offered by the press, radio, movies, and television, the content of which is intended for the broadest segments of the population. Although entertainment is not the only form of mass culture, it is universally recognized as its dominant form (Rosenberg and White, 1957; Horkheimer and Adorno, 1971). Entertainment reveals most clearly the psychological characteristics of all mass culture.

The aspect of *simultaneity of communication,* common to these forms of entertainment, is important. I refer here to both actual and fantasied simultaneity. Freud's statement quoted above underlines simultaneity as a key condition of mass psychology. Although a gathering of people as passive spectators in a theater or cinema places the individual in an actual, temporary crowd, entertainment by the press, radio, and television provides simultaneity without physical contact. These media create by implication an invisible crowd in the fantasies of each of the isolated spectators sitting in their respective homes. The taped laughter of television comedies not only punctuates the jokes, it provides an illusory crowd of spectators that contributes to an illusory sense of community (Moscovici, 1981). This feeling is reinforced when one watches television in a foreign country in a foreign language one understands—an experience that may induce, at first, a strange sense of loneliness, as though one were an intruder into a community to which one does not belong.

Reading the news in a newspaper or watching it on television also creates the illusion of being a member of a crowd; it focuses on the communication by a central figure of what is important and how one should view it, and brings us to another aspect of mass culture: pleasure to be had from passively receiving what is exciting and important without intellectual demands being made on one. Newspapers have to be read "fresh": they lose their appeal once the implicit mass of fellow readers has finished with them. And although they inform rather than entertain, any intellectual demand they make on the reader reduces their appeal. The idea that an authority is addressing a multitude of passive, implicitly equal, uninformed readers heightens the mass appeal of the communication.

In soap operas, situation comedies, films geared to adolescents or the family, war movies, thrillers, and soft porn (the level or explicitness of the pornography is relatively unimportant; its characteristics remain the same), the characters typically presented are oversimplified: they are all good or all bad, without internal complexities, immersed in their immediate reality, with obvious motivations in their interpersonal behavior. All of this permits the spectator, who has seen similar shows, to predict their actions. In fact, to be watching the developments among people on the screen or in the script whom one seems to know completely, whose motives and moves one can predict, gives a feeling of pleasure and power, of superiority and amusement: here we find a narcissistic dimension of self-aggrandizement in the viewer.

Drama is introduced by danger, which comes to the good characters through the obvious evil, criminality, violence, or dishonesty of one or several characters. This adds a paranoid dimension to the viewer's emotional involvement with the content. Villains eventually develop in one of two directions: they either become sympathetic as their motivation becomes clear and are eventually received back into the community or else, incurably evil, they are finally punished, leaving the spectator feeling morally satisfied.

Unhappiness appears in dramatic but not disturbing forms: joy, sorrow, rage, and fear are all portrayed so as to be reassuring. Expression dominates over content, and sentimentality over sentiments. Sentimentality is often conveyed by means of an implicit or explicit nostalgia for the past, for familiar forms of happiness, with a particular emphasis on universally shared symbols of innocence, trust, and tenderness that are associated with the security of early childhood (or a happy, safe, and contented old age). Nostalgia, the bittersweet longing for a lost or longed-for state of happiness, reunion, or fulfillment, evokes an idealized object of desire while implicitly confirming the possibility of its recovery.

In war movies, although some of the heroes must die, a sufficient number of centrally important characters survive so that the spectator can happily identify with a survivor. The enemy is always evil, except in movies made after the war, when an actual historical change has resulted in a formerly hostile country's becoming an ally. In this situation, there will be wise and knowledgeable members of the enemy camp who agree that war is basically bad and that it should be replaced by universal love and friendship. In the German film *Das Boot,* for example, a huge popular success in many of the former Allied countries, the audience's identification with a Nazi submarine crew is facilitated by the submarine commander's obvious loathing of the Nazi leadership.

Thrillers and films dealing with psychopathic killers are of particular interest to the study of mass culture in that the excitement of danger, the terror of the victims, the excitement of the pursuit of the criminal, and the implicit identification with the hero who finally destroys him all gratify aggressive impulses in the reader or viewer. The barely disguised gratification in fantasy of aggressive impulses as part of mass culture is central to its appeal. This is also true of war movies, but usually without the intense excitement of the identification with a particular hunter.

If violence can be enjoyed vicariously but fully under these circumstances, the same is only partially true for sex. The dissociation of erotism from tenderness is sharp and consistent in mass culture and another of its central characteristics. Little direct reference is made to the erotic aspects of love. Explicit sex, if depicted, typically occurs between individuals who have no emotional relationship or as an expression of aggression (such as rape or a group-tolerated sexually rebellious activity against conventional mores). The protagonists may indulge in sexual behavior with other characters but not with the person to whom they have a romantic link. Or the sexual aspects of the relationship between two tender lovers are presented in a veiled and romanticized style. For example, in *The Breakfast Club,* a highly popular movie with its target adolescent audience, the details of lovemaking are limited to crude sexual encounters: when two of the protagonists fall in love, the sexual details of their relationship are totally eliminated.

This basic characteristic of sexual portrayal in movies has not been affected by the apparent relaxation of film censorship. By the same token, pornographic films are usually empty depictions of mechanical sex between people who have an almost robotlike quality. The most striking dissociation of erotism from tenderness comes in connection with polymorphous perverse sexuality: this aspect of sexuality is almost entirely restricted to pornography, and totally absent in mass entertainment even in the exceptional instances wherein the protagonists are shown in bed together.

When the cinematic and television entertainment I am describing deals with so-called philosophical questions, the ideas discussed are trivial: clichés and banality predominate. The complexities of life and of people are denied. Conventional assumptions predominate over individual thinking. These entertainments offer love and compassion for the underdog, consolation for the person who loses a competition, and applause for the one who triumphs after a long and difficult effort; justice usually prevails. The world is a safe and simple place, or, at least, there are safe havens for everyone in it.

Similar characteristics are found in the news media. The perpetual focus on crime gratifies our excitement with dissociated aggression and violence, including, of course, our titillated horror at sex crimes. The subtly self-righteous, moralistic tone of oversimplified reports on world affairs is less self-evident but nonetheless present. News reporters implicitly divide the world into good and bad people, countries, and events. The stories reflect a latent assumption that the commentator's and the mass audience's views are morally superior.

There is, in addition, an aspect of news presentation of particular interest: within the general flatness of the information conveyed, we find a tendency for the program to shift between the trivial (for example, a slightly ironic description of an event that is strange, incomprehensible, amusing, or entertaining) and the dangerous (the report of something close to home that runs counter to the value system the audience is assumed to share, a deed that would require urgent corrective action—a local crime, say).

Here we find again the stimulation of both a narcissistic dimension in the receiver (our amused superiority) and a paranoid one (our justified suspicion, indignation, and revenge). The contents of what evokes fear, suspicion, and indignation, on the one hand, with what seems trivial, entertaining, and reassuring, on the other, vary quickly. The application of a simplistic morality to political and social matters, the philosophy of the situation comedy, one might say, applied to the social scene, takes the form of ideological clichés: if people of good will work together, they will solve any problem; or further study of a particular matter will make it possible for us to figure out the "right" way to view it.

If we shift from the content communicated in mass culture to its forms of artistic expression, a number of related phenomena can be detected. There is a characteristic style in the presentation. Decor, background, and objects of art are usually mass-produced articles that appeal to conventional tastes: they show a preference for either bright colors to indicate dramatic atmosphere or a uniformly dull brown for homely places, sentimentality in the art objects and, particularly, in the background music, and the prevalence of symbols evocative of carefree happiness, innocence, and childhood. Paintings are sentimental landscapes or tragicomic clowns or trivialized imitations of yesteryear's dominant artistic expressions. The illustrations on mass-produced Christmas cards are a typical expression of this style.

Taken together, the characteristics I have enumerated also define kitsch: they are appealing, comfortable, reassuring, sentimental, and overloaded expressions of a culturally dominant style that is charged with conventional symbols of wealth, happiness, romance, or childhood (Greenberg, 1946; Adorno, 1954; Moles, 1971; Deschner, 1980; Friedlander, 1984).

MASS CULTURE AND THE LATENCY CHILD

From a psychoanalytic viewpoint, the picture of mass culture that emerges is of a world that strikingly resembles the internal world of the child of latency age. In the psychoanalytic theory of child development, "latency" refers to the developmental period that begins with the consolidation of the oedipal superego and ends with the psychodynamic reorganization at the initiation of puberty. It roughly corresponds to the years between ages 5 and 10.

A first major aspect of the child of latency age is the strictness, rigidity, and overdependency on simplified conventional notions of morality of his or her superego functioning. The latency child's system of morality affirms the trusted parental authority and is characterized by an unambiguous separation of good from bad (deeds as well as people), the transformation of sadism into (superego-integrated) righteous indignation, the enjoyment of morally justified aggression, the adaptation to a social environment of peers that provides the first experience of firm, simple, stable group norms (including norms of acceptable entertainment), and the unequivocal dissociation of (denigrated) anal sexuality from tender love (for the oedipal parents). It is the reassuring morality of a well-cared-for yet misbehaving child's reconciliation with his or her temporarily angry parents before bedtime. In general terms, we have a morality of brief, time-limited sequences of misbehavior, guilt, punishment, and forgiveness. The child is "in the know," however, regarding genital sexuality and its eventual though distant fulfillment in the future.

At the same time, the latency child also harbors wishful fantasies of independence and power, along with the illusion of being independent of the parents. He or she is interested in adventure stories, with heroes and ideals that provide identification models for the future and that also gratify urges for control of the instinctual world through real and fantasied control of the social environment; the latency child is finding substitute gratifications for aggressive and sexual assertion. "Watching" adult life in reality and through cultural products is a new achievement. Illusions of independence and power are gratified by watching, with a sense of superiority, the predictable life of the "funny" grownups, while, simultaneously, fantasies of narcissistic reconfirmation are enacted by identification with supermen or superwomen, daring heroes who destroy dangerous monsters—all this within the stability of a loving and safe home. Berman's (1987) analysis of the psychology of James Bond and its correspondence to the latency conflicts of Ian Fleming provides an illustration of a psychoanalytic approach to the structure of commercial thrillers. To be entertained by striking images and displays of color, form, and motion; to be excited by violence without being threatened by it; and to feel sexual excitement without being threatened by the potential connection between erotism and love are all characteristic of the latency child's internal world.

These characteristics stem from both ego (narcissistic, erotic, and aggressive impulses framed in a latency child's perspective of ego-syntonic fantasies and wishes) and superego (a latency child's unconscious morality, which respects oedipal prohibitions and dissociates sex from tenderness). In fact, the latency child as spectator of mass entertainment is probably the prototype of the gratified consumer of mass culture.

In this situation, the consumer is watching the entertainment in harmony with his or her superego, feeling loved by his or her parents, and accepting (unconsciously) the oedipal prohibitions while indulging in fantasy the total gratification of dependency needs and enjoying an illusional sense of equality, regardless of sexual and generational differences, with his or her fellow consumers. The latency child's oral-dependent needs are gratified directly, and other sexual and aggressive needs are gratified by projection onto the spectacle and the socially sanctioned and encouraged identification with the actors. His or her psychological needs correspond to the characteristics of mass entertainment itself, the perfectly harmonious quality of mass culture that I have described.

For the latency child, exciting stories or adventures that fit these general characteristics are not simply entertainment. They are socially sanctioned, culturally transmitted confirmations and expansions of the child's universe. These experiences are major events that reconfirm superego structure, provide cognitive learning experiences, and consolidate ego skills and controls over drive derivatives (Sarnoff, 1976; Shapiro and Perry, 1976). Social conventions expand the field of strictly intrafamilial conventions; they facilitate the latency child's integration in the broader world of peers and school. For an adult, the rigid adherence to social and cultural mores that constitute the normal world of latency reflect conventionality. To the extent that adults consume mass culture, they become conventional. The question thus arises of why conventionality— the excessive adaptation to social, cultural, and aesthetic norms—is a central aspect of mass culture, and why it is attractive to its consumers.

How can we explain the consistent presence of latency age superego and ego features in mass culture? Why does it gratify, as it clearly does, most adults? Earlier psychoanalytic approaches to mass culture have focused on its conventional aspects and on personality characteristics fostering conventionality (Adorno et al., 1950). It was the conventional aspect of mass psychology that required explaining, and, secondarily, the mechanisms of the exploitation and induction of that conventional mass psychology by the "ruling classes" through the mass production of consumer goods. Before I discuss the relation between mass culture's conventionality and latency child psychology, let me review these theories briefly.

PSYCHOANALYTIC THEORIES
OF CONVENTIONALITY

As discussed in chapter 5, Adorno and colleagues (1950) considered conventionality to be a significant part of the authoritarian personality; it reflects an individual's disposition to excessive adherence to middle-class values, a consequence of instability in his own value system. Conventionality is characterized by the rigidity with which individuals adhere to popular values and with which they respond to external social pressure. Kitsch, as many theorists have pointed out, typically belongs to the middle class; and even when created for the culturally disadvantaged, kitsch conveys an idealized and sentimentalized version of middle-class values (Adorno, 1954). This is also true of "high-class kitsch" geared to the luxury trade (Greenberg, 1946). The underlying theory behind these definitions was that individuals with authoritarian personalities are overly sensitive to external reinforcement of their internal, excessively strict superego demands, and that conventionality is related to excessive submission to authority as well as to an identification with "authoritarian" aggression (aggression carried out by an authority in unfair ways that show excessive or "nonfunctional" use of power and that are rationalized or justified in the very process of abuse). The authoritarian personality would represent a prototype of identification with the aggressor, first in these personalities' developing a sadistic, strict superego, and then in identifying themselves with their own sadistic superego. Although I agree with Adorno's linkage of conventionality and over-identification with a sadistic, infantile superego, he misses the contributions to conventionality of regressive group pressures: the mass-psychology aspect of conventionality.

The views of Adorno and colleagues follow Reich's (1962 [1935]) efforts to integrate psychoanalytic thinking with Marxist theory and to explain the repressive nature of attitudes toward sexuality in Western society and in Soviet Russia. Generalizing from his understanding of German fascism, Reich proposed that the capitalist system had transformed the personality structure of all individuals by exerting authoritarian power through the paternalistic family. Where Freud thought that the repression of sexuality was the price paid for cultural evolution, Reich thought that the repression of sexuality, particularly of genital sexuality, represented the effect of a pathological superego, which in turn resulted from the social structure of capitalism. He traced a socially generalized submission to conventional mores to this same cause: conventionality was based on excessive repression of genital sexuality.

In contrast to Reich, Marcuse (1955) felt that it was not genital sexuality that was repressed by the capitalist system but pregenital polymorphous infantile sexuality. Marcuse thought that this repression aimed at restricting sexual functions to the genital so that people's unsatisfied broader erotism could be used in the service of social production. Marcuse suggested that it was the surplus repression of pregenital sexuality—a socially unnecessary repression—that constituted the main problem with the capitalist system.

In fact, however, Marcuse noted an increasing tolerance of sexuality in the Western world, particularly the United States. He therefore coined the term "repressive desublimation" to refer to what he called a pseudosexual freedom, which encouraged the individual in capitalist society to consume unnecessary goods and distracted him from the repressive conditions of his existence. In thus presenting sex as a capitalist lure for consumption that erotized advertising and created artificial consumer needs and demands, Marcuse pointed to the repressive and proselytizing aspects of mass culture, a social and economic pressure toward mindless conventional consumption.

A similar view is eloquently articulated in Horkheimer and Adorno's *Dialektik der Aufklärung* (Dialectic of enlightenment [1971]), where what they consider the degradation of culture in the hands of the modern entertainment industry is presented as a typical example of the attempt to destroy the individual's capacity for independent reasoning and making independent value judgments. Culture produced for and oriented toward the masses, they suggest, reflects how capitalist society both commercializes art and uses this commercialization to reduce the consumer's capacity to resist mass-produced, degraded art, objects, and entertainment.

The question of excessive conformity with the established social order has engaged many Marxist and neomarxist theoreticians in Western Europe since the early 1930s. It was a major focus of the Frankfurt school, of which Adorno, Horkheimer, Marcuse, and Habermas were leading theoreticians. The ascent of fascism in Western Europe and the evolution of Soviet Russia into a totalitarian state caused these theoreticians to consider the extent to which the proletariat was developing a "false consciousness." The working class, in fact, all social classes, seemed to become easy prey to the ideologies of the authoritarian regimes of the extreme Right and Left. Western European Marxists wished to develop their theory that common belief systems were created by ruling classes to ensure their hegemony over society.

Gramsci (1959) first developed the notion that hegemony was a system of power (in this case, of the capitalist class) used to obtain a level of consent from the masses via cultural institutions and the development of a corresponding ideology. Several other Marxist writers developed this line of reasoning over the years, and Althusser (1976) used Freud's concept of the unconscious to construct a new theory of ideology. Ideology, for Althusser, was an unconsciously determined system of illusory representations of reality. This system derived from the internalization of the dominant illusion that a social class harbored about the conditions of its own existence. The illusion was achieved by the internalization of the "paternal law" as part of the internalization of the oedipal superego.

In a related theoretical development, Habermas (1971, 1973) analyzed ideology as motivated by a false consciousness of social class and outlined the resolution of this false consciousness by means of a "critical theory" that would provide self-reflective enlightenment together with social emancipation. Habermas drew a parallel between the analysis of ideologies and the psycho-analytic situation, in which the patient also starts treatment with a "false consciousness" and is helped by the analyst to gain, by means of self-reflection and honest interaction with the analyst, an enlightenment aimed at freeing him or her from repression and neurosis.

Although these Marxist and neomarxist writers, in part using psychoanalytic concepts, have rightly focused on the characteristics of conventionality and the superego-mediated receptivity of individuals to the conventional aspects of mass culture, their linkage of class-determined ideology to the characteristics of mass culture is questionable. They had originally assigned these attributes of mass culture to capitalism, but they were forced to diagnose similar trends in communist cultures as well, which led to their concept of "false consciousness" (no longer attributed exclusively to the capitalist system). But in so doing they missed the historical continuity of conventionality and, particularly, kitsch, and the surprising universality of the appeal of mass culture across radically different cultures. (We see this in the appeal of Western mass culture to the youth and young adults of China, India, and South America.)

Marxist and neomarxist writers also failed to analyze the common structural properties of mass cultures that reflect opposed ideologies. Thus, for example, television soap operas in East Berlin during the communist dictatorship had the same mass-culture characteristics as those of the West. The villains differed; they corresponded to conventional communist rather than capitalist categories of good and evil. But the battle of good and evil remained the same. It is precisely the *structure* of mass culture, the structure of its conventionality, that is missed when the focus is exclusively on the motivation of the producers or operators.

Another psychoanalytic approach to mass culture focuses on the absence—in contrast to hypertrophy—of normal superego functions. Mitscherlich (1963) pointed to the cultural consequences of the absence of the father as a principle of organization at the social and familial level. He described the rejection of the father in contemporary society as part of the rejection of traditional cultural values and the replacement of such values by overdependency on immediate social influences. He also noted the intoxicating effects of mass production, with its promise of immediate gratification of needs, and a consequent fostering of a psychology of demand for immediate gratification and the lack of a sense of individual responsibility. Mitscherlich described the new "mass person" as a classless individual. He stressed the combination of the real absence of the father in the contemporary family as a consequence of the organization of work with the loss of individual functions of the father in large institutions. The primary absence of the father, whose work functions are incomprehensible, is worsened by the secondary absence of the father in massive group experiences under the effects of the immediate gratification of mass consumption and the breakdown of taboos in society at large that leads to a loss of the capacity for full sexual gratification because of the concomitant dissociation of "immediate" sexual gratification from its link with emotional intimacy. Anonymous work, Mitscherlich stated, is complemented by anonymous mass entertainment that permits the projection of internal aggression onto external mass events.

In the United States, Lasch (1977, 1978) concluded that the breakdown of the family as a moral guidance system, the avoidance of conflicts through compromise, and the accentuation of instinctual gratification all corrode the development of mature superego functions in the child. In short, for Mitscherlich and Lasch it is the failure of normal superego development, rather than the development of an excessively harsh superego, that characterizes the superego pathology that facilitates the submission to mass culture.

For the psychoanalyst interested in the study of conventionality, the individual differences in adherence to conventional values would seem to be as important as the social determinants. As I mentioned in chapter 2, Green (1969) suggests that a relation exists between the developmental level of idealization and the type of ideological commitment one makes. These levels of idealization range from earliest narcissistic omnipotence through the intermediary stages of idealization of parental objects and the final consolidation of the ego ideal. The nature or quality of the commitment to ideologies, Green suggests, is determined by the extent to which the ideologies reflect the projection of an omnipotent self or the externalization of a mature ego ideal.

In agreement with Green, I suggested that the incapacity to commit oneself to value systems beyond self-serving needs usually reflects severe narcissistic pathology. The commitment to an ideology that includes sadistic demands for perfection and tolerates primitive aggression or value judgments of a conventional naïveté indicates an immature ego ideal and the lack of integration of a mature superego. Accordingly, to identify with a messianic ideology and to accept social clichés and trivialities is commensurate with narcissistic and borderline pathology. This contrasts with the identification with more differentiated, open-ended, nontotalistic ideologies that respect individual differences, autonomy, and privacy and tolerate sexuality while rejecting collusion with the expression of primitive aggression, all of which reflect characteristics of the value system of the mature ego ideal. An ideology that respects individual differences and the complexity of human relationships and that leaves room for a mature attitude toward sexuality will appeal to those with a more evolved ego ideal.

In short, Adorno, Green, and I agree that ego and superego aspects of the personality predispose an individual to depend excessively on conventional values and attitudes. To say that the specific content of what is conventional is influenced by social, political, and economic factors is reasonable: but the universality of the structure of conventionality in mass culture and its appeal to the masses still requires explanation.

PSYCHOANALYTIC THEORY OF LARGE-GROUP PROCESSES

Granted that some individuals are more prone than others to adopt conventional values, and granted that powerful social and economic factors influence the characteristics of mass culture—including the culturally and historically determined predominance of a certain artistic style or "language"—we are still left with the puzzling question: Why are adults so prone to accept cultural artifacts, entertainment, and news that have qualities characteristic of the emotional developmental level of a latency-age child? A specific regression is involved in this process, a regression linked to the activation of group processes in the transmission of mass culture.

We have seen that Freud (1921) first described the regression in superego functions in certain mass gatherings. He suggested that the projection of the ego ideal onto the idealized leader eliminates individual moral constraints as well as the higher functions of self-criticism and responsibility that are mediated by the superego.

Turquet (1975) described how only "commonsense" trivialities permit a temporary unification of the large group, the emergence of a leader whose soothing banalities are eagerly accepted by most group members in an effort to calm the group. Those individuals who resist this banal, cliché-ridden atmosphere and try to maintain a semblance of individuality are the ones most attacked. It is as though the members of the large group envied people who kept their sanity and individuality. I described in chapter 1 how, at the same time, efforts at homogenization are prevalent, and any simplistic generalization or ideology that permeates the group can easily be adopted and transformed into an experience of absolute truth. In contrast to the simple rationalization of the violence that permeates the mob, however, in the large group a vulgar or commonsense philosophy functions as a calming, reassuring doctrine that reduces all thinking to cliché. Individuals with marked narcissistic features may provide the soothing leadership that the unstructured large group desires in order to escape from its paranoid atmosphere and give it a narcissistic quality of self-satisfaction.

Under these conditions, there is a projection of superego functions on the whole group, a projection that shows characteristics of a simplistic, conventional morality (Kernberg, 1980a, 1980c). In light of the present analysis, I propose that the temporary loss of an individual sense of identity in the large group carries with it the temporary loss of the higher level of autonomous, abstract, and individualized superego functions as well, while a regression to the functioning of the latency child superego occurs, as well as the projection of this latency superego onto the group at large.

Anzieu (1981), building on Bion (1961) and Turquet, studied the nature of evolving common illusions in groups and described some common features of the ad hoc ideologies that emerge under regressive conditions in both small and large groups. He suggested that under conditions of regression in the unstructured group, the relationship of individuals to the group as a whole acquires characteristics of fusion of their individual instinctual needs with a fantastic conception of the group as a primitive ego ideal equated to an all-gratifying primary object, the mother of the earliest stages of development.

As I mentioned in chapter 1, Chasseguet-Smirgel (1975), expanding on Anzieu's observations, suggested that under such conditions, groups (both small and large) tend to select leaders who represent not the paternal aspects of the prohibitive superego but a pseudopaternal "promoter of illusions," who provides the group with an ideology that confirms the narcissistic aspirations of fusion of the individual with the group as a primitive ego ideal, the all-powerful and all-gratifying preoedipal mother.

The psychoanalytic studies of group processes thus point to mechanisms of immediate regression of individuals in mobs and unstructured large and small groups, and explain why groups are characterized by superego regression, narcissistic orientation, paranoid developments, and a general pressure to conform. But not all regressive group formation occurs under conditions of purposefully designed unstructuredness (such as in group-dynamics groups or group-relations conferences) or of involuntary breakdown of a group's ordinary work structure (such as in organizations in crisis, when task leaders fail or are unavailable) or of spontaneous crowd formation. Group formation can also be prompted by the pleasure of the regressive experience of being part of a group process, the pleasure of the regressive fusion with others that derives from the generalized identification processes in a crowd. I am referring here to what Canetti (1960) called the feast crowd. His description of feast crowds captures my meaning:

> There is abundance in a limited space, and everyone near can partake of it. There is more of everything than everyone together can consume and, in order to consume it, more and more people come streaming in. As long as there is anything there they partake of it, and it looks as though there would be no end to it. There's an abundance of women for the men, and an abundance of men for the women. Nothing and no one threatens and there is nothing to flee from; for the time being, life and pleasure are secure. Many prohibitions and distinctions are waived, and unaccustomed advances are not only permitted but smiled on. For the individual the atmosphere is one of loosening, not discharge. There is no common identical goal which people have to try and attain together. The feast *is* the goal and they are there. (p. 62)

Here the socially sanctioned gratification of instinctual needs, their legitimate fulfillment, well deserved and unthreatened by malevolent authorities, brings us back to the psychological conditions of the latency child.

The striking correspondence between latency psychology and mass culture can therefore be reformulated. The appeal of mass culture consists in the facilitation of a group regression induced by mass entertainment that is structured to appeal to the level of latency: reality and fantasy are clearly differentiated; instinctual wishes that can be gratified directly are differentiated from those that can be gratified only in fantasy or by proxy. The oedipal prohibitions are in place, reflected by the dissociation of emotional commitment from genital erotism; genital strivings, except for direct gratification of voyeuristic needs, are gratified only by proxy, and preoedipal polymorphous perverse sexuality is either suppressed or tolerated only in a highly mechanical, depersonalized, or ritualistic fashion. Within the regressed group atmosphere of mass culture, superego functioning has regressed to a latency-phase level; it is weakened because personal responsibility is suspended or diluted when superego functions are projected onto the group (the implicit group sanctioning of the spectacle in which the individual participates as a group member: Freud's basic mechanism of the projection of the ego ideal in mass psychology). Individual thinking, decision making, value judgments, and discriminating functions are markedly reduced, together with higher levels of superego and ego functioning. The social sanctioning of mass culture and the corresponding group regression that reflects mass psychology represent the combined approval from parental authority and peer groups that provides security to the latency child. A conventionality of values and interests confirms these sanctions and approvals and ensures personal safety and security. Kitsch, with its idealized and sentimentalized activation of nostalgia, gratifies dependency longings, while the identification with the characters or the heroes confirms autonomy and power by proxy. Dependency and independence, instinctual gratification and autonomy, moral justification, and longings for peace with oneself are thus ensured in an illusion that because it is socially shared seems real.

MASS ENTERTAINMENT, GROUP REGRESSION, AND LEADERSHIP

We now have the elements for a developmental schema of regressions in groups, with particular reference to mass culture and the nature of the leadership enacted within it by the anchor person, host, commentator, or columnist. I describe two levels of regression: the first, milder level is typical of mass entertainment; the second is more severe.

The first level of regression occurs when people gather temporarily into crowds at celebrations or the theater or when they are part of an invisible temporary crowd that is created by simultaneous exposure to mass media (press, radio, and particularly, television) of individuals who are actually isolated in their homes.

At this level the threat of losing personal identity that is a feature of unstructured large groups is compensated for by the common, shared purpose. The unconscious identification with the other members of the crowd not only compensates for the temporary loss of personal identity but imparts a sense of power, importance, and security. As long as everybody else is present, the individual is doing the right thing (Canetti, 1960). Because superego functions are projected onto the large group under conditions of group regression, and because of the need to counteract the uncertainty that initially emerges in all regressive group processes, the individual becomes dependent on his fantasies regarding everyone else's opinion of the quality of the cultural offering.

When large-group leadership emerges under such circumstances, there is heightened respect for the leader as an authority and an increased willingness to accept his judgment, which is customarily expressed in simple generalizations. A benign father figure—even a firm but fair one—will strengthen the suggestive effects of conventional truth, and mild swings in either a paranoid or a narcissistic direction by such a leader will intensify the experience of group cohesion, of power and elation within the group (Kernberg, 1980a). Television anchors and newspaper columnists intuitively fulfill this function. The self-indulgent, self-satisfied, flattering attitude of the narcissistic person will produce a sense of sentimental and gratified well-being, while the mildly persecutory attitude of the leader who attacks immorality or whatever flies in the face of conventional standards will arouse righteous indignation in the group members that, in helping them identify with the leader, also strengthens their self-esteem.

At this first level of regression there occurs a generally shared projection of the oedipal superego, but the individuals still preserve an integrated self-concept and the related, integrated, realistic object representations that jointly constitute ego identity. The preservation of ego identity is ensured by a partial or time-limited activation of group processes in the context of social conditions or structures that allow the individual to maintain ordinary status and role conditions in life outside the group.

In contrast, at the second, deeper level of regression the integrated concept of the self and the integrated concept of others are threatened by the loss of ordinary role-status conditions and by the simultaneous presence of many people who reproduce the multiplicity of internalized part-object relations at a primitive level of ego development. This second level of regression occurs in large unstructured groups. It can emerge under conditions of breakdown of ordinary structure in large organizations or in the temporary formations of mobs under conditions of social tension and unrest, a "power vacuum" in a previously well-organized social structure. A suspension of ordinary social roles, the presence of many people in a totally unstructured relationship, and the inability to escape from such a frightening social condition can be induced experimentally in small- and large-group situations like those studied by Bion, Turquet, and Anzieu. But a similar regression also occurs in ordinary social organizations when the work structure breaks down, when a failure of functional leadership produces immediate regression in all task systems, and when social upheaval, external threats, the disorganization of ordinary protective social structures or extreme social isolation by a social subgroup produce the conditions these authors describe (Kernberg, 1980b).

Here, the projection of the integrated oedipal superego fails because of the lack of an integrated social structure or the loss of functional leadership on whom to project it. A regression into the preoedipal precursors of the superego and efforts at their massive projection parallels the regression into preoedipal constituents of ego formation. The regressive dependency and fight-flight groups described by Bion overshadow by far the pairing group and the remnants of oedipal sexuality; now the search is for the primitive ego-ideal leader who reflects preoedipal parental images of a wholly giving and gratifying kind. In the last resort, the leader is the pseudopaternal promoter of illusions who represents the all-powerful and all-gratifying preoedipal mother described by Anzieu and Chasseguet-Smirgel.

The mass rally of the Nazi party at Nuremberg depicted in the classic propaganda film *Triumph of the Will* illustrates these characteristics of group regression. Hitler is presented as a deity who descends from heaven and gives meaning to the life of the congregated masses. Under such conditions, the group illusion of total gratification (by the primary object represented by the leader) can be enacted as long as the minimal requirements for the earliest social-group formation (of latency) are met. The latency child's outlook on life and morality thus provide the unconscious preconditions (an unconscious "imprimatur") for an almost hypomanic, thoughtless, and irresponsible merger with the mass gathering.

The other possibility is that under conditions of social upheaval, turmoil, or stress—and in the presence of a powerful paranoid leader—the group will shift to the opposite extreme and endorse a primitive, powerful, and sadistic leader who will assure the group that by identifying collectively with the threatening primitive aggression he incorporates, they will make themselves safe from persecution by becoming persecutors themselves.

In other words, at this second level of regression, group processes activate the search for primitive narcissistic or paranoid leaders, depending on the extent to which external circumstances impose actual threats or frustration upon the group and thus reinforce the real threat of violence and the need to defend against it by projecting it outward. Under conditions of relative absence of such social threats and with the possibility of realistic gratification of primitive needs within a tolerant and flexible social environment, primitive narcissistic leadership may prevail. In any case, the swing of group emotions and leadership to either a paranoid or a narcissistic polarity of group orientation is extreme. One solution to a group's uncertain oscillation between narcissistic and paranoid orientations may be to combine primitive leadership of an extremely narcissistic and paranoid kind, which, in condensing primitive narcissism and aggression, reproduces the psychopathology of what I have called malignant narcissism.

When narcissistic group formation prevails, diffuse polymorphous erotism may be idealized and sadistic aspects of sexual interactions denied and projected; with paranoid group formations, sadistic sexual behavior may become ego-syntonic and rationalized, as occurred, for example, in Jim Jones's religious cult. In large-group formations and political masses, violent destructiveness and murder can occur at this level of regression.

What is the relation between the first and second level of regression? In the large group, narcissistic regression and leadership defend the group against a basic paranoid disposition. Are mass culture and mass entertainment "innocent" protections against more severe regressive potentials in group formation? Or is there a continuum of group regression that makes mass culture a dangerous springboard for potential further regression? The potential relation between the regressive group processes involved in "innocent" mass culture, on the one hand, and in severely regressive, paranoid mass movements, on the other—a potential relationship reflected in the commonality of many of their underlying processes—raises the question of whether mass media serve potentially dangerous or protective functions.

Horkheimer and Adorno (1971) and Anders (1956, 1980) suggested that mass culture is a malignant process leading to infantilization and the control of the masses by capitalist or communist elites. On the other hand, Brantlinger (1983) considers mass culture a small price to pay for the gratification of regressive group processes at a relatively innocuous level—a small price in return for the availability of information, artistic communication, and entertainment to large segments of the population. Moscovici (1981), paraphrasing Engels, states that "communication is the Valium of the people." The narcissistic world of the soap opera and the paranoid scenario of the thriller can be considered regressions in the service of the ego that are a far cry from the second-level, severely narcissistic and paranoid regressions in group processes and leadership under turbulent social and political circumstances.

It seems likely that the level of group regression codetermines, together with the level of individual psychopathology, the level of regression of an individual's commitment to any group-sponsored ideology. The mildly regressive group ideology fostered by ordinary mass media supports the most trivial and conventional manifestation of it, such as, for example, lip service to Marxism in communist societies, or to Catholicism in Latin American countries. These same ideologies at a less conventional and trivial level and as part of the highly differentiated value systems of autonomous individuals may be expressed in strong, complex personal ideological commitments that have a quality of independence, ethical depth, and firmness of conviction and yet openness to specific individual circumstances. At the other extreme, these same ideologies may regress into primitive, sadistic, and psychopathic forms, such as the blending of terrorism and ordinary criminality in some Marxist groups or in the terrorist groups linked to fundamentalist Islamic regimes. The transformation of mass communication and entertainment into the propaganda machinery of totalitarian regimes illustrates the dangerous nature of the potential for group regression thus activated (Welch, 1983).

Perhaps the greatest danger to the democratic political process of a pluralistic society is the effect of mass media on the political process itself. The understanding of mass psychology may be an important contribution of psychoanalysis to combating a development that can endanger intelligent participation in the political process. We do not yet know to what extent, in the long run, higher education can protect individuals against regressive group processes, or to what extent the triviality of mass culture and mass entertainment may simply illustrate a constant historical dialectic between the individual and the masses, gratifying regressive needs in socially adaptive ways and replacing historically earlier forms of ritualized social regression. Even if mass entertainment is exploited by economic and political interests, its effectiveness requires further exploration of what psychological needs it gratifies.

The regression induced by and reflected in mass culture and mass entertainment actualizes value systems and morality of latency years triggered by large-group processes as applied to the invisible group activated by mass media. These latency characteristics include the participants' projection of the unconscious superego structure of the postoedipal period onto the illusional group, the reassurance of personal identity within this group that comes when conventionality is embraced, the dissociation of sex and tenderness, and the preoedipal (narcissistic and paranoid) gratification at a mostly sublimatory level. The danger of more severely regressive large-group processes consists in the immediate activation of primitive object relations, the projection of preoedipal superego precursors onto potential leaders, and the corresponding activation of primitive narcissistic or paranoid tendencies in leadership, which may lead to violence, primitive equalization, and totalitarian control. Conventionality may be the price of social stability, but it may also indicate the ever-present danger of more severe group regression. By consciously manipulating the mass psychology activated by mass culture, political groups can expand the domain of conventional thinking or reduce that of individual judgment. For the individual, conventionality is a function of individual personality and of the activation of regressive mass psychology. Most people submerge themselves temporarily in the conventionality of mass culture for recreational purposes; for some, conventionality becomes a permanent prison.

Chapter 16 Ideology and Bureaucracy as Social Defenses Against Aggression

REGRESSION AND DEFENSES AGAINST IT IN LARGE GROUPS

In chapter 1, I proposed that Turquet's (1975) description of the loss of a sense of identity in large groups constitutes the basic situation against which both the idealization of the leader of the horde described by Freud (1921) and the small-group flight-fight, dependency, and pairing processes described by Bion (1961) are defending. I suggested that owing to the nature of the regression that occurs in groups, group processes pose a basic threat to the members' personal identities, a threat that is linked to a proclivity in group situations for the activation of primitive object relations, primitive defensive operations, and primitive aggression with predominantly pregenital features. These processes, particularly the activation of primitive aggression, are dangerous to the survival of the individual in the group, as well as to any task the group needs to perform.

Following the idealized leader of the mob blindly, as described by Freud, reconstitutes a sort of identity by identification with the leader; it protects the individual from intragroup aggression by this common

273

identity and the shared projection of aggression to external enemies; and it gratifies dependency needs through submission to the leader. The sense of power experienced by the individual in a mob also gratifies primitive narcissistic needs. I proposed that, paradoxically, the essentially irrational quality of mobs provides better protection against painful awareness of aggression than what obtains in large-group situations with undefined external enemies or in small groups, where it is hard to avoid realizing that the "enemy" is part of the group itself.

By studying large-group processes, we can recognize the threat to individual identity that occurs under social conditions where ordinary role functions are suspended, various projective mechanisms are no longer effective, and the relationships that exist among all individuals within a large-group situation replicate the multiplicity of primitive self- and object representations that predominate as intrapsychic structures of the individual before the consolidation of ego, superego, and id—and, therefore, before the consolidation of ego identity—and the regressive features of part-object relations that evolve when normal ego identity is not achieved or it disintegrates. Large-group processes also highlight the intimate connection between threats to identity and fear that primitive aggression and aggressively infiltrated sexuality will emerge. My observations from the study of individual patients, small groups, and group processes in organizational and institutional life confirm the overwhelming nature of the aggression in unstructured group situations.

The point is that an important part of nonintegrated and nonsublimated aggression is expressed in vicarious ways throughout group and organizational processes. When relatively well-structured group processes evolve in a task-oriented organization, aggression is channeled toward the decision-making process, particularly by evoking primitive leadership characteristics in people in positions of authority. Similarly, the exercise of power in organizational and institutional life constitutes an important channel for the expression in groups of aggression that would ordinarily be under control in dyadic or triadic relationships. Aggression emerges more directly and much more intensely when group processes are relatively unstructured.

In contrast to the dominant group characteristics of the unstable, threatening, potentially violent, and identity diffusing large group, small-group formation deals with the idealization-persecution dichotomy in the activation, respectively, of Bion's dependency and fight-flight groups. The activation of the pairing assumption may be considered an ambivalent effort to escape from primitive conflicts concerning aggression, primitive object relations, and primitive defenses by ambivalent idealization of the selected sexual pair.

PARANOID REGRESSIONS IN INSTITUTIONS

The two most striking mechanisms by which the large group protects itself from the threat of impending aggression are the development of an ad hoc ideology and the process of bureaucratization. The development of a simplistic philosophy as a calming, reassuring doctrine that reduces all thought to cliché described by Turquet (1975), the primitive, narcissistic ego-ideal characteristic of large-group processes described by Anzieu (1971), and the narcissistic ideology and idealization of a pseudopaternal leader as the promoter of illusions described by Chasseguet-Smirgel (1975) all refer to the tendency to a narcissistic regression into a primitive ideology that transforms the large group into what Canetti (1960) described as the typical "feasting crowd." This group is engaged, we might say, in dependent and narcissistic behavior; it correspondingly searches for a calming, narcissistic, reassuring mediocrity in its leader. Such leadership never fails to appear. In chapter 15, I described this regression as characteristic of the mass psychology of conventionality, reflecting the type of ideology characteristic of a latency child's superego and represented typically by mass entertainment.

As an alternative, as we saw in chapter 3, the large group may evolve not into such a static crowd but into a dynamic mob that is characterized by predominantly paranoid features and its selection of paranoid leadership; it is typically represented by the mass psychology of revolutionary mass formations. Conventionality, on the one hand, and violent, revolutionary movements with a totalitarian ideology, on the other, may be considered the corresponding mass psychological outcomes of idealization and persecution as basic group phenomena and, respectively, the containment by denial and reaction formation or the expression by violent acting out of aggression.

Having outlined the release of aggression under conditions of regressed and unstructured group processes, I now explore the conditions under which pathological aggression develops in the context of institutional functioning and malfunctioning, and the vicissitudes of ideology and bureaucracy as protective and corrective measures against the outbreak of aggression.

In chapter 8, following Jaques's (1976) classification of social organizations into requisite (functional) and paranoiagenic (dysfunctional) ones, I explored the nature of paranoiagenic organizations, expanding on Jaques's description of them as characterized by the prevalence of suspicion, envy, hostile rivalry, and anxiety, with a breakdown of social relations regardless of how much individual goodwill there might be. Expanding on this description, I suggested that institutional paranoiagenesis ranges along a broad spectrum, from the psychopathic to the depressive.

BUREAUCRACY

I described in chapter 8 how bureaucratic structures attempt to reduce organizational paranoiagenesis, and how the defended-against institutional sadism may reemerge in overblown bureaucratic systems. Those of us who have had to deal with members of large bureaucratic organizations as part of our leadership functions in health-delivery systems can offer innumerable examples of such sadistic behavior by inspectors, surveyors, and site visitors. One major—and on a social scale, devastating—effect of the bureaucracy's need to justify and expand its own functions is the generation of essentially nonfunctional, redundant work, which adds enormous though almost invisible costs to social organizations. The New York hospital association has calculated that 25 percent of the total expense budget of hospitals is consumed by the personnel's having to respond to bureaucratic requests of one kind or another (McCarthy, 1978).

Even without specific ideological underpinnings, the justification of bureaucratic rigidities usually includes one of three bureaucratic clichés: "We have always done it this way"; "We have never done it this way"; and "If we do this for you, everybody will want to get away with it." When, in addition, bureaucratic requirements are justified or infiltrated by an ideological system, the sadistic, moralistic, and punitive effects of bureaucratic action may assume objectively persecutory features.

The terrible consequences of the effective functioning of bureaucracies in totalitarian states, such as Hitler's Germany and Stalin's Soviet Union, on the lives of large segments of the population requires no spelling out. To a limited extent, similar types of ideological infiltration of well-functioning bureaucracies may be encountered within democratic states as well. In the United States, it is probably within the regulatory systems that affect health, education, welfare, immigration, and, particularly, justice that the ideological infiltration on bureaucratic control systems has the maximum effect of reducing efficiency, generating parasitic work, and restricting individual freedom and ordinary social interactions while increasing the paranoiagenic, persecutory regulation of the social system. Perhaps because of the immediate visibility of cost increase in the private sector of industry, bureaucratic regulations there are constrained in a dynamic equilibrium with the pressure for efficiency.

For example, within the bureaucratic hypertrophy of the judicial system, Salvador Menuchin (pers. comm., 1993) noted the disastrous effects of standard bureaucratic policies in the court system in matters of child neglect and child abuse. The appointment of independent legal counsels for the child and for the parents, in addition to a judge, and the treatment of each neglected child within a dysfunctional family as a separate court case, all combine to siphon off enormous resources into legal proceedings, to limit the authority of health-system agencies concerned with the child and the family, and to increase family conflicts by injecting into them a legal, adversarial system.

The expression of envy within large groups toward individuals whose capacity for independent thinking and autonomous functioning is resented is replicated in the bureaucratic suspicion of creative, innovative solutions to problems that are considered the bureaucracy's purview. The manifest resentment of original solutions by the bureaucrats finds a troubling, yet not surprising, resonance among the disaffected members of a regressed institution who resent the creative task performance of their own leaders. The proverbial anonymous letters that disgruntled employees send to regulating agencies are often part of this psychology. Less frequently, these letters may reflect an outburst over their own impotence by the healthy subordinates at the periphery of a paranoiagenic organization.

IDEOLOGY

Bureaucratic hypertrophy may also relate to ideology in more complex though equally destructive ways. Ideology, in the context of group and mass psychology, refers to a system of beliefs that a group, a mass, or a society share concerning the origin and functions of their common social life and the cultural and ethical demands and expectations they hold for their society. Here I note the significant discrepancies between a society's ideological commitments and its financial resources. Bureaucratic requirements mandating services that society cannot afford or is not willing to pay for may reflect an unconscious compromise between ideological commitment and practical considerations. The destructive effects of bureaucratic persecution of agencies like hospitals that are expected to produce services without adequate financial coverage leads to a worsening of the financial crisis by the nonfunctional work such persecution generates.

Underlying these contradictions lies the relations, in democratic societies, between the ideological aspirations of liberty, equality, and justice that are jointly geared to contain aggression at a social level but that may become instrumental in the acting out of that aggression. A humanistic ideology that has at its center respect for the individual and individual rights, and the aspiration for equal opportunity and equality before the law—an ideology embedded in a democratic system of government—may support the social controls that protect the functioning of organizational structures. And such control systems may protect the organization against the corruption of leaders and against the paranoiagenic deterioration that comes from the misuse of power.

The same ideology, however, may be subverted by the regressive atmosphere created in the context of large-group processes. Individual rights may be perverted within a litigious culture that artificially inflates grievances. Paranoid grandiosity becomes rationalized as individual rights. The quest for equality may be a rationalization of unconscious envy generated under conditions of regressive group processes. Zinoviev (1984) pointed to the importance of an egalitarian ideology as part of Soviet Marxism in fostering the group's envy of potential leaders; the unconscious self-assurance that came from placing mediocre individuals in leadership positions was a way to assuage such ideologically reinforced envy. I have already referred to the selection of narcissistic mediocrities as a central aspect of the transformation of the large-group situation into a static group that depends, satisfactorily, on the narcissistic leader.

In this regard, social ideologies that are tangential to institutional functioning often have a destructive effect on that functioning, particularly when individual members skillfully misuse that ideology—a painful side effect of well-intentioned efforts in the socially mandated and protected redress of grievances. The very ideal of a democratic system of government, as we have seen, may misfire when this ideal leads to another major mechanism to control the development of paranoia, namely, a democratic process of decision making.

I now examine some of the characteristics of ideological systems, some of which may counteract the regressive pull that occurs in unstructured groups. Others may foster such regressive enactment of aggression in groups, thus leading to the "return of the repressed," the enactment of aggression in the form of violence, sadistic power, and constraint of individual liberties.

From a psychoanalytic viewpoint, what is of particular interest is the extent to which an ideological system includes a worldview that, by definition, excludes all those who do not share it, declares the outcasts enemies who must be controlled or eliminated, and aspires to dominate all aspects of social behavior. These characteristics, which may be called the paranoid pole of ideologies, are found in totalitarian societies, fundamentalist religious movements, and certain cults. The division of human beings into loyal adherents and dangerous enemies may also be found in some racist and nationalist ideologies. A second characteristic of such ideologies is their invasiveness of family and intimate relationships, their supraordinate control over the relationships of couples. This is typically matched by an intolerance toward sexuality as described by Freud (1921). Family and sexual intimacy threaten the individual's complete identification with a totalitarian ideology. A third general characteristic of totalitarian ideologies is a conventional and conformist set of moral principles that regulate individual behavior, guidelines that are reminiscent of the superego of the latency years. Fundamentalist religious groups focus this morality most specifically on the sexual behavior of the individual—in effect, mounting a massive defense against individual freedom to integrate erotism and tenderness.

At the opposite end of the spectrum of ideological regression—what may be called the narcissistic pole of ideologies—we find the transformation of ideologies into social, political, and religious clichés that maintain their function of socialization within the community but have little effect on the individual's, the couple's, and the community's daily lives. I am referring here, for example, to the ritualized participation in official national, religious, or ethnic celebrations, in which the form is more important than commitment to a particular ideology, all of which may include both benign ritualization of social interactions and a reflection of historical, racial, or religious tradition. A particular type of such formalistic and essentially empty ideology is what may pervade a totalitarian society, in which the reality of daily life is in striking contradiction to the ideological system. A cliché-ridden adherence to the ideology illustrates the loss of individual liberties as well as the split between a dishonest public life and a grim private life. Kolakowski (1978b), Voslensky (1983), Sinyavsky (1988), and Malia (1994) described these characteristics of Soviet Russia as typical of its social structures during the thirty years before its collapse.

Halfway between these two extremes of ideology formation we might place ideological systems that have the following characteristics or that have achieved these characteristics at some stage of their historical evolution. Typically, they include a basis in a general humanistic value system within which individual rights and responsibilities are stressed; individual responsibilities are linked to moral demands that are expressed in the relation to the community; and individual ethical values, potential differences between individuals, and the right of privacy in decisions regarding family and sexual relationships are respected. In these ideologies, equality of rights is stressed, and it is ensured by equality before and equal access to the law, with a tolerance for differences of way of life—that is, without the imposition of an ideological egalitarianism that would significantly restrict individual freedom of decision making.

Such a spectrum of ideologies, ranging from cliché-ridden rituals, on the one extreme, to violent, restrictive totalitarianism, on the other, with a humanistic central domain may include the same theoretical system, the same ideology operating at different levels of regression. Thus, as we have seen, the cliché-ridden pseudomarxism characteristic of the Soviet Union and its satellite states may be considered the counterpart of the paranoid ideologies of Marxist terrorist groups in Cambodia, Germany, the Middle East, and Peru and the intermediate "Marxism with a human face" reflected in the ideology of some reform communist movements in Eastern and Western Europe. Similar observations may be made regarding religious systems that range throughout the spectrum in their various manifestations. The paranoid ideologies act out the aggression against which the ideology emerged as a defense; and the combination of paranoid ideologies and well-functioning bureaucracies may be dangerous to human survival. The effective bureaucracy, under these circumstances, may transform an open society into a political state.

Now we may explore the individual's contribution to the level of ideological maturity or regression that he or she adopts as a consequence of the development of individual superego functions. Here we also have a spectrum, ranging from the primitive, sadistic, conventional morality of the classic authoritarian personality to the cynical manipulation of socially accepted belief systems of the individual with severe antisocial tendencies. The individual with a mature superego occupies the central area of this spectrum.

In fact, the individual's fixation at a level of primitive superego functioning that divides all values into all-good and all-bad, that aspires for an individual "justice" which reflects a system of rationalized envy and a hatred of others' rights and belongings, and that adopts a sexual morality which maintains an absolute split between tender relations and erotic ones reflects both a severe character pathology and a consonance with the characteristics of fundamentalist ideologies. While social, cultural, historical, and economic conditions may determine the level of ideological commitment sweeping a culture at any particular time, the individual's psychopathology or maturity of superego functions will determine if and when the individual enters the historical current.

PSYCHOANALYTIC AND SOCIOLOGICAL CONVERGENCES

I have proposed that the psychology of small groups, large groups, mobs, and mass movements includes the expression, under conditions of unstructured social interactions, of primitive aggression and defenses against it that are ordinarily under control in the restricted dyadic and triadic relationships of individuals, couples, and, to some extent, families. The relationships within ordinary social networks that characterize communities also reflect in large part the dyadic and triadic relationships in which both primitive aggression and defenses against it are under control.

In contrast, in response to the liberation of primitive aggression in the group situations, regressive narcissistic and paranoid developments tend to occur; narcissistic developments in the static, gratifying, although also simplifying and at times stultifying enjoyment of group regression and the corresponding relation to narcissistic, primitive, cliché-ridden leadership. Paranoid regression, on the other hand, is characterized by the dynamic mob, mass movement, and the corresponding liberation of violence and elimination of ordinary moral constraints described by Freud (1921). Under conditions of paranoid regression, leaders with paranoid characteristics tend to take over; they provide direction, rationalization, and encouragement for the expression of destructiveness.

I have suggested that in addition to ordinary task orientation—the structural organization of groups into coordinated task or work groups within institutions—two major alternative defensive operations against the activation of aggression are represented by bureaucratic control and ideology formation. Bureaucratic control systems develop a structure; protect the individual, the group, and the organization against regressive effects of paranoid developments; and, on a broader social level, can protect individual rights and equality before the law. An ideological development that unifies the unstructured group or mass movement in terms of a relatively simple set of moral prescriptions also provides a defense against paranoid regression and the outbreak of violence.

Both bureaucratic development and ideology, however, may be infiltrated by the very aggression they are created to defend against. Bureaucratic control may acquire regressive sadistic qualities, and ideological systems may be used for the rationalization of violence and totalitarian control. Thus, major defenses against aggression may actually become infiltrated by it and reinforce its enactment. Ideology and bureaucracy may reinforce each other at both regressive and advanced levels. An ideology of egalitarianism may foster a hypertrophic bureaucracy to protect itself, paradoxically creating a privileged bureaucratic class and reducing individual freedoms. A libertarian ideology of individual rights may become a legalistic bureaucracy that transforms the defense of individual rights into a litigious and querulous relationship between individuals and the social system. Although it is easy to assert that restriction of the bureaucracy and protection of the humanistic ideology may together protect social life from the dangerous excesses of bureaucratic and ideological developments, it would be naive to assume that this is an easy task. In fact, this dilemma presented by human aggression at a social level requires constant alertness; it is unlikely to permit any permanent solution.

The positive aspect both of bureaucratic development and ideological commitments must be kept in mind. History has shown that the courage of masses can bring down dictatorships or totalitarian systems; the mass demonstrations and spontaneous uprisings in Eastern Europe against communist totalitarianism, the mobilization of the British people in response to the massive bombardments in the early stages of the World War II are illustrations of mass movements that combined a humanistic ideology with collective courage. Here the positive aspects of ideological commitment have contributed to positive historical change and stemmed the effects of destructive aggression at social, national, and international levels. Similarly, the support provided by bureaucracies created to set up avenues for redress of grievances, and the usefulness of bureaucracies in allowing optimal functioning of task systems within and across social institutions are an essential aspect of the social organization of human work.

But the ever-present dangers of ideological regression and bureaucratic sadism cannot be overestimated. Within American society, the relationship between a humanistic ideology of personal freedom and equality and a hypertrophic tendency toward litigious interactions and restrictive "political correctness" indicate the problem; and the vast, largely undiagnosed, hypertrophic bureaucratic restrictions in the area of health care are a typical expression of the evident contradiction between egalitarian aspirations and growing economic constraints derived from the development of scientific knowledge and effectiveness of health-care procedures.

Tocqueville (1945 [1835–1840]) first pointed to the danger that democracy could be transformed into a plebicitarian tyranny when public opinion was channeled into despotic laws and bureaucratic structures. He saw the risk that aspirations for equality might eventually reduce individual freedoms, although he had confidence in the social checks and balances he found in the United States, including the independence of the judiciary, the separation of church and state, the autonomy and high status of the professions, the authority of local community, and regional diversity (Nesbit, 1993).

This view was in dramatic contrast to that of Marxist theory, which assumed that the dictatorship of the proletariat, in bringing about the destruction of the bourgeoisie and the capitalist system, would by itself "disappear" and give rise to universal freedom (Kolakowski, 1978a). The development within the Soviet Union of a totalitarian and corrupt bureaucracy (Voslensky, 1983) illustrates both a fatal flaw in Marxist thinking and the danger of bureaucratization to both the socialist and democratic systems.

Weber's (1958 [1904–1905]) analysis of bureaucracy saw the rational organization of government and the economy into bureaucracies as a form of rational domination, a mode of hierarchy that supplants patrimonial, charismatic, or traditional authority by means of principles of fixed and official jurisdictional areas, governed by laws or administrative regulations. He foresaw potential conflicts between democracy and bureaucracy, with bureaucracy subverting the moral objectives of democracy. Michels (1949 [1911]) suggested in his description of bureaucracy that "the bureaucratic spirit corrupts character and engenders moral poverty. In every bureaucracy we may observe place-hunting, a mania for promotion, an obsequiousness toward those on whom promotion depends; there is arrogance toward inferiors and civility toward superiors. . . . We may even say that the more conspicuously a bureaucracy is distinguished by its zeal, by its sense of duty, and by its devotion, the more also will it show itself to be petty, narrow, rigid, and illiberal" (p. 189).

Durkheim (1961 [1925], 1933 [1893]) concluded that only moral systems that linked the individual to his or her immediate community could protect him or her from the destructive effects of authoritarian bureaucracies; depending upon the country, he saw the potential of mutual corrective influences in the protection of individual freedom by the role of the individual, by the moral systems that linked him or her with the community, and by the state. As Nesbit (1993) points out, Tönnies's (1963 [1887]) analysis of the distinction between community and society underlies all the sociologists' analyses referred to so far (with the exception of that of Marx). Tönnies conceived of the danger that community, with its specific moral systems, might be supplanted by society, that is, by a vast, atomized transformation of the relationships of individuals with one another that was caused by the democratic system of government, and the risk to the moral systems of the community by the impersonal transformation of society at large. Kolakowski (1978b) traced the contradictions in the Soviet system back to a paradox in the ideals of the French Revolution: liberty, equality, fraternity. He noted that absolute liberty denies equality, while absolute equality cannot but deny liberty; the conflict between these two ideals destroys fraternity as well.

I started from a psychoanalytic perspective of group psychology, which led me to the functional and dysfunctional aspects of ideology and bureaucracy; obviously, sociological analysts had explored the corresponding paradoxes a long time ago. I hope that our understanding of the mechanisms of individual psychology that feed into and codetermine aggressive conflicts at the social level of interactions may contribute to understanding, and perhaps even reducing, the destructive impact of human aggression in our social systems.

Chapter 17 Regression in the Political Process

Earlier, I described the processes leading to paranoiagenic regression in social organizations. I identified three types of regression, which were produced according to the personality dispositions of the individuals involved in or affected by organizational regression. In combination, these three levels of regression represent the breakdown of institutional morale.

REGRESSION IN THE PARTICIPANTS

I referred first to the *psychopathic regression* of individuals with strong narcissistic features, who lack a sophisticated autonomous value system that reflects mature integration of the superego. These individuals are especially vulnerable to this level of regression when their position within the organization promises extraordinary rewards for those who either manipulate power or submit to it, while threatening those who stand up to authority.

A second type of regression affects the large majority of the members of an organization involved in a paranoiagenic regression. They exhibit early manifestations of *paranoid regression:* going into hiding, heightened cautiousness, suspiciousness, and fearfulness in all situations they perceive as uncertain. Finally, I described a third type of regression, the *depressive regression* of the individuals whose maturity, autonomy, and strongly integrated superego functions give them a certain distance from the paranoiagenic process but who, at the same time, show a tendency to become excessively self-critical and doubtful of their own merit and value to the organization, and who experience an increasing sense of loneliness and despondency in their work.

I shall now explore the acute and usually transitory regression that is related to the political process operating in an open community rather than in a clearly delimited social institution with firm boundaries and an organizational structure determined by its primary task. Mass psychology relates to the reactions of individuals when they experience themselves as part of a large, unorganized mass. An open, democratic election can activate that mass psychology with particular effectiveness through the simultaneity of communication offered by the mass media. As the politicians vying for votes address the people through mass media, members of the open community experience themselves as an anonymous mass, as they receive this address simultaneously. I have described how this experience activates the projection of latency-level superego functions onto that anonymous mass, with regression to an infantile splitting of all value systems into good and evil. In this state, people absorb information in the context of their fantasy of how the population at large is responding to it. As a result of this process, people tend to see issues in simple terms; they become susceptible to conventional ideology and morality; and they lack the maturity and autonomy to judge the content of the information they receive independent of the imagined mass audience.

When social, economic, cultural, or historical conditions are relatively stable and safe, the democratic political process first activates a *narcissistic* level of regression. The electorate generally tends to experience politics as entertainment, observing with an attitude of amusement and superiority as politicians try to impress them.

Unstable, turbulent, potentially threatening social, economic, cultural, or historical conditions activate a deeper level of *paranoid* regression: the forthcoming election is perceived as a potential threat as well as a potential opportunity to defy and overcome a real or imagined enemy. Social subgroups become sharply divided and serve as targets for the projection of aggression and paranoid distortions. The potential for political, religious, racial, or nationalistic hostility latent in the local ideology and cultural tradition is maximally activated under such conditions.

But even under the best conditions, a more severe paranoid regression may evolve among those who are closest to the seats of power, to the decision-making process, and to the leaders involved in the political struggle. In the immediate entourage of the competing politicians and their respective committees, the paranoid regression is intensified by the relatively close relationships of all concerned. Thus a paranoid large-group process may emerge, with significant regressions in the individuals most directly involved in the election process. Within dictatorial regimes and, particularly, in totalitarian regimes, the political struggle may easily assume deadly characteristics. A relatively small group of leading functionaries exists, while the large mass of a subjugated population experiences itself as isolated from the political process. Their sense of alienation or resignation is matched only by their alertness to who's on top at any given moment. The political assassinations, show trials, and other death struggles involving small cliques within the power structure that characterized the former Soviet Union and its satellite states illustrate this process. Here the political process and personal survival were dramatically intertwined (Malia, 1994; Schabowski, 1991).

The political processes in small social organizations whose members have invested a significant amount of social, professional, scientific, or religious energy may illustrate the same psychological forces that are more dramatically and even lethally active in dictatorial or totalitarian regimes. Thus, for example, political struggles within universities, institutions dedicated to the arts, professional organizations, government agencies, and labor unions may evince regressions in the political process.

The political process may be initiated by a sharp split between the actual or potential leadership when two or more candidates compete for a leading political job. An entire leadership group may immediately be affected by this splitting process if the power of the followers in associated or secondary leadership or bureaucratic positions is at stake.

In addressing themselves to the electorate, the candidates and their supporters naturally idealize each candidate's personality, background, capacities, and potential for improving the followers' future. Without them saying a single negative word, by such a focused idealization they have already implied a subtle (or not-so-subtle) denigration of their opponent(s). The object of this devaluation experiences it as a paranoid attack, an unfair distortion of the truth, and feels the need to redress the imbalance by devaluing or denigrating, in turn, the first speaker's self-idealization. Thus, the second round of public communication usually already includes more direct attacks and, in a vicious circle, idealization of one's own side and denigration of the opposition. A gradually intensifying reactive attack on both sides shifts the equilibrium from narcissistic competition toward a paranoid social structure.

At this point, paranoiagenic conditions begin to prevail, and the three types of individual regression make their appearance. In the entourages of the respective political antagonists, individuals may emerge who have marked psychopathic or paranoid features. Undoubtedly, the most disturbed individuals show both paranoid and antisocial features. There is probably no political campaign in which there does not appear the kind of individual who spreads vicious rumors regarding the enemy while indignantly protesting the equally vicious rumors that that same enemy is in reality or in fantasy spreading about his or her own side. It is remarkable how, in the middle of an intense rumor campaign of sharply contested political battles, efforts to trace particularly malicious rumors lead back to just a few people, usually those who most violently protested about the rumors of the other side.

These intense partisans, in the grip of paranoid and psychopathic regressions, contrast with the majority of the candidates' in-group, who may be unable to avoid being caught up in the general paranoid atmosphere of the campaign but who maintain their balanced recognition of the value and decency of people on both sides. But a general paranoid atmosphere spreads throughout the groups of close adherents to the candidates, and it exerts a widening pressure on everybody in the organization to take sides. In fact, individuals who remain relatively objective and independent may gradually feel that they are being treated as "enemies" by the partisans of the feuding camps; and while paranoid pressures escalate throughout the membership of the organization, those not contaminated by the paranoid regression may experience themselves more and more as singletons (Turquet, 1975), that is, as isolated and impotent bystanders in the large group, alienated from an organization involved in a temporary madness. If organizational processes permit or require ongoing communication between all the participants concerning organizational tasks that continue throughout the campaign, personal relations may become strained under the influence of generalized projective identification. In contrast to large-group processes in which projective identification becomes relatively inoperant, ongoing specific interactions within task groups of the organization facilitate the operation of primitive defenses, so that even close personal relationships may become poisoned by the effects of the campaign. Sudden alliances, splitting of subgroups, and "treason" may evolve.

A particular type of psychopathic regression may affect some individuals in mid-level political leadership positions who could powerfully influence their own followers on both sides of the growing split in the organization, while their future would become uncertain were they to be identified with the camp seen as the likely loser. The temptation to maintain a double loyalty at all costs may lead to frankly dishonest manipulation of these people's relationships with everyone in the campaign. Sensing their dishonesty, others will react to them with suspicion, while at the same time courting them as respected opinion makers. This behavior intensifies these mid-level leaders' need to manipulate everybody. The potential for them to compromise their moral integrity, latent under ordinary circumstances, may now become activated. Often these are individuals with strong narcissistic features, who lack commitment to anything other than their own survival. This quality enables them to maintain their place in the political process, and even to ultimately achieve leadership positions themselves. Their political capability is marred, however, by their lack of moral stamina, which may become the flaw that destroys them eventually as leaders (see chapters 7 and 9).

In sharp contrast to these people are the individuals who maintain their integrity and independence while openly distancing themselves from the paranoid regression affecting most members of the organization. As a result, they may earn the grudging respect of the rest of the group and eventually contribute to the healing process of the organization, that is, help to bring individuals back together as part of a reconstruction of task groups once the organizational regression has been resolved.

So far I have not focused on the influence of the personality and behavior of the candidates around whom the organization originally split. The candidates for the leadership position have an enormous influence on the political process, and while they are subject to severely regressive forces, they may, in resisting these forces, codetermine the level of regression of the political campaign. I use *codetermine* because the other side will be equally influential in determining the equilibrium of paranoid regression. In other words, if one of two or more contestants contributes significantly to the paranoid regression, it will be difficult for the others to control this process. The more severely paranoid a candidate, the more severely paranoid the campaign will become. The fight-flight basic-assumption group in small-group processes (Bion, 1961), and the defensive efforts of large groups to consolidate in a paranoid stance, both invite and are reinforced by a paranoid leader (see chapter 5). When paranoid and psychopathic regression combine in a leader, his rewarding the psychopathic-paranoid partisans within his camp will effectively poison the entire campaign. Even a basically honest and decent, yet severely paranoid leader will implicitly reward the paranoid-psychopathic extremists of his or her camp, unconsciously conveying the message that under conditions of severe animosity and dangers for the future, all means of defense and counterattacks are legitimate.

The selection of a campaign team will be powerfully influenced by the candidate's ideological commitments and political understanding and personality. In turn the campaign will be shaped by the candidate's choice of whom to trust among the entourage of more or less paranoid, more or less ethically principled and autonomous or opportunistic partisans. Reliance on experienced, mature, politically savvy but stable individuals, who have a healthy resistance to paranoid regression, high ethical and personal standards, and a clear sense of the interests of the organization as a whole will be as important in shaping the campaign as the selection of the most violent, unscrupulous partisans. In various ways, both written and verbal communications concerning the campaign will reflect these choices of the candidates.

Probably in each camp there will be an unwavering, uncompromising, paranoid group at one extreme that contrasts with another group with psychopathic tendencies at the other extreme; both will be willing to compromise basic positions for political expedience. In between, a more rational, principled, and autonomous group may provide counsel that, at times, may appear to be politically less expedient or effective but that might be the best advice and might help change the atmosphere of the campaign.

What is tragic is that the general regression of the organization determined by the activation of mass psychology as a result of the political campaign itself will interfere with the mature, rational judgment of the majority of the voters. If, as I have proposed, the regression into a mass-psychology frame is unavoidable once a political campaign has started, the capacity for highly individualized, rational thinking about the organization is reduced among the membership in general. Practically speaking, in most organizations, a large majority of individuals experience themselves as distant from the decision-making authorities; these people may identify at varying levels with organizational goals and expect benefits from their participation in the organization without putting excessive personal investment into or much caring about the functioning and future of the organization itself.

It is the responsibility of the leaders to activate the membership so that the organization can accomplish its primary tasks. The vision that may emerge in inspired leadership can at times be quite distant from the concrete awareness by the majority of participants of where the organization stands and what its mission is. When there is a sharp discrepancy between conventional wisdom and inspired leadership, the prevalence of mass psychology creates a danger that demagogic appeals to conventional wisdom, dominant ideologies that are "in the air," and the membership's instinctive responses may become more influential than is honest information reflecting a truly challenging and valid vision.

In the context of the development of a paranoid regression, accusations hurled at the opponent that she supports views that are self-centered, authoritarian, antidemocratic, reactionary, revolutionary, elitist, petrified, ignorant, or chaotic may strike an immediate responsive chord among the voters. Under such conditions, rational analysis of the organization's positions and goals can seem intellectual, uninspiring, and cold by comparison with affectively rousing and cleverly focused clichés that feed on the dominant paranoid regression. In activating mass psychology, the political process creates the paradox that maximum participation may reduce the level and quality of the individual judgments required to make the democratic process work.

The candidates are under powerful regressive pressures. From the moment the campaign begins, the candidate's world changes from a place composed of individuals at varying levels of closeness to a place consisting of friends and enemies, where the candidate's success depends upon the opinions and decisions of an anonymous mass that is impossible to evaluate. Other people are now perceived as potential voters; all informal communication, social relationships, professional interactions, artistic or scientific work, and advisory roles are now variously contaminated by the question: "Is this person for me or against me?" The candidate now always needs to evaluate where others stand, whether and how they may be influenced, and what can safely be said and what not. A professional politician learns to feel at home with these distortions of the interpersonal environment. But a member of a professional or scientific organization can be traumatized by the temporary transformation of accustomed human relationships in the course of a political struggle.

To the extent that the normal narcissistic equilibrium of the candidate is codetermined by the views of others, her running for office may bring about a significant narcissistic regression. The candidate's future position, income, and professional role now depend on the decision of an anonymous large mass, and a situation is produced that replicates that of the period before object constancy has been achieved, when conditions of uncertainty threaten self-esteem. In other words, the massive, split-off, idealized, and persecutory representations of others affect the candidate's self-reflection and self-esteem. And, because the anonymous mass of potential threatening enemies cannot be exactly defined or controlled by projective behavior, whatever potential for paranoid regression exists in the candidate is now activated.

In fact, the potential leader is exposed to a double source of regression. First, his or her own potential for narcissistic and paranoid regressions is activated as the regulation of self-esteem is exposed to the uncertainty of the reaction of the unknown mass, while the potential for paranoid reaction to unknown enemies can grow significantly. Second, the regressive proclivities of those who surround the leader contribute to the uncertainty of the experience. The "lunatic fringe" of partisans may provide the security of their support, but they fuel the candidate's fears and suspicions about the opponent. The unconscious ambivalence of the immediate supporters may, in fact, lead them to heighten the paranoid potential of the candidate through their rumors and warnings.

The loss of spontaneity in the behavior of former acquaintances and friends is a further complication for the candidate. New friends seem to emerge from among those who are trying to ingratiate themselves with the would-be leader (a reflection of how organizations can corrupt the concept of friendship), while others appear to distance themselves, afraid of being too closely identified with their now politicized colleague. Formerly close acquaintances now seem to distance themselves in public while privately offering assurances of support; and those who were previously distant now approach with exaggerated manifestations of friendliness only to dash away at any sign of trouble. It may be that only a few close friends from the past can continue to behave as they always have, unaffected by the political situation. In short, a severe distortion in the candidate's personal network under conditions of political regression may cause a regression in his or her functioning. Such a regression is dramatically illustrated in the loss of contact with reality of East Germany's leadership shortly before the country's collapse (Schabowski, 1991). The communist politburo members were completely confused about what was going on. In any event, given the regressive potential of the situation, it is no wonder that whatever "psychopathic" potential exists in the candidate may be activated at this point, complicating the general paranoid regression in process. Paradoxically, a candidate with strong narcissistic or schizoid features may be relatively protected against regression by a reactive distancing and aloofness. That aloofness, however, beyond a certain intensity, may damage his or her political effectiveness.

Perhaps the most interesting, but also the most frightening illustration of the regressive developments in a political campaign is the emergence of a few personalities who present behaviors that are strikingly similar to those characteristic of the syndrome of malignant narcissism: a combination of narcissistic, paranoid, antisocial, and sadistic behaviors that does not seem to characterize their functioning outside the context of political campaigns (Kernberg, 1989a). Typically, these are individuals who are drawn to what they perceive to be the centers of power. They are attentive to rumor and gossip, carrying that gossip from one side to the other, often appearing to be indignant at what they proclaim to be misleading, dishonest, and aggressive distortions of the truth. Meanwhile, they help intensify the destructive effects of such messages. A surface friendliness barely hides the way they manipulate and destroy with their rumor-mongering and the demagoguery they create with their righteous indignation. Obviously, such behaviors reflect the latent personality characteristics of those involved. What is striking, however, is the explosiveness of these destructive behaviors, and the effectiveness of their regressive impact. It takes strength, maturity, and moral integrity in the leaders of warring factions to protect themselves and one another from the destructive effects of such individuals, who, as quickly as they emerged during the political campaign, may subside once political, social, and psychological stability have been reestablished.

The maneuvering to achieve positions of power, prestige, and influence complicate the relationships among the participants of the inner circle, but the existence of an "external enemy" usually keeps their conflict at a minimum. It is only after one faction has prevailed that the internal conflicts of the new group in power will emerge more strongly. Again, the quality in leaders that protects against paranoid and narcissistic regression will become crucial in controlling these potentially destructive forces within the winning group. The losers may be upset by the search for internal sources and culprits of their defeat, but usually their leader is protected from such internal fragmentation by the mutual support in the process of mourning their defeat.

Not surprisingly, the narcissistic and paranoid potential of the candidate exerts a fundamental influence on the reactions of his entire entourage in both triumph and defeat. Leadership with strong narcissistic and paranoid features is characterized by the massive use of projective identification before and after the election, and it is well known that those who are most dishonest, aggressive, and destructive are those who accuse their enemies most vehemently of the same characteristics. The Soviet show trials and the Nazi propaganda against the Jews well illustrate these developments (Bullock, 1991; Conquest, 1991; and

Dawidowicz, 1975). Severe narcissistic and paranoid pathology in the leader leads to intolerance of defeat, the inability to mourn and come to terms with the postelection reality, and an extended period of severe paranoid resentment, grudge-bearing, and desire for revenge. The same narcissistic and paranoid qualities in the victor express themselves in ongoing resentment and revenge-taking against the now defeated enemies, when what is needed is a mature effort at reconciliation, generosity, and renewed identification with the organizational tasks.

PREVENTIVE AND CONTROLLING MEASURES

The effects of an electoral process in which these regressive features have been dominant may be devastating in a small professional or scientific organization with an extended network of national or international acquaintances whose work depends on personal collaboration and on leaders working across the electoral divide. The poisoning of interpersonal relationships may carry its effects over many years, bringing about the disappointed, disillusioned, "depressive" withdrawal of some or many of the most creative and potentially valuable individuals of the organization. Therefore, preventive or controlling measures to protect the institution from the regressive effects of political processes should be built into the formal procedures of the organization before the electoral process starts.

Here, the advantages of a bureaucratic structure that protects the organization from regression into large-group processes may outweigh the usual danger of sadistic infiltration of the bureaucratic structure itself (see chapter 16). Protective regulation should include, first, limitation of the amount of time and money the institution will permit candidates to spend. Many professional organizations, such as the American Academy of Child Psychiatry, have limited their internal electoral processes to position statements given by each of the candidates that are of the same, limited length and that are published in the house organ. If a discussion of a position statement is permitted, it is limited to a specific length, and published in the same format. Ideally, letter-writing campaigns should be avoided or limited to one document per candidate, with each camp responsible for staying within the officially established limit. National or international organizations that depend on local meetings should avoid transforming these meetings into a forum for political debate. In contrast to a political party—whose task is precisely to carry out political struggles—a professional, religious, social, or cultural organization should avoid using its scheduled gatherings or time and space for political fund raising, and should discourage campaigns by other means, such as telephone appeals, electronic mail, or politically inspired social gatherings. The constitution and bylaws of the organization can provide an effective way to prevent the deterioration of indispensable political processes.

The argument could be raised that, rather than restricting the political process, broad discussion should be encouraged, for by highlighting the competing candidates' positions the electorate will be educated and provided with rational information that can lead to intelligent, informed decision making. If it is true, however, that regression is an unavoidable effect of the activation of the political process, then the electorate's capacity for intellectual understanding and rational decision making will be impaired by that regression. To put it bluntly, once an issue is discussed in the context of the large-group process, clichés and conventionally soothing ideologies will always carry the day over sophisticated, discriminating intellectual discourse.

Large-group processes inevitably activate an unconscious envy of rational leadership and induce the large group to select leaders with either dominant narcissistic and reassuring characteristics who utter calming clichés or paranoid leaders who consolidate the group in a paranoid stance.

When the candidates' communication to the electorate is limited to a brief statement, the members who care about the issues, have general knowledge of them, and maintain their capacity for independent judgment will be stimulated to give thoughtful, personal consideration of the decision they are called upon to make. The members who lack concern for the organization and have insufficient information about its history, present development, and future needs may be unable to respond to a brief position statement by making a knowledgeable judgment. But contrast this limitation to those imposed by uncontrolled political debate and ongoing manipulation of public opinion by demagogues.

For a political organization like a political party, an effort to appeal to the dominant beliefs of the electorate at large and to influence them to conform to the beliefs of the party is perfectly suited to the leadership function. In other words, the leadership of a political party has the task of defining, formulating, and convincingly presenting the current dominant ideology, its challenging or threatening aspects, and the new ideological direction in which the challengers plan to take the institution.

For a professional, scientific, or cultural organization, an appeal to a dominant, culturally accepted ideology that is tangential to the major tasks of the organization can be disruptive. The exploitation of a dominant social ideology (change, equality, economic conservatism) in order to influence an electorate that has become a regressive group can be deceptive at best and destructive at worst for an organization. What may well be a task-oriented confrontation of ideologies in the political process of open communities contrasts with the sharp focus on organizational tasks that are ideally linked to the political process in organizations with specific aims.

THE TIME SPAN OF DECISION MAKING

Let us now raise the unavoidable question: How much difference does good leadership really make? Will new leadership significantly influence the destiny of an organization? If the answer to this question is no, the entire political process appears in a poor light: it becomes a massive investment in futile agitation, a destructive consumption of resources, and a distraction from the organization's purpose. But the answer to the question depends on the nature of the organization, its tasks, and the level of freedom it gives its leaders.

The level of freedom given leaders depends, first of all, on the length of the leadership position. Professional organizations that renew their leaders annually usually do not require major changes; they consider themselves quite adaptable; and they are more concerned with maintaining the optimal functions of their component structures rather than with organizational change. If true organizational change is required, or organizational functions require planning processes over several years' time, then leaders need to be in place for a sufficient period to monitor those long-range plans and ensure functional change. For practical purposes, this cannot mean less than two years, and it justifies a serious political struggle for a leadership that will last beyond three or four years. For a major corporation where industrial planning includes ten- or twenty-year forecasts, keeping the leaders in place for five to ten years seems reasonable.

In a related process, institutions may build conservative structures into their change of leadership that permit only a gradual change in order to ensure stability. Such a slowdown may not work in times of external turmoil, which require centralized leadership as well as rapid change. Therefore, the question of whether leaders really make a difference has to be answered in the context of organizational goals, constraints, the span of decision making, and the duration of the position. If leadership at the top has a largely ceremonial function and if it ritually renews itself on a yearly basis, then optimally, the political process should practically disappear.

ORGANIZATIONAL SELF-DESTRUCTIVENESS
AND HEALING PROCESSES

The major danger in the regression that affects the political process, particularly in the case of professional, cultural, or religious organizations, is usually not the selection of a paranoid individual who reflects one extreme or the other of the political spectrum. Organizations tend to steer away from extremes except under unusual conditions of upheaval. The real danger is that the organization will select a cliché-ridden, reassuring, soothingly bland leader as part of a massive narcissistic regression that includes unconscious envy of effective leadership. The unconscious envy of decisive leadership, particularly by the middle-level bureaucratic structures of the organization, may powerfully militate against the selection of the best person available. I was witness to an election in the American Psychiatric Association at a time of severe turmoil and challenge to the profession where envy of an unusually brilliant and successful candidate brought about his defeat.

The acting out of unconscious envy that characterizes static large-group processes may be played out at the level of national and international organizations as well. The unconscious conspiracy to defeat an exceptional leader may be an expression of unconscious revenge against the envied person, disguised and rationalized in terms of a dominant ideological current that affects the entire electorate. A friendly, conventional, nonthreatening bureaucrat may be an easier identification figure for all those caught up in the narcissistic regression of the electoral process. But then at times an individual whose true capacities are hidden behind the appearance of an average person may prove to be an inspired leader. In any case, the confrontation of individual members of the organization, in the privacy of their homes, with basic, succinct information about the candidates with which to make an independent decision offers a greater guarantee that the best leaders will be chosen than decision making in the context of severe organizational regression, even though it may have the semblance of an open, extended, full political dialogue. The exploitation of mass psychology has an opposite effect to that of open communication and information sharing as part of organizational functioning.

For the winning candidate, the healthy narcissistic gratification of having won will normally rapidly turn to concern for the challenges of the new tasks. Among these is to perform the functions of a generous parent, who will do everything possible to bring about reconciliation, foster the healing process, and maintain the institutional commitments of those who lost the election. For the losing candidate, the main task is to work through the narcissistic lesion, to mourn the loss, and to avoid pathological regression into narcissistic devaluation of the organization that did not choose him or her, or a paranoid estrangement from it with ongoing resentment, blame, and desire for revenge.

Obviously, leaders with a predominantly narcissistic personality will tend to devalue the organization that did not select them, while leaders with predominantly paranoid features may maintain a grudging resentment and combative stance as the basis of their survival. For the organization, the narcissistic withdrawal of a capable potential leader is a loss, and the ongoing scheming of a defeated paranoid candidate is a potential threat to the necessary reconciliation and focus on organizational tasks. A period of mourning, of depressive withdrawal, is probably unavoidable under the best of circumstances; however, one task of a leader entering a political process is to prepare for potential defeat, a working through process that should occur silently but powerfully in the course of the institutional contest well before its denouement.

To conclude, for a leader to work with those who helped him or her to succeed in a political contest can be a source of gratification, emotional triumph, and profound satisfaction for all. To work with those who were on the other side and to build mutual trust in the context of common work for institutional goals is also a gratifying and profoundly creative experience. To achieve such creative working relationships beyond the electoral process is one of the tasks and challenges of institutional leadership.

Bibliography

Adorno, T., et al. (1950). *The Authoritarian Personality*. New York: Harper.

———. (1954). Television and the patterns of mass culture. In *Mass Culture,* ed. B. Rosenberg and D. M. White, 474–488. New York: Free Press, 1957.

Althusser, L. (1976). *Positions*. Paris: Editions Sociales.

Anders, G. (1956). *Die Antiquiertheit des Menschen*. Vol. 1. Munich: Verlag C. H. Beck.

———. (1980). *Die Antiquiertheit des Menschen*. Vol. 2. Munich: Verlag C. H. Beck.

Anderson, P. (1976). *Considerations on Western Marxism*. London: NLB.

Anzieu, D. (1971). L'Illusion groupal. *Nouvelle Revue de Psychanalyse* 4:73–93.

———. (1981). *Le Groupe et l'inconscient: L'Imaginaire groupal*. Paris: Dunod.

Arlow, J. A. (1951). A psychoanalytic study of a religious initiation rite: Bar Mitzvah. *Psychoanal. Study of the Child* 6:353–374.

———. (1961). Ego psychology and the study of mythology. *J. Am. Psychoanal. Assn.* 9:371–393.

———. (1969). Myth and ritual in psychoanalytic training: A report of the first Free Institute Conference. Ed. Charlotte Babcock. *Training Analysis,* 104–120.

———. (1970). Group psychology and the study of institutes. Unpub. ms.

———. (1972). Some dilemmas in psychoanalytic education. *J. Am. Psychoanal. Assn.* 20:556–566.

———. (1979). Psychoanalytic knowledge of group processes. Panel report. *J. Am. Psychoanal. Assn.* 27:147–149.

———. (1991). Address to the graduating class of the San Francisco Psychoanalytic Institute, June 16, 1990. *Am. Psychoanal.* 25(1): 15–16, 21.

Astrachan, B. M. (1970). Towards a social systems model of therapeutic groups. *Soc. Psychiat.* 5:110–119.

Bach, G. R. (1954). *Intensive Group Psychotherapy.* New York: Ronald Press.

Belknap, I. (1956). *Human Problems of a State Mental Hospital.* New York: McGraw-Hill.

Berman, L. E. (1987). Psychoanalytic comments on James Bond and Ian Fleming. Unpub. ms.

Bion, W. R. (1961). *Experiences in Groups.* New York: Basic Books.

———. (1967). *Second Thoughts: Selected Papers on Psychoanalysis.* London: Heinemann.

———. (1970). *Attention and Interpretation.* London: Heinemann.

Boukovski, V. (1990). *URSS: De la utopía al desastre.* Editorial Atlantida: Buenos Aires.

Bourdieu, P. (1979). *La Distinction: Critique social du jugement.* Paris: Editions de minuit.

Brantlinger, P. (1983). *Bread and Circuses.* Ithaca: Cornell University Press.

Braunschweig, D., and Fain, M. (1971). *Eros et Antéros.* Paris: Petite Bibliothèque Payot.

Britton, R. (1994). Publication anxiety: Conflict between communication and affiliation. *Int. J. Psycho-Anal.* 75:1213–1224.

Bruzzone, M., et al. (1985). Regression and persecution in analytic training: Reflections on experience. *Int. Rev. Psychoanal.* 12:411–415.

Bullock, A. (1991). *Hitler and Stalin: Parallel Lives.* London: HarperCollins.

Caine, R. M., and Small, D. J. (1969). *The Treatment of Mental Illness.* International Universities Press.

Canetti, E. (1960). *Masse und Macht.* Frankfurt am Main: Fischer Taschenbuch Verlag.

Caudill, W. A. (1958). *The Psychiatric Hospital as a Small Society.* Cambridge: Harvard University Press.

Chasseguet-Smirgel, J. (1975). *L'Idéal du Moi.* Paris: Claude Tchou.

Chasseguet-Smirgel, J., and Grunberger, B. (1969). *L'Univers contestationnaire.* Paris: Petite Bibliothèque Payot.

Colman, A. D., and Bexton, W. N., eds. (1975). *Group Relations Reader.* Sausalito, Calif.: Grex.

Conquest, R. (1991). *The Great Terror: A Reassessment.* New York: Oxford University Press.

Dalton, G. W., et al. (1968). *The Distribution of Authority in Formal Organizations.* Cambridge: Harvard University Press.

Dawidowicz, L. S. (1975). *The War Against the Jews, 1933–1945.* New York: Bantam Books.

De Board, R. (1978). *The Psychoanalysis of Organizations.* London: Tavistock.

De Mare, P. B. (1972). *Perspectives in Group Psychotherapy: A Theoretical Background.* New York: Science House.

Deschner, K. (1980). *Kitsch, Konvention, und Kunst.* Frankfurt: Ullstein.

Dicks, H. V. (1972). *Licensed Mass Murder: A Socio-Psychological Study of Some SS-Killers.* London: Heinemann.

Dolgoff, T. (1973). Organizations as sociotechnical systems. *Bull. Menninger Clinic* 37:232–257.

Dulchin, J., and Segal, A. J. (1982a). The ambiguity of confidentiality in a psychoanalytic institute. *Psychiat.* 45:13–25.

———. (1982b). Third-party confidences: The uses of information in a psychoanalytic institute. *Psychiat.* 45:27–37.

Durkheim, E. (1933 [1893]). *The Division of Labor in Society.* Trans. George Simpson. New York: Macmillan.

———. (1961 [1925]). *Moral Education: A Study in the Theory and Application of the Sociology of Education.* Trans. Everett K. Silson and Herman Schnurer. New York: Free Press of Glencoe.

Durkin, H. E. (1964). *The Group in Depth.* New York: International Universities Press.

Durkin, H. E., and Glatzer, H. T. (1972). Transference neurosis in group psychotherapy: The concept and the reality. Unpub. ms.

Edelson, M. (1967). The sociotherapeutic function in a psychiatric hospital. *J. Fort Logan Mental Health Center* 4:1–45.

———. (1970). *Sociotherapy and Psychotherapy.* Chicago: University of Chicago Press.

Emery, F. W., and Trist, E. L. (1973). *Towards a Social Ecology.* New York: Plenum Press.

Erikson, E. (1950). Growth and crises of the healthy personality. In *Identity and the Life Cycle.* New York: International Universities Press, 1959, 50–100.

———. (1956). The problem of ego identity. In *Identity and the Life Cycle.* New York: International Universities Press, 1959, 101–164.

Ezriel, H. (1950). A psychoanalytic approach to the treatment of patients in groups. *J. Ment. Science* 96:774–779.

Fairbairn, W. R. D. (1954). *An Object-Relations Theory of the Personality.* New York: Basic Books.

Foucault, M. (1978). *History of Sexuality: An Introduction.* New York: Pantheon.

Foulkes, S. H., and Anthony, E. J. (1957). *Group Psychotherapy: The Psychoanalytic Approach.* Baltimore: Penguin Books.

Franzen, S. (1982). Editorial. *Council for the Advancement of Psychoanalytic Education* 2(2): 2.

Freud, S. (1913). Totem and taboo. *S.E.,* 13:1–162.

———. (1914a). On narcissism: An introduction. *S.E.,* 14:69–102.

———. (1914b). On the history of the psychoanalytic movement. *S.E.,* 14:3–66.

———. (1920). Beyond the pleasure principle. *S.E.,* 18:3–64.

———. (1921). Group psychology and the analysis of the ego. *S.E.,* 18:65–143.

———. (1922). Two encyclopedia articles. *S.E.,* 18:235–259.

———. (1923). The ego and the id. *S.E.,* 19:1–66.

———. (1927). The future of an illusion. *S.E.,* 21:5–56.

———. (1930). Civilization and its discontents. *S.E.,* 21:59–145.

———. (1939). Moses and monotheism. *S.E.,* 23:1–137.

———. (1963 [1927]). Letter to Oskar Pfister of 10–22–1927. In *Sigmund Freud Oskar Pfister Briefe, 1909–1939 (Psychoanalysis and Faith: The Letters of Sigmund Freud and Oskar Pfister),* ed. H. Meng and E. L. Freud. Frankfurt am Main: Fischer Verlag. New York: Basic Books.

Friedlander, S. (1984). *Reflections on Nazism.* New York: Harper.

Fromm, E. (1955). *The Sane Society.* New York: Holt, Rinehart, and Winston.

Giovannetti, M. de Freitas. (1991). The couch and the Medusa: Brief considerations on the nature of the boundaries in the psychoanalytic Institution. Fifth IPA Conference of Training Analysts, Buenos Aires. Unpub. ms.

Glatzer, H. T. (1969). Working through in analytic group psychotherapy. *Int. J. Group Psychotherapy* 19:292–306.

Goffman, E. (1968). *Asylums: Essays on the Social Situation of Mental Patients and Other Inmates.* Harmondsworth, Eng.: Penguin.

Gramsci, A. (1959). *The Modern Prince and Other Writings.* New York: International Publishing.

Green, A. (1969). *Sexualité et idéologie chez Marx et Freud.* Paris: Etudes Freudiennes, 1–2, 187–217.

———. (1991). Preliminaries to a discussion of the function of theory in psychoanalytic training. Fifth IPA Conference of Training Analysts, Buenos Aires. Unpub. ms.

Greenacre, P. (1959). Problems of the Training Analysis. In *Minutes of Training Analysts' Seminar,* Chicago Institute for Psychoanalysis, November 21.

Greenberg, C. (1946). Avant-garde and kitsch. In *Mass Culture,* ed. B. Rosenberg and D. M. White, 98-110. New York: Free Press, 1957.

Habermas, J. (1971). *Knowledge and Human Interests.* Boston: Beacon Press.

———. (1973). *Theory and Practice.* Boston: Beacon Press.

Hodgson, R. C., Levinson, D. J., and Zaleznik, A. (1965). *The Executive Role Constellation: An Analysis of Personality and Role-Relations in Management.* Cambridge: Harvard University Press.

Horkheimer, M., and Adorno, T. (1971). *Dialektik der Aufklärung.* Frankfurt: Bucher des Wissens.

Howe, I. (1948). Notes on mass culture. In *Mass Culture,* ed. B. Rosenberg and D. M. White, 496–503. New York: Free Press, 1957.

Infante, J. A. (1991). The teaching of psychoanalysis: Common ground. Fifth IPA Conference of Training Analysts, Buenos Aires. Unpub. ms.

Jacobson, E. (1964). *The Self and the Object World.* New York: International Universities Press.

———. (1971a). Acting out and the urge to betray in paranoid patients. In *Depression,* 302–318. New York: International Universities Press.

———. (1971b). *Depression.* New York: International Universities Press.

Jaques, E. (1955). Social systems as a defense against persecutory and depressive anxiety. In *New Directions in Psycho-Analysis,* ed. M. Klein, P. Heimann, and R. E. Money-Kyrle, 478–498. New York: Basic Books.

———. (1976). *A General Theory of Bureaucracy.* New York: Halsted.

———. (1982). *The Form of Time.* New York: Crane, Russak.

Jones, M. (1953). *The Therapeutic Community: A New Treatment Method in Psychiatry.* New York: Basic Books.

———. (1956). The concept of the therapeutic community. *Am. J. Psychiat.* 112:647–650.

———. (1968). *Social Psychiatry in Practice.* Baltimore: Penguin.

Kaes, R. (1980). *L'Idéologie: Etudes psychanalytiques.* Paris: Dunod.

Katz, D., and Kahn, R. L. (1966). *The Social Psychology of Organizations.* New York: John Wiley and Sons.

Katz, E. (1955). Skills of an effective administrator. *Harvard Business Review* (Jan.–Feb.): 33–42.

Keiser, S. (1969). *Report of the Outgoing Chairman of the Committee on Institutes to the Board on Professional Standards*. New York: American Psychoanalytic Association.

Keniston, K. (1965). *The Uncommitted*. New York: Delta Books.

Kernberg, O. F. (1967). Borderline personality organization. *J. Am. Psychoanal. Assn.* 15:641–685.

————. (1970). Factors in the psychoanalytic treatment of narcissistic personalities. *J. Am. Psychoanal. Assn.* 18:51–85.

————. (1973). Psychoanalytic object-relations theory, group processes, and administration. *Ann. Psychoanal.* 1:363–386.

————. (1974). Further contributions to the treatment of narcissistic personalities. *Int. J. Psychoanal.* 55:215–240.

————. (1975a). *Borderline Conditions and Pathological Narcissism*. New York: Jason Aronson.

————. (1975b). Modern hospital milieu treatment of schizophrenia. In *New Dimensions in Psychiatry: A World View*, ed. S. Arieti and G. Chrzanowski, 202–220. New York: John Wiley and Sons.

————. (1975c). A systems approach to the priority setting of interventions in groups. *Int. J. Group Psychotherapy* 25:251–275.

————. (1976). *Object Relations Theory and Clinical Psychoanalysis*. New York: Jason Aronson.

————. (1978). Leadership and organizational functioning: Organizational regression. *Int. J. Group Psychotherapy* 28:3–25.

————. (1979). Regression in organizational leadership. *Psychiat.* 42:24–39.

————. (1980a). The couple and the group. In *Internal World and External Reality*, 307–331. New York: Jason Aronson.

————. (1980b). *Internal World and External Reality: Object Relations Theory Applied*. New York: Jason Aronson.

————. (1980c). Regression in groups: Some clinical and theoretical implications. *J. Personality and Soc. System* 2:51–75.

————. (1981). Some issues in the theory of hospital treatment. *Soertrykk av Tidsskrift for den norske loegeforening* 14:837–843.

————. (1982). *Advantages and Liabilities of Therapeutic Community Models*. Vol. 1: *The Individual and the Group*, ed. M. Pine and L. Rafaelsen. London: Plenum.

————. (1984a). Paranoid regression and malignant narcissism. In *Severe Personality Disorders: Psychotherapeutic Strategies*, 290–311. New Haven: Yale University Press.

————. (1984b). The couch at sea: The psychoanalysis of organizations. *Int. J. Group Psychotherapy* 34(1): 5–23.

————. (1984c). *Severe Personality Disorders: Psychotherapeutic Strategies*. New Haven: Yale University Press.

————. (1986). Institutional problems of psychoanalytic education. *J. Am. Psychoanal. Assn.* 34:799–834.

————. (1988). Identity, alienation, and ideology in adolescent group processes. In *Fantasy,*

Myth, and Reality: Essays in Honor of Jacob A. Arlow, ed. H. P. Blum, Y. Kramer, A. Richards, and A. Richards, 381–399. Madison, Conn.: International Universities Press.

———. (1989a). The narcissistic personality disorder and the differential diagnosis of antisocial behavior. In *Psychiatric Clinics of North America: Narcissistic Personality Disorder,* O. F. Kernberg, guest ed., 12(3): 553–570, 723–729. Philadelphia: W. B. Saunders.

———. (1989b). The temptations of conventionality. *Int. Rev. Psychoanal.* 16:191–205.

———. (1991). The moral dimension of leadership. In *Psychoanalytic Group Theory and Therapy: Essays in Honor of Saul Scheidlinger,* ed. S. Tuttman, 87–112. New York: International Universities Press.

———. (1992). Massenpsychologie aus analytischer Sicht. *Texte* 1:9.

———. (1993). Paranoiagenesis in organizations. In *Comprehensive Textbook of Group Psychotherapy,* 3d ed., ed. H. Kaplan and B. J. Sadock, 47–57. Baltimore: Williams and Wilkins.

———. (1994a). Mass psychology through the analytic lens. In *The Spectrum of Psychoanalysis: Essays in Honor of Martin Bergmann,* ed. A. K. Richards and A. D. Richards, 257–281. Madison, Conn.: International Universities Press.

———. (1994b). Leadership styles and organizational paranoiagenesis. In *Paranoia: New Psychoanalytic Perspectives,* ed. J. Oldham and S. Bone, 61–79. Madison, Conn.: International Universities Press.

———. (1997). Ideology and bureaucracy as social defenses against aggression. In *The Inner World in the Outer World: Psychoanalytic Perspectives,* ed. E. R. Shapiro. New Haven: Yale University Press, 97–121.

Klein, M. (1946). Notes on some schizoid mechanisms. In *Development in psychoanalysis,* ed. J. Rivière, 292–320. London: Hogarth, 1952.

Klerman, G., and Levinson, D. J. (1967). The clinical executive: Some problematic issues for the psychiatrist in mental health organizations. *J. Study Interpersonal Processes* 30:3–15.

Kolakowski, L. (1978a). The Founders. In *Main Currents of Marxism,* 1:154–178. New York: Oxford University Press.

———. (1978b). The Breakdown. In *Main Currents of Marxism,* vol. 3. Oxford: Oxford University Press.

Kreeger. (1975). *The Large Group: Dynamics and Therapy.* London: Constable.

Lasch, C. (1977). *Haven in a Heartless World.* New York: Basic Books.

———. (1978). *The Culture of Narcissism.* New York: Norton.

———. (1981). The Freudian Left and cultural revolution. *New Left Review* 129:23–34.

Lawrence, W. G., ed. (1969). *Exploring Individual and Organizational Boundaries.* New York: John Wiley and Sons.

Le Bon, G. (1969 [1895]). *The Crowd.* New York: Ballantine. (French edition: *Psychologie des foules.* Paris: Felix Alcan)

Levinson, D. J., and Klerman, G. L. (1967). The clinical-executive: Some problematic issues for the psychiatrist in mental health organizations. *Psychiat.* 30:3–15.

Levinson, H. (1968). *The Exceptional Executive: A Psychological Conception.* Cambridge: Harvard University Press.

———. (1972). *Organizational Diagnosis.* Cambridge: Harvard University Press.

Lewin, K. (1951). *Field Theory in Social Science.* New York: Harper and Row.

Lifschutz, J. E. (1976). A critique of reporting and assessment in the training analysis. *J. Am. Psychoanal. Assn.* 24:43–59.

Lussier, A. (1991). Our training ideology. Fifth IPA Conference of Training Analysts, Buenos Aires. Unpub. ms.

McCarthy, C. M. (1978). *Report of the Task Force on Regulation on the Cost of Regulation.* Hospital Association of New York State.

MacDonald, D. (1953). A theory of mass culture. In *Mass Culture,* ed. B. Rosenberg, and D. M. White, 59–73. New York: Free Press, 1957.

McDougall, W. (1920). *The Group Mind.* London: Cambridge.

Mahler, M. S., and Furer, M. (1968). *On Human Symbiosis and the Vicissitudes of Individuation.* New York: International Universities Press.

Mahony, P. (1979). The budding international association of psychoanalysis and its discontents. *Psychoanal. and Contemp. Thought* 2:551–593.

Main, T. F. (1946). The hospital as a therapeutic institution. *Bull. Menninger Clinic* 10:66–70.

———. (1957). The ailment. *British J. Med. Psychol.* 30(pt. 3): 129–145.

Malan, D. H., Balfour, F. H. G., Hood, V. G., and Shooter, A. M. N. (1976). Group psychotherapy: A long-term follow-up study. *Arch. Gen. Psychiat.* 33:1303–1315.

Malia, M. (1994). *The Soviet Tragedy: A History of Socialism in Russia, 1917–1991.* New York: Free Press.

Marcuse, H. (1955). *Eros and Civilization: A Philosophical Inquiry into Freud.* Boston: Beacon Press.

Masters, R. D. (1989). *The Nature of Politics.* New Haven: Yale University Press.

Menzies, I. E. P. (1967). The functioning of social systems as a defense against anxiety: A report on the study of a nursing service of a general hospital. In *Tavistock Pamphlet No. 3.* London.

Michels, R. (1949 [1911]). *Political Parties: A Sociological Study of the Oligarchical Tendencies in Modern Democracy.* Trans. Eden Paul and Cedar Paul. New York: Free Press.

Miller, E. J. (1976). *Task and Organization.* New York: John Wiley and Sons.

Miller, E. J., and Rice, A. K. (1967). *Systems of Organization.* London: Tavistock.

Mitscherlich, A. (1963). *Auf dem Weg Zur vaterlosen Gesellschaft: Ideen Zur Sozial-Psychologie.* Munich: R. Piper.

Moles, A. (1971). *Le Kitsch: L'Art du bonheur.* Paris: Maison Mame.

Moscovici, S. (1981). *L'Age des foules.* Paris: Librairie Arthème Fayard.

Nesbit, R. (1993). *The Sociological Tradition.* New Brunswick, N.J.: Transactions.

Novotny, P. (1971). The pseudo-psychoanalytic hospital. *Bull. Menninger Clinic* 37:193–210.

Offer, D., Ostrov, E., and Howard, K. I. (1981). *The Adolescent: A Psychological Self-Portrait.* New York: Basic Books.

Ollman, B. (1976). *Alienation: Marx's Conception of Man in Capitalist Society,* 2d ed. New York: Cambridge University Press.

Ortega y Gasset, J. (1976 [1929]). *La Rebelión de las Masas.* Madrid: Expasa-Calpe.

Parsons, T. (1964a). The superego and the theory of social systems. In *Social Structure and Personality,* 17–33. London: Free Press.

———. (1964b). Social structure and the development of personality: Freud's contribution to the integration of psychology and sociology. In *Social Structure and Personality*, 78–111. London: Free Press.

Rangell, L. (1974). A psychoanalytic perspective leading currently to the syndrome of the compromise of integrity. *Int. J. Psycho-Anal.* 55:3–12.

Reich, W. (1962 [1935]). *The Sexual Revolution: Toward a Self-Governing Character Structure.* New York: Noonday Press.

Rice, A. K. (1963). *The Enterprise and Its Environment.* London: Tavistock.

———. (1965). *Learning for Leadership.* London: Tavistock.

———. (1969). Individual, group, and intergroup processes. *Human Relations* 22:565–584.

Riesman, D. (1950). *The Lonely Crowd: A Study of the Changing American Character.* New Haven: Yale University Press.

Rioch, M. J. (1970a). The work of Wilfred Bion on groups. *Psychiat.* 33:56–66.

———. (1970b). Group relations: Rationale and techniques. *Int. J. Group Psychotherapy* 10:340–355.

Roberts, P. C., and LaFollette, K. (1990). *Meltdown: Inside the Soviet Economy.* Washington, D.C.: Cato Institute.

Robinson, P. A. (1959). *The Freudian Left.* New York: Harper Colophon Books.

Rogers, K. (1973). Notes on organizational consulting to mental hospitals. *Bull. Menninger Clinic* 37:211–231.

Rosenberg, B. (1957). Mass culture in America. In *Mass Culture,* ed. B. Rosenberg and D. M. White, 3–12. New York: Free Press.

Rosenberg, B., and White, D. M., eds. (1957). *Mass Culture.* New York: Free Press.

Rosenfeld, H. (1971). A clinical approach to the psychoanalytic theory of the life and death instincts: An investigation into the aggressive aspects of narcissism. *Int. J. Psycho-Anal.* 52:169–178.

Roustang, F. (1982). *Dire Mastery: Discipleship from Freud to Lacan.* Baltimore: Johns Hopkins University Press.

Rubenstein, R., and Lasswell, H. D. (1966). *The Sharing of Power in a Psychiatric Hospital.* New Haven: Yale University Press.

Sanford, N. (1956). The approach of the authoritarian personality. In *Psychology of Personality,* ed. J. McCary. New York: Logos Press.

Sarnoff, C. (1976). *Latency.* New York: Jason Aronson.

Schabowski, G. (1991). *Das Politbüro.* Reinbek bei Hamburg: Rowohlt Taschenbuch.

Scheidlinger, S. (1960). Group process in group psychotherapy. *Am. J. Psychotherapy* 14:104–120, 346–363.

———. (1982). *Focus on Group Psychotherapy: Clinical Essays.* New York: International Universities Press.

Scheidlinger, S., ed. (1980). *Psychoanalytic Group Dynamics.* New York: International Universities Press.

Shapiro, R. (1979). Psychoanalytic knowledge of group processes. Panel report. *J. Am. Psychoanal. Assn.* 27:150–152.

Shapiro, T., and Perry, R. (1976). Latency revisited: The age seven plus or minus one. In *Psychoanal. Study of the Child* 31:79-105.

Sinyavsky, A. (1988). *Soviet Civilization: A Cultural History.* New York: Arcade.

Skynner, A. C. R. (1976). *Systems of Family and Marital Psychotherapy*. New York: Brunner/Mazel.

Slavson, S. R. (1959). The era of group psychotherapy. *Acta Psychotherapy* 7:167–196.

———. (1962). A critique of the group therapy literature. *Acta Psychotherapy* 10:62–73.

———. (1964). *A Textbook in Analytic Group Psychotherapy*. New York: International Universities Press.

Stanton, A. M., and Schwartz, M. (1954). *The Mental Hospital*. New York: Basic Books.

Stephane, A. (1969). *L' Univers contestationnaire*. Paris: Petite Bibliothèque Payot.

Sutherland, J. D. (1952). Notes on psychoanalytic group therapy. I: Therapy and training. *Psychiat.* 15:111–117.

Tocqueville, A. de (1945 [1835–1840]). *Democracy in America*. Ed. Philips Bradley. Trans. George Lawrence. New York: Alfred A. Knopf.

Todd, E. (1990). *La Chute finale*. Paris: Editions Robert Laffont.

Tönnies, F. (1963 [1887]). *Community and Society*. Trans. and ed. Charles Loomis. New York: Harper.

Turquet, P. (1975). Threats to identity in the large group. In *The Large Group: Dynamics and Therapy*, ed. L. Kreeger, 87–144. London: Constable.

Voslensky, M. (1983). *Nomenklatura: The Soviet Ruling Class—An Insider's Report*. New York: Doubleday.

Wallerstein, R. S. (1993). Between chaos and petrification: A summary of the Fifth IPA Conference of Training Analysts. *Int. J. Psycho-Anal.* 74:165–178.

Weber, M. (1958 [1904–1905]). *The Protestant Ethic and the Spirit of Capitalism*. Trans. Talcott Parsons. New York: Charles Scribner's Sons.

Welch, D. (1983). *Propaganda and the German Cinema, 1933–1945*. New York: Oxford University Press.

Whiteley, J. S., and Gordon, J. (1979). *Group Approaches in Psychiatry*. London: Routledge and Kegan Paul.

Wolf, A., and Schwartz, M. (1962). *Psychoanalysis in Groups*. New York: Grune and Stratton.

Yalom, I. D. (1970). *The Theory and Practice of Group Psychotherapy*. New York: Basic Books.

Zaleznik, A. (1974). Charismatic and consensus leaders: A psychological comparison. *Bull. Menninger Clinic* 38:222–238.

———. (1979). Psychoanalytic knowledge of group processes. Panel report. *J. Am. Psychoanal. Assn.* 27:146–147, 149–150.

Zinoviev, A. (1984). *The Reality of Communism*. New York: Schocken Books.

Index

consensus (*see* consensus leaders); dependency needs in, 67–68, 143–44; effect of disappearance of, 32–33; effect of personality of, 52, 96, 177–79, 234–37; effect on staff (*see* staff: effect of leaders on); effects of regression in, 102; elected, 128; Freud's views of meaning of, 46; human skills of, 112; idealization of (*see* idealization: of leaders); identification with (*see* identification: with leaders); improvement of ability of, 73, 74; incompetent, 118, 133, 144, 191; intermediate, 73; morality in, 104–21; mystic, 94–95; narcissistic personality of (*see* narcissistic personality: of leaders); normal narcissism of, 112–13; obsessive personality of, 78–80, 147, 150; paranoid alertness in, 113; paranoid personality of (*see* paranoid personality: of leaders); and preoedipal conflicts (*see* preoedipal conflicts, and leadership); resignation of, 73; robot, 150; roles, 179; sadism of, 79–80, 88, 120; sadistic psychopath, 99; schizoid personality of, 78, 125, 148–49, 150; selection of, 6, 17, 89–90, 117, 135, 266, 270, 297; self-aggrandizement of, 107; self-exploration of, 177–79; sexual needs of, 63–67 (*see also* oedipal conflicts: and leaders); skills of, 176–77; technical skills of, 111–12; of therapeutic communities, 173, 176; training needs of group, 176–77; value systems of, 115–21

leadership: aggressive needs in, 60–63; authoritarian, 77, 108–9, 120; authority in, 77, 108–9, 117, 141–43; Bion on, 92–95; case study of weak, 57; characteristics of rational, 47, 59, 73, 97–103, 111–15, 130, 140, 179; diagnosis of malfunctioning, 58–60, 62–63, 71–73, 153–55; Freud on, 19–20, 44, 46, 91–92; functional, 164; illusions characteristic of group, 174–77; Marxist philosophers on, 19–20; and morality in groups, 104–21; political dimensions of, 116. *See also* preoedipal conflicts, and leadership

leadership styles, 140–55; absentee, 148–49; affective unavailability or instability, 149–51; corrupt, 151–53; narcissistic, 8, 112, 143–46 (*see also* narcissistic personality); narcissistic with paranoid features, 146–48 (*see also* paranoid personality)

Le Bon, G., 5

Levinson, D. J., 111

Levinson, H., 18, 105

Lewin, K., 10

libido, and group formation, 39–40, 44, 141

Lifschutz, J. E., 206

Mahony, P., 223

Main, T. F., 12–13, 182, 190

Malia, M., 279

malignant narcissism, 44, 115, 131, 270–71, 293

Marcuse, H., 19, 261–62

marriage, in organizations, 66

Marx, Karl, 26

Marxist philosophers: on alienation, 26; on leadership, 19–20; on mass culture, 261–63

mass culture, 42, 253–72; aggression in, 256; appeal across cultures of, 263; characteristics of, 253–58; defenses in, 271; definition of, 254; dependency needs in, 268; effect on political process, 272; enemies in, 256; father figures in, 264, 268–69; identification in, 256, 268; and ideology, 271–72; latency child in, 258–60, 266–68, 270, 272; Marxist philosophers on, 261–63; media role in, 253–54; messianic systems in, 264–65; and morality in groups, 257–58; narcissistic personality in (*see* narcissistic personality: and

Acknowledgments

I would like to thank the following publishers for permission to rework and modify material originally published in their books and journals:

Chapter 1: Adapted from "Psychoanalytic Studies of Group Processes: Theory and Application," in *Psychiatry 1983: American Psychiatric Association Annual Review* (Washington, D.C.: American Psychiatric Press, 1983), 21–36. Published with the permission of American Psychiatric Press.

Chapter 2: Adapted from "Identity, Alienation, and Ideology in Adolescent Group Processes," in *Fantasy, Myth, and Reality: Essays in Honor of Jacob A. Arlow,* ed. H. Blum, Y. Kramer, Arlene Richards, Arnold Richards (Madison, Conn.: International Universities Press, 1988), 381–399. Published with the permission of International Universities Press.

Chapter 3: Adapted from "Mass Psychology Through the Analytic Lens," in *The Spectrum of Psychoanalysis: Essays in Honor of Martin Bergmann,* ed. A. K. Richards and A. D. Richards (Madison, Conn.: International Universities Press, 1994), 257–281. Published with the permission of International Universities Press.

Chapter 4: Adapted from "Leadership and Organizational Functioning: Organizational Regression," *International Journal of Group Psychotherapy* 28 (1978): 3–25. Published with the permission of Guilford Press.

Chapter 5: Adapted from "Regression in Organizational Leadership," *Psychiatry* 42 (1979): 24–39. Published with the permission of Guilford Press.

Chapter 6: Adapted from "The Couch at Sea: The Psychoanalysis of Organizations," *International Journal of Group Psychotherapy* 34(1) (1984): 5–23. Published with the permission of Guilford Press.

Chapter 7: Adapted from "The Moral Dimension of Leadership," in *Psychoanalytic Group Theory and Therapy: Essays in Honor of Saul Scheidlinger,* ed S. Tuttman (Madison, Conn.: International Universities Press, 1991), 87–112. Published with the permission of International Universities Press.

Chapter 8: Adapted from "Paranoiagenesis in Organizations," in *Comprehensive Textbook of Group Psychotherapy,* 3d ed., ed. H. Kaplan and B. J. Sadock (Baltimore: Williams and Wilkins Press, 1993), 47–57. Published with the permission of Williams and Wilkins Press.

Chapter 9: Adapted from "Leadership Styles and Organizational Paranoiagenesis," in *Paranoia: New Psychoanalytic Perspectives,* ed. J. Oldham and S. Bone (Madison, Conn.: International Universities Press, 1994), 61–79. Published with the permission of International Universities Press.

Chapter 10: Adapted from "A Systems Approach to the Priority Setting of Interventions in Groups," *International Journal of Group Psychotherapy* 25 (1975): 251–275. Published with the permission of Guilford Press.

Chapter 11: Adapted from "The Therapeutic Community: A Reevaluation," *Journal of the National Association of Private Psychiatric Hospitals* 12(2) (1981): 46–55. Published with the permission of the National Association of Psychiatric Health Systems.

Chapter 12: Adapted from "Institutional Problems of Psychoanalytic Education," *Journal of the American Psychoanalytic Association* 34 (1986): 799–834. Published with the permission of the *Journal of the American Psychoanalytic Association.*

Chapter 13: Adapted from "Authoritarianism, Culture, and Personality in Psychoanalytic Education," *Journal of the International Association for the History of Psychoanalysis* 5 (1992): 341–354. Published with the permission of the *International Journal of Psycho-Analysis.*

Chapter 14: Adapted from "Thirty Methods to Destroy the Creativity of Psychoanalytic Education," *International Journal of Psycho-Analysis,* 77(5) (1996): 1031–1040. Published with the permission of the *International Journal of Psycho-Analysis.*

Chapter 15: Adapted from "The Temptations of Conventionality," *International Review of Psycho-Analysis* 16 (1989): 191–205. Published with the permission of the *International Journal of Psycho-Analysis.*

Chapter 16: Adapted from "Ideology and Bureaucracy as Social Defenses Against Aggression," in *The Inner World in the Outer World: Psychoanalytic Perspectives,* ed. E. R. Shapiro (New Haven: Yale University Press, 1997), 97–121. Published with the permission of Yale University Press.